Exploring Deception Pass

An Insider's Guide to
Washington's Favorite State Park

Jack

Hartt

Exploring Deception Pass

An Insider's Guide to
Washington's Favorite State Park

Jack Hartt

Exploring Deception Pass

An Insider's Guide to Washington's Favorite State Park

Jack Hartt

Copyright © September 2016 by Jack Hartt
All rights reserved

All illustrations by Jack Hartt unless otherwise credited

Local outlet sales of this book benefit the Deception Pass Park Foundation, whose mission is to protect the park and educate visitors about its resources.

www.deceptionpassfoundation.org

All the thoughts and ideas in this book are the personal opinions and statements of the author, and do not in any way represent the official viewpoints, positions, or perspectives of the Washington State Parks and Recreation Commission.
Nothing in this book is to be considered as official State Park recommendations, directions, or policy.

No state time or resources were used in the creation, production or publication of this book.

First published 2016

Made in the United States of America

Other books by Jack Hartt:

Proper Size Me
A Walk Around the Block
Two Hands and a Shovel (with Sam Wotipka)
A Walk at Bowman Bay

Dedication

To Jim Farmer

Former Park Ranger, Mentor, Unlikely Soul Mate, and Dear Friend

I had been working for Washington State Parks for over a dozen years back then, my latest park being Fort Worden Conference Center, when a new park manager took the helm. He had been at Deception Pass as the assistant ranger for many years in the Seventies, and had managed Larrabee and Moran State Parks since then. I only knew him from a presentation he had once done for rangers about signage in parks, how caring about the appearance of signs influences the behavior of visitors and certainly influences their opinion of the park.

I thought my crew and I were doing a great grounds keeping job at Fort Worden; indeed, we received many compliments how our efforts were making the park better than it had ever looked. Turns out we had so far to go.

For the next eight years, this new manager changed me. Oh, we locked horns several times as he sought to take my elementary skills and random priorities and refine them into disciplined, purposeful, and intentional acts of making a park effective at every level. He taught me lessons about how to mow (I thought I already knew, but he showed me so much more), how to look at my work through the frame of a camera, how to balance law enforcement with being human, and how to consider each and every visitor's experience each and every day. He gave all of the staff dozens of mantras to remember, including:

- Parks are forever
- It's a park every day
- The closer you look the better we should look
- Today's solution is tomorrow's problem
- Parks are for people
- Have a park eye
- Get to yes
- Keep the main thing the main thing

He had this uncanny genius to see the philosophy, the wisdom, the depth behind every decision made about the park, from where to locate a kayak campsite to choosing the colors on a building to the timing of our restroom cleaning. And if asked, he would give the deeper answer to help me see the why of what we were doing.

I remember sitting in a meeting with some special interest group wanting to do a project for the park. His discussion with them ranged through history, art, philosophy, architecture, design, poetry and science. I had never realized how much he considered for even a small request like that, let alone how he could expound upon a simple question so eloquently. He truly thought about parks as no one I had ever met before.

Over time, he chiseled and molded me enough that I started to understand some of the method behind his manners, the power of professional park management that focuses on the present and the future, on the customer and the concepts of parks as refuges for our souls, and the challenges presented to rangers as stewards of the future.

I was able to invest some of that education into my first park manager position at Riverside State Park in Spokane. And in a poor imitation I have attempted to operate Deception Pass with a similar approach, but with different personalities here modifying the direction.

Without his mentorship, I would have never grown to be able to take on the helm of a ship such as Deception Pass.

Because of Jim Farmer, I am a better ranger and and a better human being.

Contents

Preface ix
Acknowledgements xi
Introduction xv

Setting 1
Welcome 1
Features 1

Creating 7
Rocks 7
Tides 10
Currents 10
Beaches 11
Soil 12
Weather 12

Living 19
Park Habitats:
- Tidepools 19
- Eelgrass beds 20
- Sand Dunes 21
- Wetlands 21
- Forested Shorelines 22
- Dry Upland Forests 22
- Deep Soil Forests 23
- Old Growth 24
- Balds 25

Common Trees 25
Distinctive Individual Trees 28
Other Shrubs and Flowers 29
Mushrooms, Mosses, and More 31
Seaweeds 32
Invasives 32
ANIMALS 35
Between The Tides 35
Bugs, Snakes and things 36
More Small Critters 37
Birds 37
Mammals 40
Bioluminescence 42

Changing 45
First Peoples 45
European Explorers 47
Military Reservation 48
Pioneers 48

Prison Camp 50
Ben Ure 50
Fish Traps at West Beach 51
Ferry Days 51
The Years Before the Park 53
State Park Dedication 55
Civilian Conservation Corps 55
The Bridge 60
Heilman Family 63
Pass Lake Changes 64
Fish Hatchery 64
Road to West Beach 65
Cornet Bay Retreat Center 66
Amphitheater 66
New Boat Launches 67

<u>Changes in the Eighties and Nineties</u>
The Story of the Story Pole 67
CCC Interpretive Center 68
Hoypus Hill Added 69
Dugualla Acquired 69
New Entrance and Sewer Developed 70
CAMP Process 71

<u>Changes in the 21st Century, so far:</u>
Heart Lake Transferred 71
Bowman Expanded 71
Rosario Tidepools Protected 71
New Administrative Office 72
Quarry Pond Campground Added 72
Deception Pass Park Foundation 73
Hoypus Gate Closed 73
Cornet Bay Boat Launch Improved 73
Hoypus Hill Extended 74
Ben Ure Cabins 74
Kiket Island Co-acquired 74
West Beach Shelter Developed 75
Ginnett Property Acquisition 76
Group Camp Moves 76
Bowman Shelter Restored 76
New Trails, New Railings 77
Rosario Remodeled 78
More CCC Structures Restored 78
Amphitheater Rebuilt 79
Beach Restorations 79
History Timeline 81
Old Growth Forests and the People Underneath 82

Visiting 87

How to Get Here   87
Crowds   89
Seasonal Usage   89
Reservations   90
Seasonal closures   90
Fees   91
Moorage   92
Groups and Special Activities   92
School Group Tidal Visits   92
Park Rules   93
Safety   94
Navy Jets   95
Lake Quality   96
Connectivity   97
Diversity   97
Accessibility   98

Exploring 101

Park Entrance   101
East Cranberry   101
Maintenance area   102
Cranberry Lake   102
Cranberry Campground   102
West Beach   102
Swim Beach   103
Dunes   103
Amphitheater   104
North Beach   104
Underpass   104
Goose Rock   105
Quarry Pond   105
Cornet Bay Retreat Center   106
Cornet Bay   107
Hoypus Point   107
Hoypus Hill   108
Ben Ure Island   108
Strawberry Island   108
The Bridge   108
Pass Island   111
Bowman Hill   111
Bowman Bay   112
Bowman Bay Campground   113
Lighthouse Point/Reservation Head   113
Lottie Point   114
Rosario   115
Deception Island   116
Northwest Island   116
Pass Lake   116
Heilman Valley   117
Ginnett   117
Tursi Trail   117
Kiket Island/Kukutali Preserve   118
Skagit Island   119
Hope Island   120
Dugualla State Park   120
Stay on the Trail   121

Doing 125

Bicycling   125
Boating   126
Boat rentals   127
Boat tours   127
Cabins   128
Camping   128
Campfires   131
Clamming   132
Crabbing   132
Dogs   132
Fishing in Freshwater   133
Fishing in Saltwater   133
Geocaching   134
Group Camps   134
Hiking   134
Horse riding   139
Jogging   139
Kayak Rentals   139
Kite Flying   139
Metal Detecting   140
Model Sailboat Racing   140
Paddle sports   140
Picnicking   142
Picnic Shelters   142
Scuba Diving   144
Swimming   144
Tidepools   145
Weddings   145
Winter Sports   146

Happening 151

First Day Hike   151
Bellingham Series Marathon/half marathon   151
Whidbey Island Marathon/half marathon   151
Earth Day Cleanup   152
Hope Island Weed Pulling   152
Salish Sea Native American Celebration   152
Fix-it Days   153
Park Founders Picnic   153
Tri-Island MS bike run   153
Annual Open House   153
Deception Pass Dash   153
Rainshadow Runs   154
Bowman Bay Holiday   154

Learning 157

Evening Programs   157
Arts in the Parks   157
Junior Ranger Programs   157
Nature Walks   158
Guided Tidepool Walks   159
Gracie the Gray Whale   159
Visitor Centers   159
Interpretive Trails   161
Interpretive Signs   161

Serving   165
    Rangers   165
    Construction and Maintenance staff   166
    Office Assistants   166
    Park aides   166
    Camp Hosts   167
    Concessions   167
    SWITMO   167
    Volunteers   168
    Deception Pass Park Foundation   168
    AmeriCorps   170
    Beach Naturalists   170
    What About You?   170
    Memorial Benches   171
    Profiles in Service:
        Darlene Clark   172
        Gene Earnest   172
        Rick Colombo   173
        Ben Shook   174
        Mark Lunz   174
        Pat and Barry Gum   175

Caring   179
    Cornet moorage   179
    100th Birthday   179
    Kiket Changes   180
    Visitor Center   180
    Keeping CCC Facilities Alive   180
    Lake Quality   181
    Forest Health   181
    Bowman Pier   182
    Power Generation   182
    Carrying capacity   182
    Growth Management   183
    Recycling   183
    Development   183
    Finances   184
    Bridge failure   185
    Earthquake/Tsunami   185
    Climate change   185

Finding   191
    Best Places to:
        Kiss   191
        Propose   191
        Watch Sunsets   192
        Watch sunrises   192
        Find quiet   192
        Go for a hike   193
        Hike with Young Children   193
        Take a photo   193
    Suggested Itineraries   194
        for those with limited time

Park Statistics   195

Emergency Help   196

Other Local Opportunities   196
    Nearby services   196
    Other Nearby Parks to Visit   196
    Other Notable Local Sites   197
    Local Theaters   197
    Good Eats   197
    Nearby Public Golf Courses   197

In the Movies   198

Suggested References   199

About Washington State Parks   201

About the Author   205

Maps   207
    Salish Sea   206
    All of park   207
    Northern areas   208
    Southwest areas   208
    Eastern areas   209
    Hoypus Trails   210
    Kiket Trails   211
    Tursi Trail   212
    Prison camp   213
    Lake bottoms   214
    Cornet Bay Retreat Center   215
    Dugualla State Park   216

Index   218

Preface

This is a love story.

My first memory of Deception Pass State Park is as a three year old, camping at Bowman Bay with my parents and older siblings. We were in what is now site 275; I recognize it today from that memory. Our square green canvas tent smelled of mildew and adventure, mingled with the musty smell of army sleeping bags and fresh earth beneath.

During the day, my oldest brother played out in the bay in our eleven foot speedboat. My father took the rest of us to the fish hatchery nearby, and showed us concrete tanks for various fish, water swirling around they as the fish swam or hovered in place.

In the evening we watched the sun go down from our campsite; a fire crackled in the fireplace, and we sat at the picnic table and talked. Our Coleman lantern hissed and blazed brightly, shrinking our world to the reach of its light.

Eventually I went to bed, with the lantern hung with care from the pole of the tent, shadows dancing on the walls of the tent, and then the hissing of the lantern slowly fading away with the light when my dad turned it off. The sounds outside, of laughter and conversation, of waves folding onto the beach and washing back out, these also faded away with sleep and become a part of my dreams, and a part of my soul.

A few years later, I was at a summer camp on the south end of Whidbey Island. I was too young to be one of the campers, but my mom was cooking at the camp and my dad was a counselor, so I hung around with the bigger kids and felt like I was a part of them.

We took a bus one day up the island to this park, and eventually ended up in the evening at the amphitheater, overlooking the waters of the Pass and the bridge above them. We sang songs in the growing darkness, our sounds blending with each other and with the passage of water and time. Eventually we boarded the bus again and headed back to the camp, our memory of the beach like a coat wrapping us all together.

In high school, I thought that a hike up Whidbey would re-connect me to some of these roots.

I left early one morning and hiked up the island, my thirty pound pack full mostly of sleeping gear and books. My pace was getting slower and slower as the miles passed by. I wasn't sure I would make my destination of Deception Pass. But after lunch a couple days later I walked across the bridge, put down my pack, and soaked in the view. As the day wore on, I headed down to the coves on the north side of the Pass, and as it got dark I set up my sleeping bag in a secluded little grove out of sight of the normal flow of visitors.

I woke early, fully refreshed by the peacefulness of the setting. I bathed at a beach nearby, ate some mealy crackers softened with juice, and explored as much of the park as I could. I spent the next night camping in the Cranberry Campground with my dad. I was becoming a seasoned veteran of the Deception Pass State Park experience at the ripe age of 17.

At the University of Washington, I had the privilege of taking one class which focused on the shoreline management issues of Puget Sound. This was a new field back then. I became so engrossed that I latched onto one of our guest instructors as a mentor, an older gentleman named Wolf Bauer, who loved beaches as much as I did. He turned me on to the art and science of studying the shore processes going on around the Sound.

For my senior thesis for my science degree in Forest Management and Outdoor Recreation I elected to study how Washington State Parks managed its beaches. I visited every state park that touched on Puget Sound, and analyzed how effectively the park system was managing the beaches for the health of the beaches and the experience of the visitors.

The last park I visited was Deception Pass State Park. I looked at every beach in the park, quantifying the integrity of the natural processes at work, and how some of the processes were reduced or destroyed by various park developments. Compared to some parks, Deception Pass scored fairly well overall. Some of the beaches were magnificent, wild and wonderful. But I found some glaring problems, too, such as the rock wall at Bowman Bay and the creosoted beach wall at Cornet Bay.

As a grown up, now working for Washington State Parks, my growing family took occasional vacations, and sometimes came here. I took a picture of my first two children, aged two and four at the time, sitting on the rock pillar north of the bridge, the kids with toothy grins, the bridge half-painted in the background.

And we visited with our then five children on June 10, 1992, on our way to the Skagit Valley for a vacation. We stopped at Pass Island, and read the plaque on the rock there, which talks about Captain George Vancouver naming Deception Pass. The plaque mentioned that Vancouver had anchored outside the Pass when he realized it was not a river he was looking at, but swiftly flowing tidal water coming around what was apparently an island, what he would then call Whidbey Island. The date of his journal entry: June 10, 1792. We all looked at each other in amazement, and held a little celebration in honor of the anniversary.

After a long and successful tenure here, the park manager before me finally decided to retire, and several young rangers including me interviewed for the position.

During the interview, the supervisor asked what I knew about George Vancouver. (He should have asked what I knew about tides.)

I shared the story above, along with excerpts of my reading of his journals and other studies of Pacific Northwest history. Throughout the interview, the interviewers asked questions about the beaches, the staff here, the campgrounds, the tribes, my priorities for management, and the potential of the park for the future.

I answered as if I had been visiting this park for decades, and studying its life and heartbeat from within.

Because I had.

They offered me the job.

I said yes.

Over a dozen years later, I am still here, still in love with the park, and still learning something new about it nearly every day.

It has captured my imagination and my heart. I have the unbelievable privilege of visiting the park and getting paid for it, of living here and walking the trails and beaches and paddling the lakes and shorelines for fun when I am off duty, and sometimes when I am on duty, helping visitors in need or studying new projects or finding ways to maintain aging facilities.

I have seen the park in so many different moods, in full sunlight and brooding fog, in windstorm and stillness, under a full moon and naked stars, with crowds of hundreds and alone, afoot, on bike, in a kayak, swimming, crawling, climbing, and sleeping in the heart of the park.

It is a joy to share some of the highlights of the park, and some of its secrets as well. There is a depth to this park that will not be found in a hurried visit or from a distracted perspective or a map or a guidebook.

I hope through your experiences here that you will come to know the park in your own way, through your own adventures and activities, finding milestones and touchstones that connect your life with lifetime memories and meaning.

Treasure those times. You never know where they may lead.

Acknowledgements

So many people have made this book possible, by helping me care for this sacred place in our lives.

The danger in acknowledging anyone here is the guarantee that equally deserving folks will be left out. I apologize to all of you before I even start sharing names, as my life is full of people who deserve credit for the good things that have happened. I also apologize ahead of time for any inevitable mistakes you will find within

With those caveats, I plow ahead with gratitude and appreciation for everyone I know, including those listed here:

The late Terry Doran, long time Region Manager of this corner of Washington, gave me the chance to come here, though he may have later regretted it. Eric Watilo, Washington State Parks Northwest Region Director and my current supervisor, has shown extraordinary patience with me in helping guide our management of the park. His fruitless attempts to reduce the frequency of my errors is commendable. Shawn Tobin, the other NW Region Director, helped me tone down some rhetoric and keep me smiling. Many others at our Region offices work closely with us to make the park successful. These include Marsha Harvey, Heather McCrumb, Derek Gustafson, and Chris Johnson.

Ted Smith, the region stewardship manager when I first arrived here, has a love and an understanding of this earth's systems that always amazed me.

Wolf Bauer inspired me to understand beaches and help me fall in love with them as I got to know them better. One of his students, Hugh Shipman, has my other dream job of studying our state's beaches, and shares that love and knowledge with many. Dr. Rob Fimbel, State Park's resource specialist, continues to teach me about the fascinating world of forest ecology.

When I first arrived, the Seattle CCC Chapter 5 folks inspired me with their memories of the CCC days and their interest in having these stories shared with future generations. Berniece Phelps, president of the club, made it all happen with her energy and enthusiasm. Sadly, most of them have now passed on.

Much has been said about John Tursi's generosity, his kindnesses, his incredible memory, his strong work ethic and his love of this area. He has been a never-ending force for making this park and our community a better place, and he will never be forgotten.

Harrison Goodall encouraged me to see the values, problems, and potential of the historical CCC buildings that we have, and helped work on their restoration.

Sammye Kempbell may love beaches and tidepools more than me, if that is possible, and can spin a tale and enrapture the hearts and imaginations of kids from 2 to 102. Her love of Rosario continues to amaze me.

Sam Wotipka, our first AmeriCorps interpreter here, loved sharing history and loved getting his hands involved in protecting history. He still does. Jessie Osterloh, Carly Rhodes, Montana Napier, and Dominique Saks, AmeriCorps interns through the years, and volunteers Rick Colombo and Amos Almy provided enthusiasm and boundless energy and talent for sharing what they learned about this park (in a very short time) and shared that awareness and excitement with so many others.

Adam Lorio shares that same dimension of spirit, and touched mine when he worked here until budget cuts ended his position. He remains a close brother in spirit. Heather Leahy-Mack was the part-time park interpreter when I arrived, but had to leave soon after. She remains a friend of the park and an encouraging voice to me. Mira Lutz inspired State Parks to hire a full time interpreter here.

Tom Wooten, Chairman of the Samish tribe, has always been a kind and encouraging friend, as have all the Samish tribal members. Rosie Cayou and Bill Bailey, whose gift of spirit and friendship fills my soul, stand out in my mind and heart.

Todd Mitchell, Charley O'Hara, Brian Porter, Larry Wasserman, Tanisha Gobert and others with the Swinomish Tribe have helped manage the Kukutali

Preserve with Washington State Parks. They also help educate me about its values and cultural meaning.

Brian Cladoosby, Chairman of the Swinomish Tribe and President of the National Congress of American Indians, has always shared a broad smile, kind heart, deep spirit, and friendly golf story with me whenever we meet.

Barbara Bennett, the last leader of Beach Watchers before it lost its funding, always had a kind word and a helpful idea. Bruce Hanna from DNR has been a helpful friend and smiling voice.

Several of our regular volunteers for the Hope Island ventures, including Harold Mead to my right; on my left is Rick Machin, Bob Blunk, Lucie Johns, the late Susan Alaynick with her back to the camera, Let Curvers, Maggie Sullivan, and Eric Shen. Photo by Dave Wenning, another great friend of the park.

Kathleen Heilman, daughter of Claire and Amelia Heilman, shared so many pictures and stories about her heritage and home which has partly become mine.

Alex McMurry, our State Park historical preservation specialist, knows the history of our park structures as if he lived it, and he shares those stories generously.

Fidalgo Fly Fishers compiled detailed stories about Pass Lake, and they share it on their website. Brett Lunsford provided generous assistance in finding new treasures at the Anacortes History Museum.

Gayle Glass has been a kind and gracious saint in her sharing of stories and in her generosity of resources. Greg Hobson began the first park websites and offers many helpful suggestions for the park.

Brian Adams, Skagit County Parks Director, working with Jane Zillig and Molly Doran at the Skagit Land Trust, helped secure easements to expand our park's connections, as well as support me in our management of parks. Bob Vaux, manager of Washington Park in Anacortes, always has a smiling face and helpful ideas and broad perspective.

Gene Earnest, Bob Blunk, Doug Shepherd, Larry Lazzeri, Gene Joy, Joan and Duane Melcher, and my many other friends in SWITMO care about this park in practical ways, building trails and clearing trails, giving sweat equity as proof of their enduring support.

Rick Machin can always be counted on to help remove Scotch broom, assist with ranger interviews, and just keep this park looking better. He has shown great kindness to me throughout my time here. Jay Scott and Let Curvers are dedicated to the tasks of helping remove invasive species and providing smiling faces. Gene and Barbara Kiver are also frequent helping hands and hearts.

Julian and Jean Lee have provided hundreds of hours of service to the park in many special ways, helping restore historical signs, finishing the interior of the Rosario office, cleaning off the Bowman launch, paying for the repairs of park docks and roadways, and supporting many other improvements as well.

A big thank you to Liz Merriman, Brian Shelly, Rick Colombo, Barb Shaw, Estelle Johnson, Matt Klope, Jill Johnson, Terica Ginther, Steve Young, Harold Harrington, George Churchill, Barry Wenaas, and other Foundation members past and present who gave and gave, and many who still give so generously of their time and energy to make this a better park.

Brett and Terica Ginther of Deception Pass Tours deserve a big shout out as well. These two people help create the opportunities for visitors to learn about this park through their boat tours, the visitor kiosk at the bridge, and their generosity in helping support our Hope Island tours and other special events in the park.

Erik and Megan Schorr have also contributed to the recreational and educational opportunities in this park, and have helped me with their professional opinions and generous hearts.

The Skagit and Island County Marine Resource Committees provide ongoing support for making our beaches better. There are so many names to share, but I just want to mention Jay Lind for his warmth and spirit.

The Northwest Straits Foundation has also made our beaches and waters better with their ongoing work. Two people stand out: Lisa Kaufman, who can explain the reason we need to do this work as well as anyone, and Joan Drinkwin, who brought the Cornet Bay and Bowman Bay beach projects together. Without them, these improvements would not have happened.

Jan Kocian, a local diver, has monitored our underwater environment and shared what he sees each month through beautiful photographs and observations. Terry Slotemaker shared many discussions about the geology of the area. Nautilus Construction provided sensitive and professional restoration of the Rosario classroom and continues to give ongoing support of the park. Park neighbor Scott Harrison has been very helpful in digging into park history deeper and finding great stories. Eric Shen has provided ongoing financial support with Fix-It Days while helping us all transition our community to sustainability. Bud Rogers helped with many Cornet Bay stories.

I am grateful to Ron Newberry of the Whidbey News Times and Vince Richardson, Scott Terrell, and Kimberly Kauvel at the Skagit Valley Herald who have gotten the word out about the park with many of their stories.

Captain John Aydelotte helped the park many times, and helped me keep a balanced viewpoint on park plans.

Rainshadow Run coordinator James Varner and Deception Pass Dash creator Bill Walker brought these events to the park. Candice Burt created and hosts the park marathon and half marathon in April.

Jim O'Conner of North Whidbey Fire and Rescue has helped me seek professionalism in every work endeavor. Jay Brand, a park neighbor, stops by frequently to share a book or encourage me in some way. Vince Streano has shared his skills in photography and photo production with us for several years, creating many of the photos on display around the park. The Mount Erie Fire Department, led by Mike Noyes and assisted by Bob Parmley, has always been there for us as well, as have the many folks at North Whidbey Fire and Rescue. To all our local emergency services and law enforcement brothers and sisters, thank you for being here.

Bill Overby, my predecessor as manager of this park, still carries the aura and well-deserved reputation of being the ultimate professional ranger and leader of this park. I could never fill those shoes.

Rick Blank, assistant manager for the park for more than twenty six years now, sparkles in his love of this park and his skill at taking care of it. His right hand leadership with me has been invaluable and essential for taking care of the details of this park each and every day.

Many other park staff have also been at the park longer than I have, including Jim Aggergaard, Jeri Lancaster, Bill Ruh, Ben Shook, Mark Lunz, Marvin Wold, and Darlene Clark. Talk about low turnover at a job! These people love what they do and they are good at it. More recent arrivals include me, Todd Harris, Jason Stapert, John Whittet, Bryce Watkinson, Doug DeYoung, and Paige Ritterbusch. Rick Colombo has become a mainstay as well, wearing many hats and fulfilling many roles.

It was Brian Evans, a park aide here for a couple years, who suggested that we needed a short and simple guide to the park. Sorry, Brian, this book is neither short or simple. But you had a good idea. Maybe somebody will do it someday.

There are so many more dear people who fill my life with joy and who have made my experience here full of meaning. I am sorry I have not named you all. I can only hope you find your investment in me reflected in the thoughts and ideas expressed within, and for that I offer my thanks.

And finally, Susannah Hartt, and our children Jordan, Taffy, Bryan, Lindsay, Charlie, and Ben have all enjoyed the chance to live here or at least have weekends or holidays here, along with our grandchildren Elora, Audrey, Kataleya, Naomi, and JJ. They all bless me beyond words and beyond the reach of time.

Introduction

Deception Pass is iconic. It is epic. It is among the most scenic and yet accessible wonders of the State of Washington.

You may have visited here before, in which case you remember the majestic sweep of beauty as you first see the bridge, or the magical moments of walks on the beach or of hikes to the headlands.

If you have never been here, you are in for a special treat. The park is the most popular state park in Washington for many reasons. It offers stunningly dramatic vistas a step or two from your car door; it offers deep solitude on trails through old growth forests; it offers miles of windswept shorelines, acres of wildflower meadows, quiet lakes and busy playgrounds.

It has several cabins and hundreds of campsites in three different campgrounds and on several islands nearby.

Those looking for fishing can choose between two trout-filled lakes or the rich salt waters of the Pass, accessible by beach, dock, or boat. Hikers can climb hills or descend to hidden pockets along the water; they can walk hushed forests or windy ridges.

Eagles and seagulls call this place home; it is also home to rich stories of tribal life and historical structures still in use.

Those who come will never forget having been here. The experiences touch our soul. The memories linger long after the smoke of the campfire or the colors of the sunset have faded away.

I have learned much about this place, and I have seen the love that millions of others have in their hearts for this park too.

I wrote this book to help introduce the magnificent features of the park to those who have never been here, and to open up some of the hidden gems to those who know the park already.

The more we learn about this place, the more we respect, appreciate, and value its heritage and marvelous wonders. I hope the ideas here will inspire some to become active in helping protect the park for the future, whether as a visitor, volunteer, employee, or friend.

A word of caution:

The history chapter reminds me in black and white that minor changes will happen every year, affecting which campsites are open, or where trails may lead, or how much it costs to visit, or when a facility is open.

Future editions of this book can update those changes. But that doesn't help you plan your visit today if the change just happened yesterday.

So please refer to the appropriate websites if you need to know the current fees, the most recent facility upgrades or area closures, or to avoid any other possible monkey-wrench to your plans.

Change is inevitable. I marvel at the changes that the park has seen just in the past 200 years, with tribal life becoming pioneer life, many of the park's forests being logged, the lands being farmed and mined, and ferries giving way to bridges and communities and modern life.

And although the setting of the park remains fairly constant in the span of our lifetimes, the operational details and facilities change frequently.

But parks are forever, if we protect them. And the values of the park will bless our grandchildren and beyond if we manage our parks as inviolate legacies of the past, opportunities for re-creation in the present, and magnificent treasures for the future.

Give this park your care.

Setting

"To stand at the edge of the sea, to sense the ebb and flow of the tides, to feel the breath of a mist over a great salt marsh... is to have knowledge of things as nearly eternal as any earthly life can be."
--Rachel Carson

You will remember the moment, that first time that you encounter Deception Pass. You come to the edge, the earth falls away at your feet, and there before you is a gaping hole in the planet with a bridge arching gracefully across the expanse.

Then you see the surrounding landscape, of black-green trees framing the bridge, of waters rushing underneath, and of bold headlands book ending the sweep of log-strewn beaches. The swirling water stretches beyond jewel drops of islands all the way to the horizon, with distant mountain ranges becoming the backdrop east and west.

It takes a few minutes to begin to take it all in.

I still have that sudden intake of breath every time I come to the Pass, and I have done that nearly every day for over a decade. No, it never gets old or less than amazing. In sunlight or fog, day or night, howling winds or quiet calm, it never ceases to touch my heart and spark my imagination.

Welcome

The Pass is central to Deception Pass State Park, but it is only one facet of the many places to explore, of the many stories to hear, and of the many lessons to learn.

With dramatic headlands, tranquil forests, windswept beaches, and colorful meadows, the park captures your imagination and invites your exploration.

Spanning the tips of Whidbey and Fidalgo Islands, the park is treasured for its spectacular scenery, rich history, and diverse recreational opportunities.

The park is also respected for its sacred values which set this park apart from everyday life.

This area has been home to Coastal Salish tribes who never forget the beautiful world that gave them being. Even the rocks along the silent seashore thrill with memories of past events as part of the life of the tribes.

Spanish explorers visited the area in the late 1700s, leaving behind many Spanish names that we still use today, including Rosario Beach and Fidalgo Island.

In 1792, Captain George Vancouver of England also explored the area, and gave the name "Deception Passage" to the waterway that is now the namesake of this park.

The United States Government set aside the land around the Pass as a military reservation shortly after the Civil War. Hidden from public access, the land remained protected from the buzz of pioneering activity taking place throughout this area over the next few decades.

With no future need for shoreline forts in the area, the federal government gave the untrammeled land to the State of Washington in 1922 for public recreation, creating Deception Pass State Park.

During the Depression, the Civilian Conservation Corps built the roads, shelters, and trails of the park for visitors to be able to use and enjoy. Since then, the park has grown in size, in popularity, and in the memories and dreams of all who visit.

The park welcomes you. I hope this book helps you discover its many secrets and pleasures. Explore its hidden treasures. Get close to its wild heart of life. Share it with friends and family, or experience it in quiet solitude.

Adventure awaits you.

Go.

Explore.

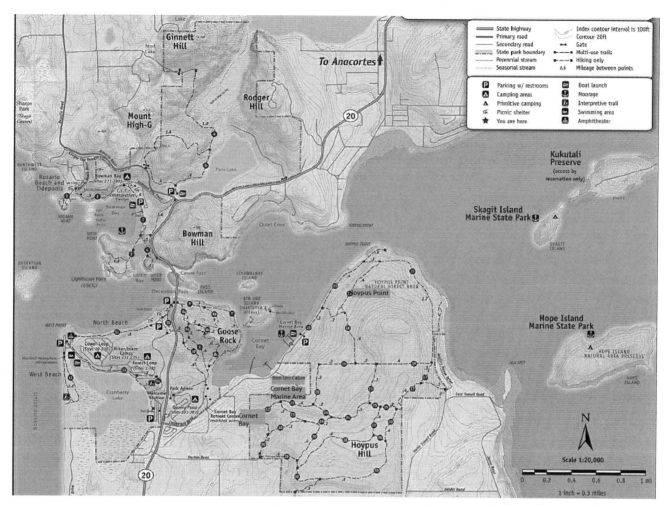

This excerpt of the topographic map of the park and its trails is available in full color as a two-foot by three-foot folding map. I highly recommend the map for hiking on the park's trails. You can pick it up for a couple dollars at the park store. The map can also be found on every bulletin board in the park. It is also available online at the Foundation website, at www.deceptionpassfoundation.org (This version of the map does not show the new addition of land on the east side of Hoypus Hill.)

Features

Like an octopus with multiple arms, the park has several named areas, shared around the common hub of the Pass. Each of these areas ties back to the center of the park, and each is also distinct from the centrality of the bridge experience.

Each area of the park is united by the connecting waters of the Pass. Together they form the complex simplicity of the park as a whole.

Rosario sits off in the far northwest corner, quiet and subdued yet alive in mystery and beauty.

Bowman Bay focuses on the quiet waters of the bay and the recreational opportunities on its shores, with camping, picnicking, kayaking, and special events sharing the space with the hub of several trails.

The Pass Lake area now includes not only fishing and boating on the lake but also the miles of trails through forested lands and meadows beyond, a gateway to sites seldom seen, earned by each step along the trails.

Goose Rock rises above the bridge as a short but memorable hike for those willing to climb above the crowds.

Below, North Beach offers quiet majesty near the flowing of the waters of the Pass, while around the corner, busy West Beach beckons swimmers and storm lovers, picnickers and strollers.

Sandwiched between those two beaches, the Cranberry Campground becomes home to thousands of campers every night during the busy season. It echoes with the laughter of kids playing and the Rockwell pictures of families gathered around a campfire.

Lying just the proverbial stone's throw from the waves of the Salish Sea, Cranberry Lake provides a peaceful freshwater alternative to the miles of saltwater framing the park.

On the east side of the highway that bisects the park, the Quarry Pond Campground offers year round camping and cabin sites.

East of that, tucked away from the busy activities elsewhere in the park, the Cornet Bay Retreat Center lies separate and hidden from the rest of the park, but open and inviting as a gathering place for large groups. The retreat center has room for 200 overnighters in cabins both rustic and modern, some with beds and most with bunks, as well as a lodge with a modern professional kitchen and other meeting spaces and play areas.

Further east leads to the Cornet Bay boat launch area, and beyond that to a couple square miles of forest at Hoypus Point and Hoypus Hill.

Several islands dot the waters of the Pass, offering wildlife a haven safe from people on some, and offering people a haven safe from modern concerns on others.

The newest addition to Deception Pass State Park, Kiket Island, lies farther east of the Pass, adding even more opportunities for protecting our natural heritage around the Salish Sea and providing low-impact recreational activities in a culturally rich and meaningful area.

Almost unknown to most visitors to the area, and even to most locals, Dugualla State Park lies a few miles south of Deception Pass, and offers a square mile of quiet forest and remote beach, much of it untouched by human hands.

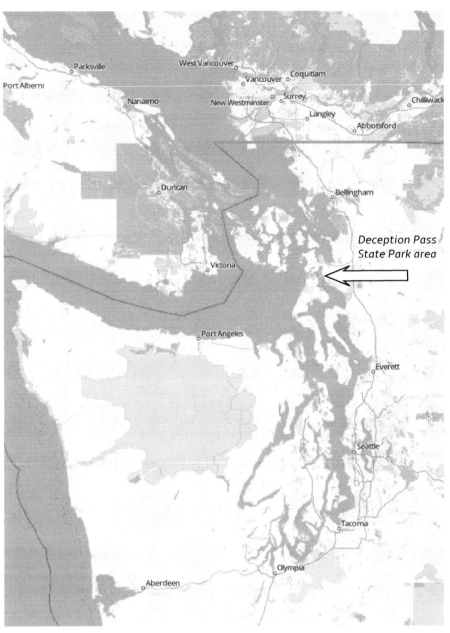

These and other park features are explored in detail in the following pages.

Explore this grand park as you have time and interest. New discoveries await around every corner, in all weather, throughout the seasons of the year.

Share what you find.

Experience the ecstasy of each and every discovery, each moment of life that we can enjoy, each step of exploration in a park waiting to be discovered anew.

The white arrow points to the Deception Pass State Park vicinity in its relationship to the towns, parks, and waterways of the Salish Sea of Western Washington and southwestern British Columbia. The park lies south of the Fidalgo Island town of Anacortes and north of the Whidbey Island town of Oak Harbor. The park fills part of the south end of Fidalgo Island and the north end of Whidbey Island, along with several islands in the waters nearby. Image courtesy of OpenStreetMap.

So there I am.

It's my first spring at Deception Pass. It's a gorgeous April morning, and it's freezing cold. Still, how often do I get a chance to see the bridge at sunrise on a beautiful morning like this. I never have before. I drive into the park and down to North Beach, at the amphitheater, figuring the sun will rise directly behind the bridge as seen from here.

I wait in the cold early dawn, watching the midnight blue turning to deep blue then to a powder blue or chiffon yellow now. My fingers snap a few pictures, then I quickly put them back into warm pockets. A sailboat motors in from the west as the eastern skyline grows lighter and more golden. The sailboat gets close to the bridge, and the skyline behind spills a box of crayons mixed together with purples and golds and blues and greens and yellows and oranges and reds. The bridge silhouettes in black, an umbrella above the sailboat now going under. I click a few more pictures.

This is a memorable experience, I feel. Glad I got up early and saw this new perspective. Glad the sun cooperated so well. Glad my fingers are back in the warm pockets again. I head home.

A couple years later, our agency wants to have icon pictures for each park that they can develop into images for shirts or posters or whatever. I send in four or five pictures, including this one of the sunrise. A couple months later we get the sailboat-under-the-bridge-at-sunrise image back as a complete icon package, in black and white and color, in round, square, and rectangle, with the name of the park around the edges. I like it.

My boss isn't sure – the bridge is not part of the park, he says. True, the bridge isn't technically part of the park.

But seriously, the bridge is part of the iconic memories and emotions we all share about the park. People see the bridge and they think "Deception Pass". Having the sailboat gives it life, and having the headlands on each side gives it context. And having a sunrise makes me smile. And having the park surrounding the bridge gives us a place where images like this are possible.

That was over a dozen years ago. The logo graces the sweatshirt I am wearing as I type this. And I remember that morning.

My fingers would have appreciated the pockets on this sweatshirt.

Come to our entrance station, campground store, or the visitor center at the bridge for items you can wear, such as sweatshirts, polos, t-shirts, fleece coats, hats, mugs, or other useful ways to keep you warm. Your financial support contributes to the educational programs and presentations at the park.

Wear the logo with joy and pride. And keep your fingers warm.

Creating

"Earth and sky, woods and fields, lakes and rivers, the mountains and the sea, are excellent schoolmasters, and teach some of us more than we can ever learn from books."

– John Lubbock

One way to get to know the park is by exploring it from the ground up, discovering how these landforms were created, and looking at what continues to shape and affect our lands today.

Rocks

Our earth is formed with a central core, solid and liquid, surrounded by a couple thousand miles of mantle, on which ride our oceanic and continental crusts. The crusts are broken into plates which move around the planet bumping into each other to create the landforms that we see today.

In this corner of the planet, the eastward moving, heavier Juan de Fuca oceanic plate is sinking beneath the westward moving and lighter North American continental plate. Meanwhile, the Pacific Plate beneath most of the Pacific Ocean is sliding northwestward, creating further tensions in the area.

Eons ago, ocean waves lapped a shoreline somewhere near today's Idaho border. A mass of land came in and docked against the older North American plate, moving the shoreline westwards. Much later this happened again, this time creating the North Cascades, and moving the shoreline westward to what is now the foothills of the Cascades. More pieces of plates arrived over time, creating landforms such as the San Juans and Olympics.

Over time, this area became a sandwich of subsurface igneous rock mixed with layers of sedimentary rocks from the oceanic crusts, volcanic rock formed from the melting of the plates, and metamorphic rock layers changed from their original structure to new forms due to pressure and heat.

The multi-layered sandwich then tilted from the pressures of moving plates. Fidalgo Island and northern Whidbey Island are thus a famous blend of volcanic ocean crust with remnants of the earth's mantle as its base.

At Rosario, the climbing wall east of the parking lot shows volcanic basalt and other versions of basalt. Most of Rosario Head itself and an area near Lighthouse Point have pillow basalts, molten rock that comes in contact with cold ocean water.

Rock Types

Our planet's surface has three basic sources of rock development:

Igneous: *magma, or melted rock, that has cooled and hardened. If it forms underground, it cools slowly and forms a course grained rock. If it cools rapidly at the earth's surface, as in a lava flow, it has fine grains.*
Common examples: basalt, granite, andesite

Sedimentary: *formed from the accumulation of sediments, such as sands, mud, or plant or animal materials. They become cemented together by chemicals, and show layering parallel to the way they were deposited.*
Common examples: shale, sandstone, limestone

Metamorphic *("changed body"): rock that has been subjected to pressures so intense or heat so hot that the rock structure is transformed into a denser material, an entirely different composition from the original rock.*
Common examples: slate (from shale), gneiss, schist.

Ribbon chert on the northwest side of Rosario Head, above the tidepools. Deception Island and the Olympic Mountains can be seen beyond.

Rosario Head also has a great example of ribbon chert, a combination of shale and rock formed from the silica skeletons of plankton.

Rosario Head actually belongs to the San Juan Island rock formations, distinct from the rest of Fidalgo Island! When the San Juan rocks and local rocks collided, the ribbon chert got folded and turned on edge, forming distinctive tight ridges like rope above the tidepool area.

The nearby Ginnett area has a rock quarry composed of tuffaceous argillite, a mixture of clay and fine-grained volcanic fragments. The rock comes in two colors in the park, a brick red and a gray-green.

The Deception Pass Bridge rests on siltstone and greywacke at the north end. These are sand and clay rocks mixed with grains of volcanic fragments.

Goose Rock rises above the landscape as a monolithic volcanic rock.

Nearly a mile of ice blanketed the entire Salish Sea area just a few thousand years ago. Most of the ice came south out of Canada, and most of Whidbey Island shows north-south scouring. However, toward the end of the glacial period, glaciers from the Cascades crossed north Whidbey, moving westward, leaving east-west landforms and striations in the rock and burying most of the area in glacial debris carved from the earth as the glaciers moved.

Kiket, Skagit, and Hope Islands, however, still show their bedrock base on the north, west, and south sides, with glacial outwash covering the centers of the islands.

Hope Island's bedrock originated in the Jurassic age, with serpentite and other rock types exposed very clearly, making great bald habitats. Kiket has sedimentary rocks that were changed by pressure and chemical action, now clearly exposed where it is not covered by the glacial debris.

A granite erratic sits on the south side of Rosario Head, dumped by the glacier and now totally out of place with the other rocks there.

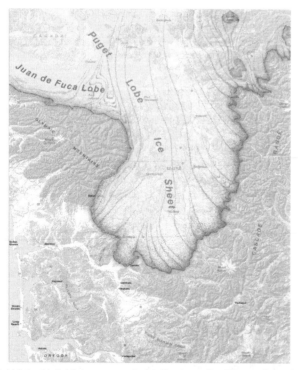

A thick glacial lobe scoured out the trough of Puget Sound, burying the land under thousands of feet of ice. Courtesy of Washington's Department of Natural Resources.

When the glaciers retreated, they left behind scattered boulders that they brought down from Canada or the North Cascades, looking completely out of place with the local rocks because they are so different. These odd droppings are called glacial erratics, and can be found in odd places on the landscape as if they just dropped out of the sky, or to be exact, melted out of the glacier. Usually they are distinctive because they are salt-and-pepper granite, sitting on the bedrock of gray basalt, as on the south side of Rosario Head, in the tidepools, near site 41, and in various other places throughout the park, too.

The glaciers also left behind a mixture of rock, gravel, dirt, and clay. In some places the melting left behind solid layers of clay, and then a gravelly soil on top, creating a potentially unstable foundation for anything built on top of this ground. Hoypus is a deep mess of glacial outwash, with layers of clay holding water near the surface over much of the hill, creating muddy conditions on trails and places of slippage near Hoypus Point.

Lidar image showing the terrain of Island County, with Deception Pass at the very top. Notice that the striations from glacial scouring run north - south over most of Whidbey and Camano Islands except at the north end, where the most recent glaciers out of the Skagit Valley area carved the land in an east-west direction.
[Image courtesy of Joe Sheldon, Whidbey Audubon]

A significant fault line runs east-west south of the park near the naval airbase and Dugualla Bay. A branch of this fault apparently runs through the Pass toward Lopez Island to the west. The Pass itself could be strong evidence of a crustal shifting line, subject to future earthquakes.

Geologists love the many stories that can be found in Deception Pass and around Fidalgo Island. The plates are still in motion, and the landscape of today will be shifting in the future, creating new stories yet to be told.

Tides

The moon and sun are always pulling on our planet. Because the moon is so close, the difference between how it pulls on one part of the planet is different from how it pulls elsewhere, giving us tides as the moon rotates around the earth.

At Deception Pass, we generally have two high tides and two low tides every day. One of the high tides is usually higher than the other, and one of the low tides is usually lower than the other. The tidal range can be more than fifteen feet between low and high tide.

Springtime and summer have minus tides (below zero, which is the average lower low tide) in the morning. In the fall and winter the minus tides are mostly at night. The best time to visit Rosario's tidepools is when it is a minus tide, as this is when you will see the lowest and richest portions of the tidepools.

When the moon and sun are aligned, during a full moon or new moon, the tides will be higher than average and lower than average. When the air pressure is lower, or the wind blowing onshore, or there is extra rain or melt-water in the Skagit River, we get super or king tides, higher tides than predicted. Occasionally king tides can flood the parking lot at Cornet Bay or the amphitheater at West Beach. If a storm blows through at the same time, the beaches can change quickly and dramatically.

Currents

Because the moon and sun are pulling water around the planet, we get currents. And because Deception Pass is a narrow channel for that moving water, we get fast-moving currents through the Pass.

Most of the water from the east side of Whidbey Island has to go through the Pass as the tide ebbs, and then return through the Pass on the flood tide.

These currents can race through at speeds of over eight knots, or nine miles per hour. This is obviously far faster than anyone can swim or paddle.

As the water ebbs, it piles up on the east side of Pass Island, as the water cannot get through as quickly as the moon is pulling it that way. Water on the west side has

An ebb tide races out the Pass like a river in flood stage, flowing at the narrow channel at up to nine miles an hour. No wonder Vancouver was deceived!

ebbed quickly through the wide channel of Admiralty Inlet. Water east of Whidbey struggles to catch up, and remains at a higher level, like a wall, to the east of Pass Island.

As the water churns through the Pass, it creates eddies and whirlpools. These whirlpools can be dangerous to small craft such as canoes or small rowboats; the churning water can turn them so quickly that they capsize. However, many kayakers love going into these eddies and whirlpools to play in the rapids and slalom on the rushing water. Sometimes we get calls to 911 concerned that a kayaker has flipped under the bridge. Oftentimes it is just a well-trained kayaker having fun, and they will pop back upright again in a few seconds.

However, this is not a play area for inexperienced paddlers; we have had to rescue many boaters from the waters of the Pass when they encounter conditions that are over their head.

As the tide changes from ebbing to flood, or flood to ebb, there is a short amount of time when the water is not moving. This is 'slack tide', and lasts about an hour on average. Interestingly, slack tide actually occurs about an hour before the tide is at the highest or lowest point in Cornet Bay. In other words, when the tide is at its lowest point at Cornet Bay, the water has already been flooding into the Pass for over an hour, gaining speed as the tide rises. The slack tends to match up with the high or low tide at Bowman Bay on the outside of the Pass, not the high or low on the inside at Cornet Bay. The time difference between these two locations, only a mile apart, is nearly an hour. It takes that long for all the water backed up inside the Pass to escape out the narrow opening, and visa versa.

Divers and kayakers sometimes get caught by this difference. They may expect to be in a slack tide, and then find themselves caught by the change coming earlier than expected. Being unable to swim or paddle as fast as the current, they are pulled through the Pass.

The current is less strong the farther you are from the Pass, with average maximum currents of three knots at Deception Island and Hoypus Point, and two knots at Hope Island and Rosario.

Beaches
(How they were made)

One of the outstanding attractions at Deception Pass is the multitude, depth, and variety of its beaches. There are over seventeen miles of saltwater beaches and headlands around the park.

The beaches have been created -- and continue to be created -- by the active forces of winds, waves, rivers, tides, and current. The predominant wind around here is out of the southeast. Waves carve into the headlands of Whidbey Island, filling the water with sand and gravel. The south wind pushes the sand and gravel northward, creating the long strand at West Beach.

At one time, centuries ago, Cranberry Lake may have been a salt marsh, open to the sea. The longshore currents from Whidbey pushed enough sand and gravel across its mouth through the years to close off the connection and leave a freshwater lake that now drains through miles of beaver habitat to an outlet near the Navy airbase.

The Skagit River east of Whidbey Island pushes millions of tons of sand downstream each year, which then heads past Hope and Skagit Islands toward the Pass. Some of the sand gets stuck in Cornet Bay, creating a muddy beach of almost quicksand texture. Most of the sand flows out the Pass, then gets pushed northward by the southeast winds and tidal action to settle out in Lottie Bay, all around Deception Island, in Bowman Bay, and in the waters around these areas. Although the Pass itself is over 180 feet deep in places, the deposits have created a sand bar only 25 feet deep near Deception Island.

In summer, the winds come mostly out of the north, so this Skagit River sand gets pushed onto West Beach during the summer, creating a sandy playground for the busiest beach in the park at its busiest time.

Rosario's beach does not get the benefit of Skagit's sand. Instead, the rocks around Rosario have been worn down by tides and storms over the years to create a steep beach composed mostly of flat black volcanic stones, perfect for skipping across the bay. Just off the beach, however, the bay itself is buried in the thick sand of the Skagit.

Hoypus has the benefit of weaker tidal currents, and is protected from most storm winds, so the beach is a mix of sand and gravel, ideal for clams and beach walks.

North Beach, on the other hand, is scoured four times a day by tides that can range from a couple miles an hour to nearly nine miles an hour in each direction. This leaves a cobble and rock beach where sand has a hard time sticking around.

Kids playing volleyball between Cranberry Lake and West Beach. The sand came here from the bluffs to the south by the winds and waves of past millennia, eventually building this popular beach.

The many islands of the park have beaches that reflect the nature of the islands themselves. Northwest, Deception, Pass, Skagit, Ben Ure, and Strawberry are rocky outcroppings with basically no beaches at all, with small exceptions. Kiket and Hope have good beaches facing south toward the conveyor belt of sand from the Skagit River. The cove on Hope's northern side is muddy at low tide, but pleasant at high tide.

Each beach tells a story, a story of where it came from, and how it is best protected. Seawalls and other obstructions have damaged a couple of the park's beaches, but with good science and good sense, the damage is being reversed and those beaches are becoming healthy again.

Soil

Much of what you will discover about the habitats and associated plants and wildlife you find at Deception Pass is determined by the soil.

Look around at the ground you walk on, and mentally note how it compares with other places based on some of these concepts:
- Material: rocky, sandy, clay, course or fine, gravelly, forest debris mixed in?
- Porosity: dense or porous?
- Moisture: wet, moist, or dry?
- Slope: flat or tilted?
- Depth: Deep or shallow?
- Density: loose or compact?
- Cover: covered in duff (needles, leaves) or bare?
- Light: open to the sun, partially shaded, fully shaded?
- Odor: rich, smelly, light, or none?

Based on these observations, see how the soil affects what lives there. This park has a host of different soil types based on the ground beneath, erosion, water movement, and the plant growth all around.

Some of the soil is thin and fragile, taking hundreds or even thousands of years to accumulate even an inch or two. Other soils here are many feet deep, rich and capable of supporting tall forests. Poke your finger into the ground as you walk. See how they compare.

Weather

How would you like to live next to a refrigerator with its door open? In much of the country, summers are hot and relentless. Standing next to the open door of a refrigerator may sound pleasant for a few minutes or even for a day or two. And in the winter, when it may be well below freezing outside, having the air like the inside of your refrigerator sounds more comfortable than the freezer.

It never gets hot here. Or cold.

The Salish Sea is a refrigerator, with its waters averaging about 47 to 52 degrees F year round. In the summer, when Seattle is in the upper 70s or 80s, and much of the rest of the country in the 90s or more, Deception Pass is in the upper 60s or 70s at most, with a cool breeze off the water in the afternoons. If it gets really hot inland, you can almost guarantee that within a day or two, fog will roll across the Pass every morning and keep temperatures down in the 50s until late in the day, especially in mid to late summer. And in the winter, when snow and ice freeze much of the rest of the nation, Deception Pass has that moderating Salish Sea softening the colds into cool temperatures just above freezing. Snow is rare and short lived. Ponds seldom freeze over, and never for any extended periods of time.

The park lies partially in what is called the 'rain-shadow'. Winter storms come from the Pacific Ocean west of us. Blocking the path of those storms is a massive mountain range, the Olympics, which catch much of the moisture on the west side and create a drier zone immediately northeast of the mountains. The park lies at the east end of that shadow; the total rainfall at the park averages about 24 inches, compared to the 36 inches in Seattle, and not even comparable to the boot-busting amounts of 10 or 15 FEET that drench some places on the west side of the Olympics.

So why does Seattle in particular and the Pacific Northwest in general have a reputation for being rainy? It's not the quantity of rain, it's the frequency. While New York may get 45 inches in a year, and Miami over 60 inches, they get their rain in bunches. When it rains in those places, it pours. When it rains at Deception Pass, it rains for hours or days on end as a light mist becoming a mild rain then back to a mist, then holding off for a few hours, then back to a mist, then a light rain again, back and forth for days or weeks on end. A local resident at Cornet Bay said to me that this is the only place where it can rain all day and you might never get wet.

Clouds or fog can be counted on to be a part of the scenery much of the time. The United States as a whole averages about 205 days of sunshine a year. This park receives almost two months fewer days than that, barely getting 150 days a year.

Snow, on the other hand, is a rarity too. The park averages 4 inches a year, total, all year long. We haven't had more than a half inch for the past several years. Maybe we are due. Maybe we are getting even less now with the climate changing the way it is.

Rain drenching the woods in a steady drizzle; sometimes these last for days on end.

Wind? Yes, it blows here. Being next to the Strait of Juan de Fuca and other large bodies of open fetch, the air is seldom still. Winter storms can be frequent, but rarely becoming destructive. Some memorable storms include the Columbus Day storm in 1962, when winds exceeded 80 miles per hour; the December 28, 1990 windstorm that came out of the north, a most unusual direction that caught trees unaccustomed to the new direction and left much of the park's north-facing forests horizontal instead of vertical; and the Hanukkah Eve storm of 2006, when winds toppled trees in the campground like match sticks.

We get gale force winds several times a year, mostly out of the southeast. When they turn out of the west, or north, we expect damage. To protect campers from these expected hazards, we close the most heavily forested campgrounds in the winter season, with just the Quarry Pond campground available, providing greater safety for our campers and greater peace of mind for the park manager.

Commonly, the winter winds are out of the southeast, and the summer winds out of the northwest. Southerly winds tend to be warmer than northerly winds, for obvious reasons, but also wetter, as they bring in the storm fronts from off the ocean.

One other unusual feature of the Pacific Northwest in general is the summer drought. When most of the central and eastern parts of the nation receive considerable rainfall in summer, the west is dry, very dry, comparatively. Although it may be cool and cloudy, it is rarely wet during the height of summer. The soils dry out, picnics are usually predictably rain-free (remember that qualifier word 'usually'), fire danger increases dramatically, and we play outside a lot.

Fog rolling through the Pass at about noon on a summer day.

Having said all that, I must add that people from most other parts of the United States say that Pacific Northwest weather is nothing compared to the winds, the lightning, the snow, the rains, the hail, the ice, and everything else that they deal with almost routinely.

They are right. Things are mostly pretty mellow here.

So how to best prepare for the weather? Expect anything, but it probably won't be very severe.

Regardless of the season, bring a light raincoat, a sweater or sweatshirt, a warm shirt, a t-shirt, long pants, shorts, a hat for sun or rain, and boots and tennis shoes and sandals. Yes, it's okay to wear wool socks in your sandals around here.

Rainfall in inches for most of the state of Washington. The very light color at the north end of Puget Sound shows the rain-shadow effect from the Olympic Mountains. This park gets about 24" annually. Eastern Washington is also drier. Map courtesy of the United States Geological Survey.

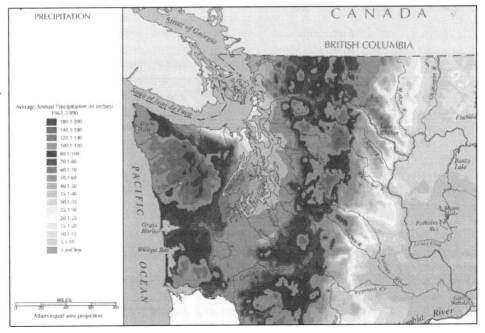

Waves from a summer storm pound the rocks at West Point.

miles per hour, perhaps with gusts approaching 80 or more. It was not only the speed and ferocity of the wind, it was also the direction -- out of the north. Our trees are accustomed to strong winds from the south, or maybe the west on occasion, but not with this speed from the north.

Trees fell like matchsticks anywhere exposed to the north wind. North Beach was a jumble of tree trunks down everywhere. The Cranberry Campground was hit hard, losing dozens of trees.

January 20, 1993: Inauguration Day Storm

Freakish low pressure brought 60 mile per hour winds and more to the Whidbey Island area, knocking out power for several days for many people.

We sell many sweatshirts here in the summer because Seattle area campers did not expect to be playing near the open door of a refrigerator.

If you are tenting, consider bringing a tarp or a good rainfly to cover your tent, and one for the picnic table too. I don't care if it looks sunny outside, be ready for anything.

Remember that Bowman Bay will stay foggy in the summer longer than the Forest Loop and far longer than Quarry Pond, so choose your campsite depending on whether you want warmth or character.

If you want pictures of fog coming through the bridge, a classic shot from the north side of the bridge will be available as the fog begins to break up, usually toward noon, but it can happen whenever conditions are right. It is particularly photogenic if there is an early morning fog with low light coming through the pass.

Recent Windstorms

October 12, 1962 Columbus Day Storm

I was 7 years old, and remember the wind singing through the wires in Seattle. Wind speeds were in excess of 85 to 90 miles per hour on Whidbey Island, but the island was spared some of the brunt of that storm. Still, the park had to have a logging sale to remove thousands of board feet of fallen trees.

December 28, 1990 Arctic Blast

The latter part of December that year was cold, bitterly cold, with temperatures in the teens. Early in the morning of the 28th, pressure gradients brought arctic air out of the Fraser River valley down across the San Juans, slamming into Deception Pass with winds exceeding 60

January, 2004, "Truck Against the Bridge-Railing" Storm

At about 6 a.m., with the wind screaming out of the west at my house on Pass Lake, I ventured outside. In the dark of early morning, I saw sparks rolling like bicycle wheels down my driveway, the result of downed but living power lines on my long driveway, flipping circles in the wind and sparking as they moved. My basketball hoop was on the ground, and I knew I was not going to be driving to work this day.

But the State Patrol called me to say there was a truck versus truck accident on the bridge. I asked another ranger to pick me up at the end of my driveway. I walked to Highway 20 and he and I drove from there to the bridge.

What a mess. There wasn't yet a lot of traffic; southbound cars were backed up from Pass Lake to the bridge. We drove around them onto the bridge to find a semi-truck facing south, leaning scarily on the eastern metal railing, its cab over the railing and the box trailer well above and beyond the railing. The wind was deafeningly loud and hitting like a freight train out of the west. The semi-truck had slid along the railing for dozens of feet, finally stopped by a small white truck going the opposite direction, now scrunched in its front end by the large front end of the semi.

I found the semi-truck driver, standing semi-dazed nearby. I had him sit in the cab of our ranger truck, and asked him what happened. He said he was driving south across the main span of the bridge when he was hit by a gust that pushed him into the opposite lane, then up against the final railing of the bridge. He looked out his cab window and down at the water below as he slid along the railing, expecting to be blown over the railing at any moment. The other truck stopping his forward momentum may have saved his life. He said when he got out of the cab (on the passenger side) he walked away and will never get back in a truck cab for the rest of his life.

It took more than five hours before the wind subsided enough to have tow trucks safely pull the trailer off the railing and move everything off the bridge.

December 14-15, 2006 -- Hanukkah Eve Storm

We knew the storm was coming. We asked campers to leave our Forest Loop, as large branches might come down and hit their trailers. One camper stayed in site 19.

That night, the wind tore through the park and across all of Western Washington. I went to work early the next day, the 15th, uncertain what I would find, hoping everyone was okay. There was no power anywhere. When I got to the Rosario intersection, I could see why. Huge firs lay across the power lines in the intersection, making it nearly impossible to get by. The wind continued to howl above us.

I went across the bridge. Trees buried the entrance and exit roads to the Cornet Bay Retreat Center. I went into the campground. The area from site 12 to site 19 was a tangle of pickup sticks made out of four and five foot thick trees piled on top of each other, obliterating campsites, tables, the dumpsters, and the road. One pile of trees was over twelve feet high.

To a lesser degree this scene was repeated throughout the campground and park. Over a hundred trees buried the Cranberry Campground, trunks down across campsites, restrooms, and roadways.

The camper in site 19? He had heard trees crashing down all around him in the night and fled the area. Amazingly, the trailer he left behind was untouched.

Nearly every park staff person came to work that day, even on days off, to see how each of them could help. We worked at it for the next several weeks to create some semblance of order.

It took months for authorities to authorize us to remove the trees by selling the wood to a logging company. The campground didn't open until late May.

So many old-growth trees fell during the Hanukkah Eve storm that they piled on top of each other like over-sized matchsticks. Maintenance specialist Marv Wold stands in front of site 15, which lies buried under all those trees.

August 29, 2015 -- Mid-summer Madness

We knew this one was coming too. And it was coming on a summer weekend, with a full campground. And salmon fishing from North Beach was nearing its peak, filling that lot early in the morning. And the trees were in full leaf, creating sails that would catch every gust. And we were in the middle of a three month drought, stressing trees further.

We warned every camper to consider moving somewhere safe for the storm. But few did.

By 10 a.m., the winds were rising, and we lost power as lines went down along Highway 20. I drove to North Beach, and as I drove small branches pelted my truck like rainfall. I got to the beach and told everyone to leave. They understood, and started packing up. Park staff closed the gates to the park.

Then things started happening in the campground. A tree fell across the entrance to a campsite, trapping the campers. I gave the order to close the campground and move everyone to West Beach or Cornet Bay. We drove around the campground (235 campsites in the Cranberry loops) telling everyone to leave. Some did not want to. I told them they did not have a choice. It helped confirm my point when a tree fell across the top of one of the restrooms in front of some campers as they questioned my direction. Then more trees fell. People began to leave quicker and with no convincing necessary.

By noon we were at the peak of the storm. Trees fell across the West Beach road, blocking camper traffic from entering or exiting that beach. A tree fell across my Pass Lake driveway, blocking my family in.

By two in the afternoon, the winds reduced their intensity. Campers returned to their sites, but because there was no power, many of them decided to go home. Power wasn't restored until late on Monday. The park wasn't restored for a week as we cut trees and opened up roadways again.

March 10, 2016 – The Highest Tide

And we knew this storm was coming. What we didn't expect is that during its peak, it would bring higher storm surges at high tide than anyone around here had ever seen before.

The past few months had been wetter than ever. The previous week was windy and wet. The soil was saturated, tree roots were weak.

The wind blew for hours on end at speeds of well over 30 miles per hour sustained, and gusting to well over 50, sometimes hitting 60 mph in places. The park lost power for a few hours. We closed the park and evacuated our campers to the Quarry Pond campground.

The morning of the 10th, staff were cutting trees off the roadway at Bowman and elsewhere so that people who were there could leave. I arrived before daybreak, hoping to see Cornet Bay, which I knew would be flooding. But when I investigated park roads, I realized I would be busy helping get the roads open again.

I didn't get to Cornet Bay until an hour after high tide. There I found a huge pile of driftwood had buried the parking lot, and left its new high tide line of debris just a foot from the restroom, just inches from being able to go in the doors.

The south wind blew log debris from the Skagit River northward in Skagit Bay toward Kiket Island. The storm surge pushed the driftwood piles higher and higher on the tombolo, onto the first causeway well up the driveway there, and smashing the fence along the roadway. At the west end, the driftwood buried the trail going out to Flagstaff Island two feet deep, making the trail impassable. The high tide even put debris onto the old boat house foundation just north of that tombolo, where a building had stood for forty years with no issues from high tides.

From the conversations I had with park neighbors, this may have been the highest tide in anyone's memory.

Storms and events such as these capture our interest because they affect our life experience. They are rare.

And there will be more.

What I find amazing is how our life experience can be just as affected by the joys of the common days, the drizzle of a gentle May morning watering the rhody flowers on Goose Rock, or the splash of sun after the fog lifts from Lighthouse Point, almost blinding in beauty as it makes its surprise appearance and paints the earth in golden light.

Every day shares its beauty, every day gives a gift of time to experience another facet, another common sight given uncommon depth because it is today.

	High Temperature (F)	Low Temperature (F)	Precipitation (inches)	Days with precipitation	Hours of sunshine	Snowfall (inches)
Jan	47	37	3.58	18	69	0
Feb	50	36	2.32	14	108	1
Mar	54	39	2.32	16	178	0
Apr	58	43	1.93	14	207	0
May	64	47	1.89	12	253	0
Jun	69	51	1.5	9	268	0
Jul	73	54	0.87	5	312	0
Aug	74	54	1.02	4	281	0
Sep	69	51	1.54	7	221	0
Oct	60	45	2.76	13	142	0
Nov	51	40	4.69	18	72	1
Dec	46	35	3.43	17	52	1

Above: *Anacortes average monthly climate data.*

Below: *Anacortes average annual precipitation and temperature graphs.* Both charts adapted from the National Oceanic and Atmospheric Administration.

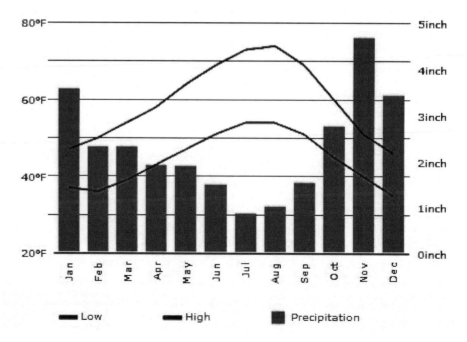

So there I am.

I'm heading out to Hope Island with my new boss, my first spring at Deception Pass State Park. He had asked me to find a good time to go out there that considered the tides, as the bay where we land goes dry at low tide, and we don't want to get stuck. I grew up on the water, I knew tides fairly well I figured, and so I say sure.

I check the tide tables, find Bowman Bay's schedule, and find a day where we could land just as the tide was coming back in so that we wouldn't have to worry about the bay going dry while we were tied up there.

We land. The bay is just as I expect, with just enough water to land the boat. I tie it up, keeping it tight so that as the tide rises, the boat won't be slack very soon. Then we hike around the island a bit to look at things and learn about what I could do there as the new manager.

Then we return to the boat to go back to Cornet Bay. The boat is high and dry. My boss looks at me at the same time that I look at him, only I have that "I don't understand what went wrong" look and he has that "I don't understand how you goofed on the simple task of picking the right time for the tide" look. Or it may be some other look, but I don't want to imagine what that could mean.

We sit there, the two of us. A long time. I try to make a joke about it, but my boss fails to see any humor. The tide goes out for another hour, then takes another hour to turn and get back to the boat, and a little more time before the boat is floating again. We get on board, and I quietly motor back to Cornet Bay.

A few years later, I am asked to teach about tides for the Beach Naturalist class. Not sure why they ask me; maybe they think I might learn something if I have to teach it. Enough time has passed, and I laugh in class about my mistake. The class goes well.

For some reason, I am asked to teach about tides at the Sound Water Stewards event on Whidbey Island called Sound Waters, and then at the Fidalgo Shoreline Academy class, and a few other places. It's a popular class, because tides can be confusing.

But at least we all laugh at the story of me

Hope Island's northern shore, looking east from the bay. A family rows out to their boat anchored nearby.

using the Bowman Bay tide table, a bay outside the Pass, to predict the Hope Island tides, an island inside the Pass. There is a difference of well over an hour.

We can learn from our mistakes. And serve as a bad example to help others. But mistakes like that are not a good way to impress your new boss.

Living

"When we try to pick out anything by itself, we find it hitched to everything else in the Universe."
-- John Muir

Some people want to know "what is that flower called?" or "what's the name of that bird?" It helps to be able to have a name for the different species that live among us, just like it is good for you to know the names of people living in your community.

But over time, you want to get to know your friends and neighbors on a deeper level, to learn why they live where they do, and what makes them who they are, and what kind of relationship you will be able to develop.

The same is true for the natural world. After we learn names, we want to learn why certain species live where they do, how they adapt to their specific environments, and how they connect to other species on this planet.

The following information does not delve into the depth of knowledge to be gained from studying our fellow species. But it does help you understand what you can find, and why it is there.

Hopefully by getting to know some of these friends, you may learn more about them in years to come and appreciate their character and gifts. We are all interconnected in the strands of fabric that weave our lives together.

Park volunteer extraordinaire Rick Colombo points out some special creature to a group of students at the Rosario tidepools.

PARK HABITATS

Deception Pass lies in the heart of a classic vegetative life zone, where the associated plants form communities that are readily identifiable and fairly well understood in general and in some detail.

Plant life here, like human life, grows and thrives in communities. We have several communities in the park that live side by side but with distinct community members and appearances.

Tidepools

Most of Puget Sound's beaches are a mixture of mud, sand, and gravel. From Olympia up to Seattle and Everett, Bremerton, and Port Townsend, the predominant beach type is a gentle rise of mud, sand, or gravel, or all three.

That is what makes the tidepools at Rosario so special. Rosario is the closest place for lower Puget Sound's population to go where bedrock is finally exposed, creating a diverse environment of rocky slopes, pools, mini-canyons, and ridges. Rosario's pools are not very large; in fact, the entire rocky area to explore is under an acre in size, but that's enough to be the home for an eclectic mix of tidepool critters.

Intertidal life faces the challenge of being at home in the salt water but being out of the water for a portion of each day. Some species are better adapted for being out of the water for a longer time than others.

Thus you will find different species high in the tide zone, reached only by the highest of the tides, than you will find low in the tidepools, exposed only when the tides are at their lowest. This layering is called tidal zonation. At Rosario, the zones are distinct with the different heights of rock side by side.

We find the highest zone inhabited by small periwinkles and barnacles, critters that can close up their home at a moment's notice and stay that way until the water returns hours later. An isopod may be found hiding in various cracks in the rock, and jumping insects may be feeding on detritus left by the previous high tide.

Lower down we start to see larger specimens and fuller coverage of the rocks. Rockweed covers much of this zone at Rosario. Once upon a time it was far thicker than it is now; our restoration efforts are watching for the return of rockweed as an indicator of success. Many other algaes live in this zone as well, colored green, red, and brown, providing habitat for many species of animals. Limpets, carpet-type sponges, larger barnacles, larger snails, and chitons make this area their home. Several species of smaller green anemones can live here too.

Toward the zero tide line the rocks are covered with water most of the time, so life can grow larger and be more diverse. Here we find mussels, larger chitons, purple shore crabs and others, nemertean worms, and occasional seastars living on the open rocks or in a forest of red algaes, sea lettuce, sea sacs, and

A Clown Nudibranch as seen underwater, observed at Rosario Beach. – Photo by Adam Lorio.

rockweed, denser than above. More varieties and larger sizes of anemones can live here as well.

Below the zero line, exposed for only an hour or two at the most every couple of weeks, we find the greatest abundance and variety of life. Feather boas and sea palms, among others, stand tall here, protecting a cornucopia of species, including lovely nudibranchs, sea cucumbers, sea urchins, even an octopus perhaps in the crevice of a rock.

The tidepools trap outgoing water in a natural aquarium to allow lower species to survive higher in the zones. Rosario displays several tidepools at a plus two tide that help us see what is living out of sight below.

Please respect all of these creatures as a guest in their home.

Eelgrass Beds

The Skagit River brings down silt and sand to fill some of the numerous bays here with an ideal environment for eelgrass.

Eelgrass is not seaweed; it is a flowering plant, actually related to pondweed. It grows in extensive beds where conditions allow, creating a forest-like habitat critical for the life cycles of plankton, invertebrates, forage fish, salmon, and birds.

When the sun brightens the water in spring, roots grow downward, stems spread out, grass-like shoots sprout up, and flowers form. When the days shorten again in fall, growth slows, storms break up the plants, and its seeds are dispersed.

An astounding assemblage of plants and animals make their homes within the dense cover of the eelgrass meadow. Each blade of eelgrass is a small food factory.

Eelgrass creating a forest-like canopy for a healthy and diverse habitat.

Diatoms, bacteria, and detritus (decaying plant and animal matter) gather on eelgrass leaves. This detritus provides food for many invertebrates. These invertebrates make eelgrass beds rich feeding areas for fish and marine birds. The density of the eelgrass beds provides safety for marine life as well, a hide-out from predators swimming above.

During low tides, eelgrass shelters small animals and plants from extreme temperatures. On tideflats, eelgrass beds hold moisture like a sponge, offering additional protection for small creatures. Many animals use eelgrass beds for nursery areas; others swim or walk among the leaves, or burrow in the sediments.

Deception Pass hosts several eelgrass beds at Cornet Bay. The existing docks over the bay reduce the light reaching the bedlands, damaging some of the eelgrass beds. New docks are in the works to be installed further offshore to avoid the beds. And the new docks will be covered with grating instead of solid decking to allow light to go through the docks, giving the life-giving eelgrass a better chance to survive.

A mother and son wander the trail among the grass-covered dunes at West Beach.

Sand Dunes

Deception Pass has a rare natural sand dune environment, the only significant dunes in the Puget Sound area. Located south of West Beach, between Cranberry Lake and the saltwater, the dunes spread out over twenty acres, with classic fore dunes, secondary dunes, and back dune woodlands.

Winds and waves from the west took the sandy material moving north along the beach and pushed it landward to form the dunes. Over time, specially adapted plants and eventually trees stabilize the dunes. Without them, the sand would just keep blowing. Sand does not hold moisture and lacks nutrients. Add drying winds, drought, and salt air and very few plants can survive on dunes. Those that do are slow growing and deeply rooted.

Typical grasses in the dunes include Elymus dune grass, seashore bluegrass, and European beachgrass.

As plants become established, they stabilize the sand with their spreading root systems.

Behind the fore dune, beach strawberry, sand verbena and others establish beach heads, so to speak, but are unable to stabilize the sand entirely. Between the fore dune and the secondary dunes, the hollows experience reduced winds and increased moisture, allowing a denser growth of vegetation. Flowers found here include yellow sand verbena, seashore lupine, beach peavine, black knotweed, and gumweed.

Check out how each flower adapts to this harsh environment, using hairy leaves to reduce moisture loss or hugging the ground to stay out of the wind, or having seeds that use the wind to scatter them, or spreading by roots rather than seeds.

If the dune plant life is damaged, the dunes are put in jeopardy by the eroding winds. We ask you to stay on the paths to avoid harming these fragile dune plants.

Behind the unstabilized dunes, the next micro-environment shows some stabilization, with a somewhat denser plant cover.

Under these harsh conditions, even the normally stately Sitka Spruce tree is stunted and grows more like a low rambling shrub. This also explains the small size of the old growth trees in the woods near the lake.

Inland of these dunes, the back dune can become established with larger plants and denser growth, eventually allowing salal, ocean spray, and even trees such as Douglas fir and Sitka spruce to rise up tall.

Wetlands

Wetlands are like sponges: they hold water, slowing down its movement; and they filter water, separating out solids such as sands and other particles. They offer food, shelter, water, and a stable home.

Coastal wetlands are declining in the Salish Sea, in both number and quality, due to the overwhelming impact of human resource use and development. These critical environments deserve our utmost protection.

Although difficult to explore because of the wet, muddy, and brushy conditions, our wetlands play a large role in feeding, supporting, and protecting a large amount of wildlife and the web of natural processes.

If the soil is sufficient, the dominant tree will probably be alder, with Sitka spruce also seen in some of our

Life thrives in the wetlands on the east edge of Cranberry Lake. It's messy, diverse, and productive.

wetland areas near the coastline. Western redcedar love damp areas as well, and can be a significant part of the biomass on the edges.

Salmonberry, red elderberry, Nootka rose, Pacific willow, and other willows fill the shrub layer, along with many other species. Sedges and rushes clearly indicate wet habitat. Skunk cabbage blooms in March in some of our wetlands. Nettles and sword fern may be abundanat in these habitats.

There are a few minor saltwater wetland examples at Deception Pass, including a small remnant at Bowman Bay, Lottie Bay, Cornet Bay, and at the Kukutali Preserve.

Freshwater inland wetlands can be found in Heilman Valley, the north shore of Pass Lake, along the Discovery Trail, in the Quarry Pond campground area, behind the Cornet Bay moorage parking lots, the Hoypus Hill area, and a couple large wetland complexes in the uplands of Dugualla State Park.

Forested Shorelines

When forests overhang beaches, they contribute important organic materials such as leaves, twigs, and insects to the marine environment. Insects from this vegetation are an important part of the diet of juvenile salmon species. Shading from these shoreline forests have also been shown to be essential for summer spawning surf smelt and sand lance, as it keeps the temperatures down on otherwise hot days. These forage fish spawn in the upper third of a beach, so it must have a healthy upper shoreline to allow their spawning to be successful.

The Salish Sea has lost nearly all of its original forested shorelines, severely weakening the health of the sea.

A variety of tree species come down to the water's edge at nearby Dugualla State Park, providing food and shade for marine life in this forested shoreline.

Deception Pass hosts miles of still-intact forested shorelines. Some of the classic examples are on both sides of Hoypus Point, North Beach, Goose Rock, Lighthouse Point, and all of the islands in the park. And Dugualla has a mile of classic Salish Sea forest hanging over its beaches.

The tree species found along our shorelines depends on the soil and location. Dugualla has an eclectic mix of alder, bigleaf maple, Douglas fir, grand fir, cedar, hemlock, and spruce, creating a mosaic of great variety. Bowman Bay has madrone and Douglas fir on the north shore, spruce on the northeast side, alder on the southeast, and back to Douglas fir again on the shaded south side of the bay.

Dry Upland Forests

Some of the most dramatic landscapes at Deception Pass are framed by a forest standing on rocky ground or

A classic dry forest environment at Deception Pass, with shallow, rocky soil supporting madrone and Douglas fir trees and a salal understory. This example is on Ben Ure Island.

sandy well-drained soils. Here you will also find grassy slopes, brushy areas, and moss-covered rocky knolls. Wildflowers put on a show from March through June here; in the winter the ground is carpeted with emerald mosses and ferns.

On south or southwest facing slopes we find shallow, rocky soil supporting species that out-compete other species by not needing as much water. The soil is shallow because plant life cannot produce as much biomass without water, which limits how much material is added to the ground throughout the year; therefore the soil stays thin.

Several species live here, and several do not. You will find madrone here, growing tall and angular, hanging out over beaches, holding onto rocks by tenacious root systems.

Lichens festoon a Douglas fir on West Point.

Douglas fir also grows here, not tall and stately, but with character. In this challenging environment, often lashed by winds because of their exposure, and parched by a lack of water, the trees become distinctive individuals. Lichens such as Fishnet lichen may hang from the branches.

In very dry locations exposed to the warmth of the south, such as the south slopes of Hope and Skagit islands, we even find juniper, and if you look closely, perhaps a cactus or two.

Common shrubs below the scattered trees include snowberry, dense pockets of salal, ocean spray, Oregon grape, Nootka rose, and thimbleberry. Stonecrop and strawberry hug the ground.

Some of the more typical examples of this habitat in the park include the hillside north of Bowman Bay, the south side of Lighthouse and Lottie Points, West Point, and the south sides of Deception, Ben Ure, Kiket, Skagit, and Hope Islands.

Deep Soil Forests

Many areas of the park have deeper soils, usually because they are in moister areas and support a greater density of plant life. North facing slopes have less direct sunlight, allowing more moisture to remain in the soil. Areas that have underground seeps or deep pockets of soil may also retain moisture, allowing vegetation to take root and grow with abundance.

Douglas fir is still the most common tree in our deep forest woods, sometimes achieving diameters of well over six feet and heights of over 200 feet. Their thick bark can withstand ground fires, and in centuries past fires occurred here every few decades or so. You can see fire-blackened bark on many of the large Douglas fir in the park.

In their shade, western hemlock and grand fir take root, growing slowly but steadily to eventually become dominant trees in a century or two. Pacific

Insider: Lichens

Diversity improves our options and adaptability. One family of plants makes a practical example of that idea. An algae and a fungus join forces to create a different family of plants called lichens.

The dominant partner is the fungus. Fungi are incapable of making their own food. They usually provide for themselves as parasites or decomposers. The lichen fungi cultivate partners that manufacture food by photosynthesis. Sometimes the partners are algae, other times cyanobacteria. Algae can photosynthesize, creating food out of sunlight and water. Cyanobacteria can take nitrogen gas from the air and turn it into usable compounds, so lichens with cyanobacteria can make major contributions to soil fertility.

"Lichens are fungi that have discovered agriculture", quips lichenologist Trevor Goward.

They are pioneers covering rocks, fence posts, sand, tree bark, even old barn siding. Most lichens look like peeling paint or strands of dead branches. Lichens grow in the leftover spots of the natural world that are too harsh or limited for most other organisms. Able to shut down during heat, cold, and drought, they may appear dead, but they are just waiting for conditions to improve to snap back into action.

All they need to grow are light and moisture, clean air, and freedom from competition. Most lichens grow very, very slowly, often less than a millimeter per year. Some lichens are thought to be among the oldest living things on Earth.

One species stands out at Deception Pass; it's hard to miss when you see it. It flows like a long beard, or a drapery of fishnet from the branches of trees close to the water. It has the understandable name of fishnet lichen. It picks up the moisture from foggy winds blowing through the trees, and stays protected from direct sunlight by the shade of the trees above them.

They give a mysterious and ancient feel to the forest as you walk among trees draped with this living fishnet. Find them at West Point, on the eastern half of the Dunes Trail, and along a handful of other shoreline locations.

And celebrate their partnership in diversity.

Sunlight filters through a foggy old growth area near North Beach. Young cedars and Western Hemlock trees thrive in the muted shade.

yew is uncommon but distinctive, looking more like a gangly tall shrub. Big-leaf maple may take hold where sunshine allows, such as the south side of Kiket Island.

Shrubs are dependent on the soil and exposure, with salal, currants, and Oregon grape in drier soils, sword fern and elderberry in wetter soils.

Deep soil forests can be found on the back of Ginnett Hill, north Bowman Hill, the north side of Goose Rock and Hoypus Point, North Beach, the north side of Kiket and Hope islands, and scattered locations around Dugualla.

Old Growth

Deception Pass is blessed with thousands of acres of forests, some of which have never been logged. Small pockets of these forests are true old growth forests. Healthy forests contain large live trees, standing dead trees, and downed logs, and a diversity of species, tree ages, and understory plants.

Alder and Douglas fir tend to be pioneer and early forest species after a disturbance. Over many decades and even centuries, hemlock and grand firs grow in their shade and eventually dominate the mix. Cedar and sword ferns grow in areas that have more moisture.

There is no exact definition of old growth. It is not just the presence of old trees. One commonly accepted description from Spies and Franklin states: "Old-growth forests are ecosystems distinguished by old trees and related structural attributes ... that may include tree size, accumulations of large dead woody material, number of canopy layers, species composition, and ecosystem function."

"If we've learned anything in the last 30 years," Spies says, "it's that our understanding of ecosystems will change, just as our understanding of old-growth forests changed during the late Twentieth century. We have also learned that the diversity of nature frequently defies our attempts to put it in nice boxes, either with words, scientific models, or plans. Natural systems are complex and our cultural responses to them are complex as well. Given the natural and social diversity, it would seem prudent to recognize as much diversity as possible in how we understand, manage, and plan for forests of the future whether they are old or young."

Some of the living trees in our forests show scorched bark, exhibiting the evidence of century-old forest fires, a natural part of this forest ecosystem. Old growth forests cycle energy, nutrients, and water more slowly and efficiently than a young forest. The forest canopy intercepts rainwater, thereby reducing the flow of water

Allison Alderman, former assistant manager of the NW region of Washington State Parks, tries to wrap her arms around an old-growth Douglas fir near North Beach.

down slopes, which helps stabilize the soil and decreases erosion.

So rather than try to define where old-growth forests can be found at Deception Pass, let's look at where we can find tremendous diversity. Most of the park has been disturbed to some degree by historical and pre-historical cultural practices. What we have today is a mosaic of many forest types, all of which have been changed by human activity.

But for diverse ecosystems, we have several good examples to study, explore, and enjoy. Check out Hoypus Point, North Beach, the east slope of Dugualla, the north side of Kiket Island, and the north half of Hope Island.

As this park's years of time become centuries, more of the park will display even greater diversity. These include the Ginnett Hill areas, Hoypus Hill, Skagit Island, and all of Dugualla.

Our future generations will thank us.

Balds

Near the top of Goose Rock, a wildflower garden provides a rainbow of beauty in the sunlight and shallow soil.

No, not the appearance of some of our visitors.

Balds are glacier-scraped bedrock areas in the park where the soil is too shallow to support shrubs or trees, so they are mostly covered with mosses and meadows.

The exposed bedrock prevents a thick accumulation of soil, making them extremely vulnerable to erosion and damage. This environment supports a great diversity of grasses, forbs, small shrubs, and vascular plant species, and serves as an important forage source for a variety of animals.

That is a fancy way of saying you will find colorful and beautiful wildflowers in the meadows framed by native grasses such as Idaho fescue and others. Grass widows, onions, and camas bloom in March and April, followed by a host of other flowers in May and early June.

Deception Pass has several classic examples of balds around the park. The best example is also off-limits to visitors at the present time, just to protect this rare and endangered habitat. It is on Flagstaff Point, at the west end of Kiket Island. Wildflowers grow here in great abundance, untrammeled by invasive boots or weeds. Please keep it that way.

Other great examples are at the top of Goose Rock, with smaller sized balds scattered on Lighthouse Point, Rosario, near the John Tursi Trail, and on Deception, Strawberry, Pass, Skagit, and Hope Islands.

Common Tree Species

To know the forests of the Pacific Northwest, you need to know a few key trees. The ones listed here are distinctive and common, so with a little effort they will become old friends.

Western redcedar

This classic tree likes very moist soils. You will find it scattered throughout the park, but primarily near fresh water lakes or in draws and valleys. The leaves are scales; the bark stringy.

The wood is so straight-grained it can be split into long pieces, ideal for roofs or siding on buildings. Western redcedar supplied many of the Samish and Swinomish lifestyle needs. They use it for making hats, diapers, canoes, longhouse roofing and siding, story poles, chests and other furniture, fishing nets, clothing, and more.

The wood is extremely durable and insect resistant. In Western culture it is popular for fence rails, shingles, and shakes.

The branches bow down then curve up again at the tips. The leaves have a yellowish-green cast, standing out from the darker blues of spruce and green-blacks of Douglas fir. They grow up to 200 feet, and often become hollow in their older age.

Another common name is "giant arbor-vitae", or tree of life, a reference to many mythical stories we know, based on the tree's medicinal values and decay resistance. You cannot forget the distinctive fragrance of their foliage, or of the wood when it is split open.

Western hemlock

Appointed as the state tree of Washington, the **Western hemlock** has short needles, generally flattened on each side of a branch. The cones are very small as well. The tops of hemlocks have no strength so they droop.

They love shade, and therefore may become the dominant tree in stable forests. Slow and steady can win the race. Seedlings will sprout anywhere the ground is moist. They will then grow slowly until they eventually take over a forest environment, or until the next disturbance starts the process all over again. But with the frequent winds around here, disturbances happen often.

Douglas fir

Doug fir is the dominant tree throughout the park. The needles are an inch to an inch and a half, and generally grow all around the branch. It reaches heights of 200 feet or more, and diameters of well over six feet.

The cones are distinctive with three pronged bracts alternating with the scales of the cone.

The bark is distinctively thick and deeply furrowed. This bark helps protect the Douglas fir from ground fires, and you can see many of these trees with blackened trunks from fires. One obvious fire-scarred tree is just north of the entrance station.

Douglas fir trees frame most of the views around the park, and get distinctive shapes when sculpted by the wind. Adaptability is a positive trait, and Doug firs are true champions in the forest world. They are long-lived, tough, and durable, and regenerate quickly following disturbances.

Grand fir

Halfway between the hemlock and Douglas fir in appearance, with longer, fatter needles than the hemlock but still flattened on a branch. The thin bark is nondescript, with minimal ridging. The tree is not very strong, and branches or whole trees break without much warning.

The cones grow upside down and disintegrate as they mature, so you rarely find true fir cones on the ground. It grows well in shade. It has a distinctive shape with a very dense crown, and often has multiple trunks, leading to further points of weakness and failure.

Sitka spruce

Solid trees with scaly bark that grow very close to the salt water. The wood is strong and light; this wood was used in fighter planes in World War 2. It's cones are about two or three inches long but without bracts. The needles,

Touching the needles of the Sitka spruce very gently!

however, are unforgettable. If you touch one, you will see why they are called 'needles'.

Nearly all the spruce in this park can be found within a hundred yards of saltwater. Look for them at the shoreline of Bowman Bay, along North Beach, and along the shores of Cornet Bay and Hoypus Point.

Seaside Juniper

Seemingly out of place until you look at the habitat it enjoys, junipers do well on dry, south facing slopes in a few places in the park, such as Hope Island, Skagit Island, and a handful on the south side of Ginnett Hill.

They form pyramidal bushy little trees in these places, some growing to thirty or forty feet, most in the ten to twenty range.

Big-leaf Maple

One of two major deciduous tree in the park is the Big-leaf maple. Related to the sugar maples of the east coast, our Big-Leaf has truly big leaves, hand-shaped leaves with five digits (like the flag of Canada) but over a foot long. They turn a bright yellow in fall and drop enormous amounts of vegetation to carpet the woods or to be raked up off pavement. They are abundant at Bowman Bay and Kiket Island where the soil is moist.

A solitary madrone celebrates life on the rocky shoreline along Cranberry Lake.

Madrone

The only common broad-leaved evergreen tree in Washington is a favorite for many people. The bark is a blaze of red and orange that peels away in patches from the trunk; its flowers are bright white in April, and the berries a bright barn red in summer. The leaves are evergreen, which means they live for a year and a half, dropping off in mid-summer after the new leaves have sprouted to take their place.

They are only found where they have access to full sun, so look for them on any south-facing slopes, such as the north end of the bridge, the north shore of Bowman Bay, and the south side of Goose Rock, Ben Ure, Skagit, Hope, and Kiket Islands.

Left:
My hand looks child-sized compared to a Big-leaf maple leaf.

Red Alder

Alder trees are found in dense patches, as they are the pioneers that reclaim any open ground. They build soil by fixing nitrogen from the air. The leaves are plain, somewhat ribbed, about four to six inches long. These are deciduous trees, but don't wait for fall to see them change color. The leaves just slowly turn a dull brown before falling off.

They are abundant in a few places. Look for them along the trails at Dugualla and Hoypus Hill where logging took place, the shores of Cornet Bay and Bowman Bay, around Pass Lake, and many other places in the park.

Distinctive individuals

- On the Dunes Trail, an ancient tree with massive arms reaching out in all directions (Douglas fir - see text and illustration below).

> "For over 850 years, this Douglas Fir has stood witness to the forming and changing of these dunes. Thick bark and strong wood have served well against storm, fire, drought, and disease. Through all of this time it has offered generations of people its leaves for shelter, limbs for climbing, and branches for sitting. Its bark is strong, but thinning from so much climbing.
>
> "Love it gently. Look on it with thought for the times it has seen. Find its stillness while you listen to the forest, dunes and sea. Wonder at what forces sculpted it so. Reflect on the ways its relatives touch your lives. Love it gently and it will live to shelter your children and theirs, as well."
> -- interpretive sign illustration and text for the ancient tree on the Dunes Trail.

The solitary tree, one of my favorites in the park, sits on a narrow point of land just east of Rosario.

- Just east of Rosario heading toward Bowman, on a point of land, a solitary tree stands in silhouette (Douglas fir - see photo above)
- On the North Beach trail, not far from the bridge, near the rock wall along the trail, a particularly wind-blown tree frames the view northwest (Douglas fir)
- At the top of Rosario Head, in a wind-carved t-shape (Douglas fir- see the sunset section pictures.)
- At the divide in the trail on Lighthouse Point, a hollow Western redcedar.
- On the southwest side of Kiket, a bright red ganglion of majesty overhanging the beach (Madrone).
- Where the road begins to drop down to North Beach, a hall of old growth trees that may be the largest in the park (Douglas fir and cedar).
- On the main Kiket trail, halfway out, the largest yew tree I have found here, although one on the perimeter trail near Goose Rock may be larger.
- On the Big Cedar Trail west of the John Tursi trail, as you climb west out of Heilman Valley, a huge specimen of Western redcedar.

Rhododendrons

Women in Washington State organized a statewide election in 1892 to select the state flower. Eager to display a flower that would represent their state at the 1893 World's Fair in Chicago, more than 15,000 women cast a ballot in the election. The Coast Rhododendron emerged the winner.

The Coast Rhododendron grows naturally along forest edges and in clearings created by tree falls and fires.

The shrub generally reaches 6-8 feet tall at maturity; however it can reach heights of 20-30 feet. The flower's dark green leaves extend between 3 to 6 inches long and up to 3 inches wide. In springtime, the showy flower displays a colorful array of large, tubular blossoms. The flowers usually range in color from pale pink to darker pink.

The biggest patches I have found in the park are on the south slope of Goose Rock and along the western side of Hoypus Hill, on the North Fork Trail.

Other Shrubs and Flowers

Hundreds of species of plants make this park part of their home turf. Botanists have spent years making lists of everything found here. You can find these lists in scientific files and reports.

Some of the commonly found plants listed below can be the foundation for being able to recognize familiar friends throughout the park. Many serve as key indicators of the kind of habitat you are in.

Ocean Spray

Fast-growing ocean spray is also called ironwood because of the strength of its stems. They were often used for digging sticks, harpoons, arrows, and furniture. Clusters of flowers cascade down the plant when they bloom in May and June, turning a hillside into falling waves of white. Some of the tallest examples I have found are on the south end of Lighthouse Point, but they grow nearly everywhere in well-drained soils. (See page 123 for a photograph of Ocean Spray.)

Salal

Salal fills the understory throughout the park where the soil is dry and well drained. The gangly plant grows for decades, reaching heights of over ten feet where conditions allow, such as on Lighthouse Point. It's large dark evergreen leaves contrast grandly with the white flowers of late April. In late summer it sports small black berries that can make a great tasting jam (add sugar).

Flowering Currant

One of the earliest flowers in spring, especially on south-facing slopes, flowering currant gives food to hummingbirds and beauty to the forests after months of winter gray. There is one clump just south of the bridge that warms my heart in late February or early March when it starts to bloom, transforming the rocky hillside into a splash of joy.

Sword Fern

The dominant ground cover in moist soils will often be clumps of the distinctive sword fern. New growth in spring uncurls like fiddleheads to eventually replace last year's fronds. Sword fern can cover the ground so thoroughly that little else grows with it. Find it throughout the park where the ground is moist, but in some places it feels like all you see is a carpet of sword ferns below a canopy of trees. It makes the forest feel a little like you are in an Ewok scene.

Salmonberry

The deep pink flowers of the salmonberry bring the rufous hummingbird back to the northwest in the spring. It's golden to salmon-colored berries feed many animals and park visitors in late spring. The plant has a rich history of use by local tribes. It does well throughout the moist areas of the park.

Nootka Rose

Nootka rose graces many of the beach slopes and forest edges around the park. This fragrant pink flower grows in thickets near the seashore at Rosario, Bowman, and West Beach, and along Cranberry and Pass Lakes. In May, take the time to put your nose close to the flower to enjoy its heady fragrance. Actually you don't even have to be close – it fills the air all around.

Red Huckleberry

Although not a true huckleberry, the red or native huckleberry grows in scattered locations throughout the deep woods. For some reason, they love to grow in old stumps or on rotten logs.

Their light spring green leaves brighten the dark woods on a drizzly day. Their berries splash red in the forest in late summer. Their leaves are deciduous, unlike its cousin the evergreen huckleberry.

Skunk Cabbage

Skunk cabbage have the biggest leaves of any plant in the park, each leaf big enough to shade a small child. One of the earliest flowers of the year, sporting a yellow light-bulb-shaped flower in February, this is not one you want in a bouquet – its smell gives the plant its name. Find it in marshy soil such as at the Cornet Bay Retreat Center, the Cornet Bay Road west of the boat launch, at Dugualla's wetlands, and deep in Heilman Valley.

Stinging Nettles

Nettles must be known by every hiker who ventures an inch off the trail in any of the park wetlands. The tiny hairs on the stems and underside of leaves will break when touched, exposing a needle that injects a cocktail of painful chemicals into the porous parts of your skin.

Conversely, they make a great tea when they are young and tender, and a great cooked green, a little like spinach. Find them wherever the soil is moist and recently disturbed, such as along the wet portions of trails at Hoypus, Dugualla, and other damp areas.

Camas

Camas provided a starchy staple for the diets of the local tribes. The bulb pushes up a dark purple flower in early spring. Nearly every meadow and bald in the park sports a carpet of camas in April. **Death Camas** looks almost the same as camas after the flowers die away. It's flower is creamy white and shaped quite differently. Like its name suggests, death camas must not be mistaken for camas in your diet.

Starflower

Starflower catches my eye in April when I hike through dense woods. It seems to like shady ground covered with duff where little else grows. The floor of the forest becomes a little carpet of stars in a bed of dark green leaves.

Gumweed

Gumweed looks like a weed in many ways. In fact, as we were seeing the new beach plantings at Cornet Bay become established, one of our volunteers felt proud of the work she did in removing truck-loads of just-planted gumwood out of the beach areas! The thick plant grows a couple feet high, and in late summer shows off a bouquet of yellow dandelion-like flowers that are very sticky, hence the plant's name. As a late bloomer, it is a critically important source of pollen for bees. You can find it along nearly all of our sandy or gravelly beaches. (It has returned to Cornet Bay.)

Stonecrop

Stonecrop graces places that have virtually no soil. We find them on nearly every rock face in the park, hanging on to the side of cliffs and steep rocks, with waxy bulbous leaves and small yellow flowers.

Mushrooms, Mosses, and other things
we overlook because they are small

We have barely scratched the surface in looking at the plants of Deception Pass State Park. Many hundreds have gone unmentioned here.

Indeed, whole families of plants have not even been alluded to. The closer you look, the more you will see.

For mushrooms, your best bet is to get in touch with the Puget Sound Mycological Society. Every fall they have a 'foray' into our woods, and then exhibit the dozens of species they have found that year. Check out their website at www.psms.org

For mosses, find a great book, of which their are many, and spend the time getting to know all the details that make them distinctive and important to this environment.

Even the common diseases of our trees, another field of fungi study, provide years of interesting and practical education as you see what's causing problems to our forests and threatening our facilities.

A lifetime of exploration awaits you if you pursue the chance to get to know our native plant species.

The Enemy Beneath

Trees share their resources among themselves. In a typical healthy forest, you will see trees of all ages, sharing a habitat. What you will not see is under the ground, where each tree's roots tangle and intermingle with the neighboring trees, creating pathways that allow the trees to share water and nutrients. Those with an abundance share with those in need, even among different species.

This characteristic of sharing helps build stronger forests in a given habitat. It also leads to the destruction of the trees in that habitat when a pathogen uses that same internet-like network of connections to spread a deadly fungus from tree to tree, species to species (except the western redcedar). The pathogens can weaken and eventually kill a tree, then spread out to all the trees nearby, weakening and killing them too, then spreading in an ever-widening circle of destruction.

Root rot is one of the most common diseases to take advantage of this security flaw in a forest grove. The disease kills the roots of trees, leaving them standing with all the appearance of being in full health, while beneath the ground their roots have died from the pathogen. The tree may fail and fall at any time.

These pockets of pathogens are called "root rot pockets". They are distinctive once you recognize one. As you walk through a forest, you may come upon an opening where sunlight is pouring in. Fallen trees lie in the middle, weakened trees stand on the edges, and healthy trees are all around with few defenses against the slowly encroaching attack. Picture fairy-ring mushrooms growing in a lawn, with brown grass inside the ring and the line of mushrooms expanding outward in an ever-widening circle.

A root rot fruiting body at the base of a large Douglas fir. This tree fell over a year later.

With time, these sunny pockets grow small plants and shrubs, and new, resistant trees become established on the site. This is one way that the forest environment is recycled and re-energized, creating diversity through a mosaic of forest composition.

You can find pockets scattered around the park. They occur naturally, a part of the life of the forest. Unfortunately, some of the pockets are growing near park facilities, such as the former group camps near North Beach. We closed the group camps rather than risk having campers spending the night where trees are under attack from the hidden enemy.

Seaweeds

Our intertidal zones host dozens of species of algae, in colors of green, red, and brown. Each of them have fascinating stories to tell and life styles to study. Find them wherever there are rocks exposed at low tide. For smaller crowds and more abundant marine life, try the rocks between Rosario and Bowman Bay, or find a boat and go exploring where few have gone before. Just respect the life you find wherever it may be.

Here are two seaweeds you must know:

Bull Kelp

Imagine the growing pains from growing sixty feet in one year. Bull kelp is an annual plant, starting deep under water each year and reaching the surface with a light-bulb sized head, then spreading fronds out from the bulb for photosynthesis. In late summer, the fronds stretch out for dozens of feet along the edges of the shoreline, showing mariners where rocks lurk below the surface.

Then in fall they break off, creating a rich nutrient field on our beaches for bugs and other critters, which further contribute to the health of the Salish Sea. Kids (many of whom are big enough to be called adults) have been known to take the long stalks and use them as whips, or to cut the stalks and play them like a trumpet.
You can see them in late summer particularly in the water under the bridge and at Rosario, but anywhere that we have rocks a couple dozen feet under the surface, you will find a forest of bull kelp.

Rockweed

One of the "must know" seaweeds on our rocks, rockweed covers rocks in the lower to middle tidal range, providing a forest haven for small intertidal animals and some protection from heat, dehydration, and predation.

Olive green to slightly brown, the algae grows from a small button of a holdfast to branch out and branch out again, creating a many-fingered wrack that has bulbous air-filled sacks at each tip.

Invasives

It's a military term, right? These enemies have every intention and ability of taking over any ground they can conquer. Some have succeeded in sizeable areas.

They out-compete native species, reproduce or spread prolifically, and reduce food sources for native animals.

You can find many non-native species here, but these listed below stand out for their visibility, success, and danger to the environment.

Spurge laurel, or Daphne

Noxious as well as invasive, daphne looks innocuous but spreads through dry forests by roots and seeds. They are tough to pull out of the ground because of their long taproots, and they are smelly and slightly toxic to cut.

We see them in nearly all our south-facing forests, such as Hope Island, Hoypus, Ginnett, and the north shore of Pass Lake.

Himalayan Blackberry

Although we have some native species, the Himalayan blackberry creates a massive tangle of impenetrable growth that overwhelms any other plants in an area, and left unchecked will keep expanding.

Yes, the berries are delicious, and small animals such as rabbits can use their cover for protection from predators, but without nearby food, even those species soon lose out.

Our worst areas are recently disturbed areas such as the hillside facing the beach at Rosario, the Forest Loop near Cranberry, the Fidalgo land of the Kukutali Preserve, and the north shore of Pass Lake.

Purple loose-strife

Not as well known because it grows in the wetlands on the south end of Cranberry Lake, it is a pretty but terrible invasive, taking over vast areas if left unchecked. We have tried to remove it, but success takes time and thorough removal; we are short on time.

Holly

The Christmas decoration grows slowly but relentlessly, brought in by birds depositing seeds that they have eaten, and spreading by their roots.

We see these throughout our forest areas, sometimes as large trees. The largest I know is just north of the old entrance on Highway 20, a tree of over thirty feet now. You can find holly scattered in nearly all of our forests.

Scotch Broom, or Scot's Broom

WCC crew members remove Scotch broom plant by plant on Bowman Hill.

This plant can take over an entire meadow in just a few years. It produces seeds by the gazillion which can lay dormant but viable for decades. It kills the plants beneath, overshadowing them with its course body that adds basically no value to the environment.

Large swaths of the broom cover the hills above Rosario, the shoreline between Rosario and Bowman, on Bowman Hill, on Pass Island, and the south side of Hope Island. We have our annual removal battle on Hope Island one day every spring. Come help us reclaim the wildflower meadow there.

English Ivy

A particularly dangerous enemy, ivy spreads by its roots to blanket the ground it grows on, and climbs any trees it encounters to find sunlight, weakening and eventually killing the trees.

Our worst infestations are at the north shore of Pass Lake, an expanding patch on Ben Ure, and several places at Rosario, although one massive patch west of the Maiden has been eliminated by volunteers, thanks especially to the work of the late Susan Alaynick.

Another patch near the field classroom has almost been removed by other volunteer parties.

Some of the **other common invasives** in the park include herb robert, aka "stinky bob" (which unfortunately fills our entrance beds of all places!), tansy ragwort (along Cornet Bay Road and at Dugualla), yellow archangel (at Bowman and along Cornet Bay Road), spartina (showing up occasionally in Cornet Bay), and water hemlock (near the water's edge at Bowman and elsewhere). There are many others as well.

Although this is a long list of plants, and our losses are many, volunteers have done a great job fighting back and reclaiming our natural environment. Left unchecked, these plants will dominate their new ground. But through vigilance and hard work, we will prevail.

Burning Concerns

We are overdue.

Actually, we get minor fires every year somewhere in the park, on the beach from an illegal fire in driftwood, or along a trail or near a campsite from careless or illegal campfires. But we have not had a large scale fire for over a century. Our forests still show scars from that fire (see photo below).

Our forests used to get their woody debris cleaned out on a periodic basis by fires that swept along the ground, burning brush and dead branches while leaving scars on thickly-barked Douglas fir. This opened up the woods for new growth and renewed energy and opportunities for plants and animals.

By faithfully suppressing all fires in parks, we have created conditions ripe for potentially catastrophic fires which will not only clear out the underbrush, but will climb the accumulated forest debris into the crowns of the trees and then spread tree to tree, killing everything in its path.

We could reduce the ground fuels and "ladder fuels", debris that allows fire to climb into the crowns of trees. But that kind of work is expensive, time consuming, smoky, and disturbing to see. We could start small controlled burns in the off-season, but again the smoke and expense limits our options. We do try to maintain fire access roads, and there have been discussions about thinning out some of the unnatural buildup of ladder fuels.

For now we maintain a readiness to fight any fire that may get started, whether by lightning, accidental spark, campfire, or intentional. Park staff are trained in fire fighting, some more than others. We have small pumps ready to go for an initial attack, and the support of North Whidbey Fire and Rescue on the Island County side and Mt. Erie Fire Department on the Skagit side. The Department of Natural Resources also responds to any wildland fire in the park.

The question is not if, but when. Are we ready?

So there I am,

walking outside early one fine September morning, with the sun just rising and the dew already evaporating as another summer day begins. I smell the lovely fresh air -- only it is acrid with an intense odor of wood smoke. We are in the middle of a statewide fire ban because it hasn't rained around here for months now; the forest is tinder dry. Smelling any smoke at all is a bad sign.

And it is so strong I think my house is on fire. I look all around my house, but it just looks sleepy. I see no smoke anywhere, but the odor is so strong I know a fire is close.

There is no wind blowing. I wander around to the east, and the smell lingers but fades slightly. I wander west toward Ginnett and the Heilman Valley and the odor gets a little stronger, then it disappears completely. I don't smell anything now. I wander north toward a different part of the valley, but still smell nothing. I wander in circles for a half hour, looking for smoke, sniffing for smoke, but now there is nothing, just the fragrances of a late summer morning. It's just gone now.

I assume someone had a fire going briefly somewhere and then put it out. (You may be noticing a trend in my stories -- I'm good at wrong assumptions.) I go about my day, a day off, and I head to town to enjoy the day there.

At 2 p.m., I get a call from a ranger that they are looking for a fire somewhere near Ginnett. Oh, no, I say to myself, it couldn't be.... He calls again a short while later to say they see a column of smoke rising on the south side of Ginnett Hill, deep in the woods. He says several park staff, the Mount Erie Fire Department, and DNR are all responding. I head back to the park. It's a very warm day. I see the wind has now picked up, blowing steadily from the south. A fire on the south side of the hill getting a south wind will get pushed up the hill and can grow quickly that way. My imagination plays through scenarios that are not pretty.

I finally get there and find DNR crews laying out 900 feet of hose, all that they have, from the Ginnett overlook area down the trail into Heilman Valley. I hike down the trail to find Ranger Shook, Mount Erie Fire Department staff, and DNR staff digging a fireline around a quarter acre fire, and hosing down hot spots. Flames are still flaring on tree stumps. Trunks are charred, bushes are toasted black.

At the edge of the trail, the remnants of a small campfire remain intact-- a small circle of rocks, a burned beer can inside the ring, along with the burned remains of food wrappers and foil. The hillside is steep here, and laden with rock. This wasn't a campsite, it was a party site for locals from the night before.

I had smelled the now-unattended campfire in the cool morning air as it crept into nearby duff to give the sharp smell of smoldering woods debris. The light dawn winds must have changed as the sun rose, taking away the only clue that we had. When the afternoon winds began sweeping up the hillside, it ignited the smoldering duff into active flames which started to climb the hill, fortunately sending clear

smoke signals as an alarm as well.

Thanks to an efficient emergency response team in the area (and no thanks to me) the fire was extinguished while it remained fairly young. You can still see the evidence of this fire halfway between the bottom of the Heilman Valley and the Ginnett overlook area.

ANIMALS

"Are there any special animals here in the park?"

Visitors ask this question of me all the time. I am never sure how to answer. What is or is not special?

We have what you would commonly expect, like deer, raccoons, squirrels, mice, bats, lizards, snakes, frogs, butterflies, crows and seagulls. I think they are all special.

There was a period during the Sixties when various people reported sighting "Deception Pass Sea Serpents" playing in the waters off West Beach. One park ranger reported that he saw it coil and dive. That might be special.

In September 1963 the remains of a strange 'monster' washed up on West Beach. A local periodical reported that the remains "were about 25 feet long, with a horse-like skeletal head. It's rubbery hide had distinctive spots from which hair grew, and gristle-like flesh clung to its bones." It may have been a basking shark, unusual for this area, but since no one made a positive identification, it all just remains a mystery. That's not special.

But let's talk about what we know is here. That makes each of these animals special. Seek, and you may find.

Between the Tides

Information about the abundant tidepool animal life here fills numerous books. Some of these books are referenced in the back.

I want to highlight some of the animals living here because they may very well have been a part of your earlier explorations, or a worthy subject for future explorations at our beaches.

There are so many others to get to know as well, each with fascinating stories. Come to the tidepools when our Beach Naturalist volunteers are there to learn more and catch their enthusiasm!

Barnacles

Picture life standing on your head, using your feet to gather in food as it drifts by. Then for half of each day, imagine having to lock your doors up tight because your idyllic world has changed to a deadly environment, threatening to kill you with heat, cold, dehydration, or predators.

That is the life of those animals living in the sharp little white shells on the park's rocks. You know, the ones that keep you from slipping on the rocks by giving your foot some traction, but which also slice your skin if you fall on them.

Barnacles secrete a glue that binds them to the rock forever. Then they stand on their head and wait for food to drift by, which they capture with their feather-like feet.

Gumboot Chitons

Chitons are like snails stretched straight and laid out in a line. They still have a shell, but it is broken into 8 pieces that articulate with each other. Separately, these shell pieces look like little calcified butterflies.

Our beaches shelter several species of chitons, but the largest in the world is found here, the gumboot chiton, also called the Giant Pacific chiton. They can grow over a foot long, and look somewhat like a football cut in half, or the skull of a Klingon if you have a nerdy mind like me. It's Haida name is 'sgiidaa', which translates roughly to 'lying face down forever' a sad epitaph for an interesting creature. They creep along the tidepools, eating algae as they crawl along.

Look carefully for gumboots in the rocky tidepool areas. Please leave it be. Living face down forever is enough of a challenge in life.

Anemones

"Animals that look like flowers, with soft petals and a sweet life, just sitting there all pretty like."

That's how many people describe anemones. But once you get to know them, there is nothing soft or sweet about them. Those 'petals' on the top are deadly tentacles, with harpoons that fire into an unsuspecting prey and release a toxin. Once paralyzed, the pray is drawn into the mouth in the middle and dissolved whole.

People can gently touch these tentacles and get a feel for the effect, though our thick skin protects us from a terrible end. But small fish or crabs will not survive an encounter with these lovely plant-like animals.

Find them in the mid to lower levels of the tidepools, and also on piers and pilings around the docks.

Purple Shore Crabs

To me, these little creatures provide a reward for patient tidepool observation. Two inches across at the most when full grown, these common little crabs fill the crevices under rocks and in the tidepools. Although out of sight, they are busy feeding on algae and any dead animals they come across.

Many people turn over rocks to find them, and there they are – a dozen sometimes of various sizes, now scurrying over to the next rock to get away from you.

They have mottled shells that are purple and with several other earth tone colors splattered around. Their claws are small, but be careful if you choose to pick one up – there's a right way and a painful way.

Better yet, wait for them to appear in a tidepool, and just enjoy them without having to touch them and upsetting their day.

Insider: Finding Life Without Causing Death

Move a rock to see what's underneath, or leave it be? It is true that the life under small rocks on the beach outnumbers the life on top of the rocks by a large factor. However, there is no way to move that rock without causing damage to those living there. And imagine if everyone moved that rock at low tide, and the other nearby rocks.

One otherwise well-written book I read said to just pick up any medium size rocks at the water's edge to find the small life beneath. If you do, you expose hundreds of animals to danger, and then threaten their lives even more when you put the rock back down again, because many of them will be crushed, or perish because they are no longer protected in the same way.

Please refrain from changing this fragile environment during your visit. Just go slowly and observe.

Check out the life in a tidepool instead, where the animals feel more protected and put on a better show anyway. Or just crouch close to the ground and watch. Wait. You will be amazed at how much more you will see.

The Seattle Aquarium shares these pointers for visitors to tidepools:

- *Walk carefully; there is life beneath your feet.*
- *Touch gently with one wet finger.*
- *Observe animals where they are and avoid picking them up.*
- *Only move rocks that are small enough to be moved with one hand.*
- *Carefully return rocks to the exact position you found them in.*
- *Do not remove anything natural from the beach.*

Clams

Yes, they live at Deception Pass, and no, I'm not going to tell you the best places to find them.

But I will say that most clams prefer intertidal areas that are not stagnant and muddy (don't look in Cornet Bay or Bowman Bay), but areas that have mixed sand and small gravel (don't try Rosario, too rocky), with water that is replenished every tide with fresh nutrients, and not a lot of wave action (forget West and North beaches). One hint: Kiket Island is closed to harvesting except for Swinomish tribal members.

That should be all the clues you need.

Bugs, Spiders, Snakes, and things

With healthy ecosystems throughout the park, we are blessed with an abundance of insects, salamanders, newts, and other critters rarely seen and little understood by most of us. Many books on the market can help you find and identify these species.

But there are some animals that everyone knows and talks about because they interact with us in direct ways. These are the species that get in our food, under our skin, and into our imagination.

Hornets: We have yellow jackets and bald faced hornets. When the weather turns dry, they turn hungry and mean. Park staff do our best to eliminate any nests that we find, or that visitors find and tell us about. Keep your food safely contained, and expect to see them in July through September if you have sugar drinks or a chicken wing on your picnic table.

Mosquitoes: Yes, they are here, but not to the annoying level of other places I have been. We see them March through August primarily, heaviest in the May to July period, depending on the weather. I find the Dugualla, Hope Island, and Hoypus Hill areas to be the buggiest. Okay, I must be honest, the mosquitoes on some of these trails can rise to the annoying level, and maybe a couple levels beyond.

Snakes: We have quite a variety, but you will probably never see any unless you are truly exploring the woods on your hands and knees around here in moister locations. None of the snake species are poisonous, or hazardous unless you try to get bitten.

Ticks: The March to April season brings these critters into mind as they wait for passing victims in high brush or grasses. If you stay on the developed trails you will probably never encounter any. I find them when I go off trail in brushy areas. Check your body thoroughly when you get home or back to your campsite if you have gone wandering through the brush for any length of time.

More Small Critters I Love

Banana Slugs

Did you know we have the second largest slug in the world, living right here, in abundance? It grows up to 10 inches long, although it is most commonly about 6 inches, and lives up to seven years. They may be yellow with black spots, or greenish, depending on what it eats and other factors. As scavengers, they eat small dead animals or detritus, as well as leaf litter and fungus, turning it all back to soil and fertilizing our forest floor.

Since they depend on moisture, they enjoy the nighttime for activity, but they may be about during the day on moist ground such as logs, stream banks, or shaded woodlands.

They tend to be solitary creatures. You might be too if your best defense mechanism consisted of slime, which also helps retain moisture and allows for movement across dry ground.

Frogs

The Pacific treefrog is the smallest but most commonly seen and heard frog in Washington, heard far more often than it is seen.

The "song" or call of the male treefrog, designed to attract females, is a loud, two-part *kreck-ek*, often repeated many times. This calling stimulates other males to join in, and the chorus of these frogs can be heard far away.

Male treefrogs call mainly in the evening and at night, although they often call sporadically during the day at the height of the breeding season. When male treefrogs are in a dry place away from their breeding ponds they call out a slow single-note *Krr-r-r-ek*.

I love the sound of frogs in springtime as they bring a background of hope and love in their songs. Hear them in park wetlands, such as at Bowman Bay, Lottie Bay, the center of Hope Island, the wetlands at Dugualla, and the shores of Pass Lake and Cranberry Lake.

Painted Turtles

Painted turtles are seen in great numbers basking on logs and rocks in our lakes and ponds in the summer, but they are shy and quickly slide into the water when approached.

These turtles have a wide diet including water plants, insects, crayfish, fish, tadpoles, and dead animals.

As suggested by their name, painted turtles are ornately colored. They have black to olive skin with red and yellow stripes. Their lower shells are mostly yellow with varying shapes and sizes of other colors, like red, black, and/or reddish-brown. They have smooth, flattened, and oval upper shells ranging from green to black.

Look for them along the shores of all the lakes in the park. Approach the shore slowly and low to the ground, or else the only sound you will hear is a small splash as several turtles jump into the water and disappear out of sight.

Birds

Find a good bird guide, whether a book or a person, to learn more about our fascinating world of avians. The park is rich with bird life, in part because of the diversity of its habitats, also in part because of the health of our habitats, and also because the park is in the middle of the Pacific Flyway.

The Whidbey Audubon Society has several guided outings in the park throughout the year. Check them out at www.whidbeyaudubon.org; you can also find detailed bird lists at their website.

Below is quick summary of where you will see our more common and easily identifiable species.

Bald Eagles

See them sometimes on a snag on the northeast side of Canoe Pass, on the east and west side of Kiket Island, hovering around Rosario Head, at Cornet Bay, at Hoypus Point, and along North Beach and West Beach at times. We have a handful of nesting sites that they rotate through on a regular basis.

I have been engrossed just about every year by a pair of eagles tag-teaming against a lone duck on Pass Lake. The eagles will take turns diving toward the duck, which goes under the surface to avoid the attack. With the barrage of never-ending approaches by the eagles, however, the duck eventually tires of holding its breath and stays on the surface a little too long. I have never known what cues the eagles to attack a particular duck, but the results are nearly always the same.

Canada Geese

Although native to the area, their numbers have increased exponentially to the point that they are destroying habitat, reducing lake quality, and making a mess of any lawn in the park that is near water. They nest around Cranberry Lake and love to be at the swim beach there. If they gather too often or in large numbers, people complain about park staff not picking up "dog waste". Canada geese can poop a pound a day!

They also nest on Strawberry Island and come to Cornet Bay or the Retreat Center to eat lawn grasses, leaving behind their calling card where children play.

Cormorants

Large black birds that fish for a living, they enjoy Cranberry Lake, especially in winter or whenever the lake is stocked; and at Cornet Bay. Sometimes you will see them flying west under the bridge at sunset, and east in the early morning.

Great blue herons

Common at Cornet Bay, at the wetlands at Bowman Bay, along Lottie Point and Lighthouse Point, and with several in the forests along the beach at Dugualla, and a couple in the lagoon at Kiket.

Approach these areas slowly so as not to disturb them, if you can. Otherwise they fly off giving a squawk that sounds like it's from the Jurassic age.

Kingfisher

One family loves Sharpe's Cove near Rosario, another lives near Flagstaff Point, and another near Lighthouse Point. You often hear them before you see them, when you hear their chattering as they fly.

Owls

Although very common, they are rarely seen, though you may hear them in the evening or early morning.

As nocturnal hunters, owls have big eyes to gather light, in the front of their face like humans so that they can have a three-dimensional perspective. Unlike humans, their eyes are fixed in their sockets, meaning it has to turn its head to see to the side. And because of that it can turn its head nearly all the way around!

They can also fly silently – their flight feathers are fringed to muffle the passing air. They capture prey with their large talons, feeding mostly on rodents, and eating the prey whole. They can also catch prey using only sound as a clue.

Their hoots and other sounds allow them to communicate with others of the same species. Each species has a distinctive set of sounds.

Many different species live here. You may be lucky to see one, but if you listen carefully, it is very possible that you will hear one or two species. I have been blessed to hear each of the calls listed below at some time somewhere in the park.

Owl Calls

Since they are heard more often than they are seen, here is a guide to what you may hear in the evening or pre-dawn hours.

Great horned owl: a series of four or five deep, resonant hoots given in various rhythms by different individuals: "hoo-hoo-hoo... hoo...hoo" ("who's a-wake, me too"). Occasionally two or more owls can be heard hooting, seeming to respond to one another.

Barred owl: a clear-voiced series: hoo-hoo, hoo-hooooo, hoo-hoo, hoo-hoo-o-aw. Given in words: "who-cooks-for-you, who-cooks for-you-a-all," ending with a <u>descending</u> note.

Western screech owl: a slow but <u>accelerating</u> series of short mellow whistles, tooooo-toooo toooo-tooo-too-to-to-to-to, that is slightly lower at the end.

Northern saw-whet owl: low, whistled toots (about two per second): too-too-too-too-too-too, like a backing truck alarm, only faster.

Northern Pygmy-owl: a soft, hollow toot (one note every two seconds).

Barn owl: a long hissing or raspy scream, cssssshhh which sounds similar to a canvas being ripped. Not a pleasant sound.

To hear these owl sounds at home, visit http://www.owlpages.com/owls/sounds.php

Olive Colored Flycatcher

You may not ever see it, but I bet you will hear it if you spend time in the woods. It's call has been described in many ways with many phrases, such as "Quick, THREE beers", but the one I hear is "Mc-GY-ver" or "eXavier!" Or "It's RAI-nier" (Once you recognize the call, it almost starts to get annoying, as the bird will repeat it every five to ten seconds.)

Oystercatchers

Find them along the rocks at Rosario, Flagstaff Point, Lighthouse Point, and West Point.

Pacific wrens

I adore their cheerfully melodic song be it winter or summer. They abound in the forests around the park sharing their joy from high up in our forests, the song improvising melodies for ten or even twenty seconds at a time.

Purple martins

Boxes have been built for them at the park dock west of the Cornet Bay moorage docks. Larger than swallows, it is comforting to know they are comfortable in their little houses at the dock.

Ravens

One of my favorite birds, they can often be seen or heard near Ginnett and at Bowman Bay, among other places. Larger than crows, and deeper voiced, somehow I hear "wild" when their croak echoes across the hills.

Red-throated loons

Hundreds may gather in the Pass near North Beach during the winter just as the tide starts to ebb. The loons are enjoying a feast of forage fish caught in the swiftly flowing tidal waters coming out of the Skagit Bay area. Join with our local Audubon societies to learn more about them and see them up close during winter explorations.

Swainson's Thrush

To me, the call of the Swainson's thrush is a key sound of wilderness. I know the environment is healthy when I hear its rising circles of sound from some place deep in the woods of the park. The **varied thrush**, a cousin species, sounds like a hum and a whistle sung at the same time, the duo-toned note lasting a couple seconds. Try doing that. You'll get it.

Western Grebe

A bird you will probably not see, and unfortunately probably not hear anymore either. Growing up along the shores of Puget Sound, the 'kree-ree' call of the grebe from far out in the water somewhere still fills my memories of walks after sunset along the beach. Now their song is a rarity, as their population lost 95% of their numbers from a few decades ago. What has changed?

White Crowned Sparrow

The song this sparrow sings along the seashore from April through September has become a part of the life of the spirit of the Pacific Northwest. The little brown bird with white stripes on its head crowns the music of a quiet summer day at the beach. It sounds kind of like "Hey, now, listen to the earth: ssshhhh." It's a lovely sound, the sound of summer, the sound of the the outdoors.

Mammals

Bats
These nocturnal "flying mice" are insect eaters that do their job very well, eating several hundred every night. They leave their roosts in the early evening to find a mega-meal of insects. Sit quietly if you know where they roost, and you can enjoy the marvelous sight of dozens or maybe hundreds of bats heading out with their radar-guided flight.

They rest in the winter, finding a safe roost with just the right temperature and humidity. Some live in houses, some in caves, some in tree trunks. The most common bat around here has the distinctive name of Little Brown Bat (yes, that's the official name). Another common bat is called the Big Brown Bat. Creative, eh?

A special bat that calls this park home is the Townsend Big-Eared Bat. It winters in the caves above the Pass on Bowman Hill, where the temperature and humidity stay relatively constant year round. Please do not disturb them here, especially as they are susceptible in the winter to hunger and disease. This species is one of several that are listed as a "Species of Special Concern".

Bear
A black bear in Heilman Valley scared a young pioneer at the turn of the twentieth century. Pioneering neighbor Joe Lynch found it on Rodgers Hill and killed it. We have not seen any bears since. They were reported in the early pioneer days as living on Whidbey Island as well. Not now.

Beaver
Over a dozen live in the Cranberry Lake area, eating the trees around the lake and living in dens along the shore. Watch for them in the lake near Cranberry Road early in the morning or late in the evening if there is little traffic to disturb them. You can also find evidence of their work in the numerous tree stumps along the east, north, and west shores of the lake.

Cougar
Once abundant enough on Fidalgo Island to have been hunted near the Rosario area, we thought they no longer roamed our woods here. The same pioneer Joe Lynch that killed a bear in Heilman Valley killed two cougars at Cougar Gap, inspiring the name of that area.

But then a camper at Bowman Bay in 2016 gave us a credible, plausible story about seeing a cougar chase a raccoon up a tree, then give up and descend the tree and slink off toward – yes, you guessed it – the Cougar Gap area. She described the very long and bushy tail, agile walking style, and overall large size of this tawny-colored cat, so we believe her report to be valid.

Wouldn't that be an awesome addition to the 'special' animals living in the park?

Coyote
More often heard than seen, they will serenade us once in awhile, reminding us of who this park really belongs to. Hearing them howl is almost the call of the wild.

They live anywhere they can find food in the park or surrounding neighborhoods, which means they live pretty much everywhere.

Deer
Although common to the area, they are mostly endangered by the abundance of cars on Highway 20. They are commonly found near the entrance to the Cranberry area, where they stop traffic by munching meals right next to the road; near Cornet Bay; at the Cornet Bay Retreat Center; on Kiket Island; at the park office enjoying the rain-garden offerings; and along the east side of Pass Lake.

Douglas squirrel

Also called the chickaree, these active tree dwellers are brown to dark gray on top, with orangish chests. They are not shy – they will scold you mercilessly if you interrupt their busy day.

In the fall, they cut green cones from our trees and bury them in middens. If you are standing near a tree and see Douglas fir cones dropping down on you from above, you may be intruding on a squirrel's plans for the winter.

Killer Whales or Orcas

Although these are rarely seen near the park, we do get the occasional sighting as they cavort off Rosario or West Beach. Rarely have I seen them in the Pass, but one of their journeys through brought us a treat of several pod members jumping and breaching as they headed west toward the bridge and the open sea.

Porcupines

These nocturnal animals are rarely seen, but they are around, munching on trees or waddling along the ground, their coat bristling with pointed barbs.

River Otter

These long, lithe creatures are secretive, but gregarious with each other. William Dietrich describes them as the playground kids of the animal kingdom.

River otters make their den on land, but seem to live to play in the water – salt or fresh. Sometimes people misidentify them as sea otters, but those are distinctly different creatures that live in our coastal waters.

Otters are most commonly seen at Bowman Bay near the pier, at Cornet Bay near the docks, and at Pass Lake and Cranberry Lake. You may see them sprinting across the ground, or swimming in the water, but wherever they are, they seem to be having fun.

Seals

Harbor seals are frequently seen in all of the waters around the Pass. You can see them from the bridge if the lighting is right. Better yet, get on the water and see them up close just about anywhere.

They are curious creatures and seem to enjoy popping their heads up and just looking at you, the same way you are looking at them. Soon they get bored and dive down again, more interested in finding a meal than being photo-bombed in a selfie.

River otter feeding at the water's edge. Photo by Adam Lorio

Insider: Please Don't Kill the Babies

Every late spring and early summer, mother seals encourage their newly born pups to rest awhile on the beach while the mom goes fishing.

These pups look like they have been abandoned, much as a baby child will look abandoned as it rests in its crib. In other words, mom is being a good mom, and the baby is just resting.

When we hear about a seal pup resting on the shore, we will post signs at least 100 feet away telling people to stay away, as it is the law and it also is best for the seal. But unfortunately, people see the sign, find the seal, and out of curiosity and compassion try to help it.

They see this pup seal on the beach, being cute with its googly eyes looking at them, a creature which many people have never seen before. So they pour water on the pup, take selfies with it, pet it or try to move it back into the water.

Mom is probably watching from nearby, and seeing her baby assaulted by people, assumes it is a goner and never comes back for it. The end result: the baby dies of dehydration and starvation a couple days later, right there on the beach in front of everyone.

Visitors get mad at park staff that we didn't do anything to protect it, feed it, or care for it.

Please, let the momma seal care for it. Stay away. Let it live.

Insider: Bioluminescence

It's magical to me. After dark, you stir the water of the sea, and stars ignite all around. I scoop up a handful of water in my hand and I'm holding galaxies of starlight, or an explosion of fireworks, or a northwest gathering of fireflies.

Bioluminescence has a factual basis as well, perhaps even more exciting to researchers than the simple thrill of handling living light.

Darwin observed it while at sea, though he could not understand how it happened. Apollo 13 astronaut Jim Lovell mentions it in his story about finding his way back as a Navy pilot to his aircraft carrier. Tom Hanks portrays the story in a classic scene in the movie "Apollo 13".

Many plants and animals around the world use bioluminescence, a complex chemical reaction. Fireflies, glowworms, jellyfish, some bacteria and some fungi exhibit the captivating light. Several species of dinoflagellates, a tiny one-cell form of marine plankton, cause the phosphorescence in the surface layers of the salt water here.

They are most abundant and active when the weather and water have warmed up, if you can call it 'warm'. So look in the late spring or summer.

To find it at Deception Pass State Park, find a dock or some other way to get out into the salt water. I have always considered the float below the pier at Bowman or the dock at Sharpe's Cove at Rosario to be my favorite places for bioluminescence.

For either of those, you need to either be camping in the park or park outside the gate and enter after dusk with permission. Then go to the dock (please be quiet if there are boaters sleeping on their boats at the dock, or invite them to join you if they are up) and move the water.

Stirring it vigorously works, but it sends all the plankton elsewhere. Just holding a handful brings my palm alive with the cold glow of stars in my hand.

I have been unable to get a quality picture of it. If you can, I would love to see it.

Star trails above the bridge as seen from North Beach. Photo courtesy of TakePacific Photography

So there I am,

my very first day on the job, in 2003, and I'm in a meeting with several others talking about the Rosario tidepools. What are we going to do to protect the intertidal life, everyone asks? Rosario has always been popular for school visits during low tides in spring. A few years earlier, however, 1500 students and teachers descended onto the tidepools throughout the day, with no purpose other than to 'experience' the beach on a spring day. They pulled seastars off the boulders, urchins out of crevices, shore crabs from under rocks, and anything else that could be moved and removed. Bucketfuls of life ended up dead on the beach or in the parking lot. The tidepools resembled a moonscape rather than a seascape. Visits like this had been happening on a frequent and increasing basis. It is now time to do something about it.

We decide to require all schools to register with the park ahead of time so that we can manage how many people are in the tidepools at one time. We also ask them to visit for the right reasons, to learn about the fragile intertidal environment and from that knowledge help become citizens who care for all of our home planet.

But for the next few years this is not enough. The life in the tidepools does not return. Annual studies show no improvement in diversity or density of life.

Meanwhile, up on Goose Rock, we have a similar problem. The meadows are being trampled to death. Where there used to be rainbows of wildflowers across the balds we now see mostly weeds and grass, and even those are not healthy, trampled down to their roots, bare soil replacing what used to be rich fields. We decide to designate a trail across the top of Goose Rock, with low cedar railings outlining the trail. We put up little signs on the railings that say simply "respect the meadow, stay on trail". The railings are only six inches high. Anyone could step over them and walk through the meadows. But hikers respect the intentions of the railings and signs. In two years, flowers are again growing in the meadows adjacent to the trail, and the balds are deep and green with new life. I am thrilled.

Seeing that success, interpreter Adam Lorio and I meet to talk about our options for the tidepools. We discuss several alternative with many specialists and interested people. Ideas range from giving up trying to do anything to fencing it off entirely.

Adam studies other beach areas to see what they do, and we find alternatives ranging from guided hikes to raised metal walkways to publishing pleading brochures to allowing visits by advance reservation only for everyone.

We choose a fairly benign approach as our first attempt: lay out a rope through the tidepools to delineate a trail for people to follow, a route that goes through all the intertidal zones as a sacrificial area that then allows all the other acreage of the tidepools to be free of wandering feet and inquisitive hands.

We also post signs that encourage everyone to look but not touch except with one wet finger.

It takes several years to teach people that we are serious about recovering the life of the pools, giving the plants and animals a chance to live. And it takes us some time to figure out how to be there to encourage appropriate behavior without making visitors feel scolded or unwelcome.

For the first couple of years the work mostly falls on just one dedicated volunteer, Sammye Kempbell , and she begins to burn out from the effort. So she recruits others to join her, and then organizes a system of classes to teach these new volunteers how to share their new knowledge with visitors. The program takes off and becomes our Beach Naturalist program, growing stronger every year. Sammye continues to volunteer hundreds of hours each year, but she is now supported by over a dozen other dedicated volunteers who also contribute many, many hours.

And what becomes of the intertidal life?

The most recent transect studies indicate that the density of growth has increased 30% since the rope was first installed. It's coming back! That is the kind of result that makes me want to dance with joy. After all these years and all the volunteer effort, the life at Rosario is coming back.

Changing

"We are made wise not by the recollection of our past, but by the responsibility for our future."

— George Bernard Shaw

First peoples

With a history of human occupation in this area spanning many millennia, and an incredible richness of life all around, it is not surprising that the tribes who occupied the area had and continue to have a complex and well developed hunting-gathering-fishing culture.

They lived in large villages during the winter, building expansive plank houses for multi-family residences. They used large canoes for transportation across miles of open sea. During the summer they lived in various encampments that followed the seasonal cycles, gathering from the mouths of rivers and streams where salmon could be found, the shorelines for shellfish and forage fish, the marine waters for larger fish and sea mammals, and the inland forests for wild game and berries in season.

These tribes had sophisticated social, artistic, and technological traditions. They were notable for being one of the few cultures to develop sedentary villages without practicing agriculture.

The Pass area was home to several tribes, including the Swinomish and Samish. The Swinomish (pronounced (SWIN-a-mish) probably had a small village site near Cornet Bay, and perhaps along the banks of Cranberry Lake and North Beach. The Samish occupied the Fidalgo shores, with longhouses in the Bowman Bay and Rosario areas and elsewhere. Shellfish middens, areas strewn with village detritus, are found in all of these locations.

The tribes shared a similar life-style oriented toward fishing, hunting and gathering, as well as creating the implements necessary to be successful in these activities. Salmon was the most important food, the cedar their most versatile resource. The dugout canoe was the primary means of transport.

A typical village was located near a beach, and composed of a small number of large cedar-planked longhouses--each giving shelter to several related families.

As part of a larger Coast Salish cultural complex the Samish and Swinomish formed a village community, which consisted of several important social groupings: the family, the house group, the villages, and the entire tribe. Tribal members married outside of their groupings, so as to create a network of "kinships."

These kinships regulated both the internal and external relationships between the families, the house groups, the villages, and the tribes. The tribe relied on these relationships during bad times in order to be able to access areas of food and shelter that were not currently in their home territory.

Linguistically and culturally, the Samish tribe is grouped as Coast Salish, speaking a dialect of Coast Salish known as "Straits Salish," while the Swinomish speak the Lushootseed dialect, a different language but somewhat related.

White settlers to this continent brought two elements in particular which changed tribal culture forever. We brought diseases to which the tribes had no immunity, including smallpox, measles, and tuberculosis. These deadly diseases may have killed 90% of the population of the tribes, moving from the east coast to the west coast faster than the settlers did.

The second disruptive element to the tribes was the white concept of private ownership of land, completely foreign to the culture of the tribes. In 1855, tribal leaders from thirteen tribes, including the Samish and Swinomish, gathered at Mukilteo to sign the Treaty of Point Elliott.

Governor Stevens arbitrarily lumped tribes together for treaty-signing purposes. The 1855 Treaty of Point Elliott created the Swinomish Indian Reservation to include March Point and the southeastern side of Fidalgo Island, including Kiket Island. The Samish lived in the March Point area along with the Swinomish. March Point was arbitrarily and unilaterally removed a short while later from the reservation.

The Dawes Act of 1887 allowed tribal members to own parcels individually, and as owners, they could also sell their parcels to non-tribal members. This resulted in the loss of much of the original reservation land.

The tribal way of life could not exist in a world where a people who once freely roamed the Salish Sea had now become a people without a home at all.

In 1969, the Bureau of Indian Affairs (BIA) revised its list of recognized Indian tribes. A BIA clerk dropped the Samish Tribe off the list, for no reason. Based on the list, the BIA started treating the Samish Tribe as unrecognized and denied federal benefits to tribal members.

In 1992 a federal court overturned the BIA denial of Samish federal recognition and ordered a new hearing.

Finally, in 1996, the Samish Tribe re-recognition was listed in the Federal Register.

The tribal cultures are living cultures, with a rich past and strong presence for the future.

That the Samish and Swinomish have been able to re-establish an authentic tribal lifestyle for their people is a testament to their dedication and commitment to their ancestors and to their future national legacy.

It would be inappropriate for me to tell the stories and detailed history of these people. I leave that to the reader to research and discover from those who know the stories the best, the tribal elders.

However, one of the Samish stories has been shared by the tribe for the express purpose of letting others come to know the story and learn from it. The depth of the story comes out when told by an elder.

The Samish tribe has graciously consented to display the story in signs at the Rosario area of Deception Pass.

Image courtesy of Joni Polig and Sarah Rivers

The Story of Ko kwal alwoot

Ko Kwal alwoot and other maidens were gathering food from the shore. As she reached into the water for a shellfish, a hand grasped hers.

A man's voice spoke out "You are safe. I just want to behold your beauty."

Ko Kwal alwoot returned to the water's edge many times after that to talk with the man. They talked of many things and shared deeply.

After many meetings, a young spirit man emerged from the water. The man went to Ko Kwal alwoot's father to ask to marry the young maiden. The people noticed a chill and icy wind when the man was in the village.

When he asked to marry Ko Kwal alwoot, her father said "No, my daughter would die in the sea."

The young man exclaimed "I will give her eternal life, as I love her dearly."

But if the father refused, the man warned, there would be a great scarcity of all types of food. Even the streams would dry up if the young maiden did not marry him.

This came to be.

After some time Ko Kwal alwoot went to the water. There she called to the man, begging for food for her people.

He replied, "Only when you are my bride will food be plentiful once again."

Her father reluctantly gave his daughter so that the tribe might survive. He asked that she be allowed to return to her people once a year, which the man accepted.

Ko Kwal alwoot wrapped her garments of cedar about her and walked into the sea until only her hair was seen floating in the current of the sea.

Once again food was plentiful and the tribe prospered.

Ko Kwal alwoot returned to her people every year. Each time she returned she appeared more like the sea life that is the life force of her people. She was unhappy to be out of the sea. At last her father suggested that she not return unless she wished to.

The story pole at Rosario has two sides representing the two lives of Ko Kwal alwoot, one as a human, the other as a spirit.

As you watch the currents flow back and forth in the waters of the Pass, imagine the Maiden's long hair drifting gently with the tide.

European Exploration

Juan de Fuca (Ioánnis Fokás) of Greek descent may have been among the first of the European explorers to this area, allegedly visiting here as a passenger on a ship in the late 1500s. He wrote a record of his vist when he returned to Europe, which may describe some of the features of the area, including the Strait that now bears his name.

In May 1790 Salvador Fidalgo made a voyage north to visit the Russian outposts in Alaska, while Manuel Quimper examined the Strait of Juan de Fuca. Quimper's pilot was Gonzalo López de Haro. Some of the important sites found and charted during Quimper's expedition include Neah Bay, Esquimalt Harbour, Admiralty Inlet, Haro Strait, Rosario Strait, and Deception Pass.

Further exploration voyages were undertaken in 1791. In early May, Eliza set out in command of the *San Carlos*. The *San Carlos* was accompanied by the small schooner, the *Santa Saturnina*, nicknamed *La Orcasitas* and under the command of José María Narváez, with Juan Carrasco as pilot.

At the start of Narváez's voyage the *Santa Saturnina* passed Admiralty Inlet, the entrance to what is now Puget Sound (called "Ensenada de Caamaño" by the Spanish). Narváez saw that it was a large channel leading to the south and planned to explore it after returning from the north.

On July 1, 1791, Narváez and Carrasco sailed north, up present-day Rosario Strait. He gave the name "Boca de Flon" to the present-day Deception Pass. They named Fidalgo Island for Lieutenant Salvador Fidalgo who was present off the shore of Vancouver Island and in the Strait of Juan de Fuca in 1790. They then headed into the Strait of Georgia.

But the Strait of Georgia proved larger than expected and Narváez ran out of food, the *Santa Saturnina* being very small. They never returned to explore Puget Sound. The Spanish thus missed the opportunity of preempting the British exploration of Puget Sound, which took place a year later by the English explorer, Captain George Vancouver.

Vancouver's voyage in the H. M. S. Discovery started out soon after the mutiny aboard the H.M.S. Bounty, with the result that a consort, the armed tender Chatham under the command of Lieutenant William Robert Broughton, was sent to accompany the Discovery. George Vancouver and William Bligh had served together on Captain Cook's third voyage, Bligh being the sailing master. There is no doubt that the mutiny on the Bounty influenced Vancouver's attitudes toward his officers and men. Vancouver had also been present when the natives in Hawaii killed Captain Cook, and that undoubtedly colored his attitude toward native peoples.

Vancouver entered the Strait of Juan de Fuca in the spring of 1792. He spent several months exploring the area. We still use the names he gave to many of the features of the area: Puget Sound, Admiralty Inlet, Mount Rainier, and Mount

The Spanish artist Cardero sketched this depiction of three ships in Guemes Channel being met by Samish tribal members. Mt. Baker rises in the distance. Image used by permission of Museo Naval Espana.

Baker. His surgeon-naturalist, Archibald Menzies, marveled at the verdant vegetation he found here. He is credited with naming many species, including madrone, bigleaf maple, and western hemlock.

Vancouver explored the western and lower end of Puget Sound in May, then headed up the east coast of the Sound. He named an inner waterway Port Gardner and Saratoga Passage having explored that from the south. He sent a small boat under the command of Master Joseph Whidbey to explore further north. Whidbey reached the northern end of Saratoga Passage and explored eastward into Skagit Bay, which is shallow and difficult to navigate. He returned south to rejoin Vancouver. It appeared to him that Skagit Bay was a dead-end and that what we now call Whidbey Island and Fidalgo Islands were just a long peninsula attached to the mainland.

Then Vancouver sailed up Admiralty Inlet, arriving a couple days later off the mouth of what he thought was a substantial river. His surgeon, Archibald Menzies, gushed about "...*the enchanting variety of the surrounding scenery where the softer beauties of landscape are harmoniously blended in majestic grandeur with the wild & romantic to form an interesting and picturesque prospect on every side.*" This place is known to generate that kind of poetic prose in people.

Vancouver again sent Whidbey in a smaller boat to explore this area. Peter Puget narrated their travels.

"*June 8, 1792: That evening assisted by a strong flood tide we arrived off the first opening tending to the eastward but it was so narrow that we imagined it almost impossible it would communicate with any other branch. A short time however convinced us of our error for the tide of ebb came down with such force that its rapidity checked our utmost efforts and effectively stopped our progress for the night.*"

They camped on North Beach, probably near where the amphitheater is now. Puget then continues:

"*On Saturday 9th we again proceeded to the examination of this branch through this narrow channel. By nine Mr. Whidbey was perfectly satisfied of its communication with the arm he surveyed when dispatched on that service. Therefore we have now determined this intervening land between the branch in the NE arm in the NE shore of the narrows to be a large island which Captain Vancouver named after Mr. Whidbey.*"

Whidbey had sailed through Deception Pass, and realized they had nearly circumnavigated what was actually an island, and that the flow of a 'river' was actually ebbing tidal currents. He returned to the ship which was waiting outside the Pass on June 10, 1792.

Vancouver, feeling that he had been 'deceived' as to the nature of his Port Gardner and this other passage, wrote of Whidbey's efforts: "*This determined to be an island, which, in consequence of Mr. Whidbey's circumnavigation, I distinguished by the name of Whidbey's Island: and this northern pass, leading into [Skagit Bay], Deception Passage*".

Vancouver described it as "...*a very narrow and intricate channel, which, for a considerable distance, was not forty yards in width, and abounded with rocks above and beneath the surface of the water. These impediments, in addition to the great rapidity and irregularity of the tide, rendered the passage navigable only for boats or vessels of very small burthen.*"

A monument on Pass Island now commemorates this visit of over 200 years ago.

The Wilkes expedition came up the coast in 1941 with the express purpose of mapping the territory and conducting scientific studies. Lieutenant Charles Wilkes is credited with assigning many of the geographical names, many from non-local sources. The names of Yokeko, Hoypus, and Kiket may be from indigenous tribes in California! His strict leadership style may have inspired the character of Captain Ahab for author Herman Melville.

He sailed his brig the "Porpoise" through the Pass, perhaps the first large sailing ship to attempt the feat.

He named Fidalgo Island Perry Island, after Commodore Perry's famous battle on Lake Erie. And he named the tall mountain on the island Mt. Erie. That name survived, but a few years later, another explorer, Captain Kellett, changed Perry back to Fidalgo in his efforts to restore the original Spanish names.

Military Reservation

Shortly after the Civil War, military planners recognized the strategic military values of the Pass as a backdoor entrance to Puget Sound. They set aside 1760 acres from both sides of Deception Pass for future harbor defense needs. President Andrew Johnson officially withdrew the land from public use on September 22, 1866.

The only fortifications ever built here took place during World War One, when a search light tower was in place at West Point (the foundation still remains as a popular sunset-watching seat) and three-inch guns were installed at Gun Point, between North Beach and Little North Beach. The guns came from Fort Casey, but they were never used. The soldiers had a cookhouse and platform tents where the North Beach parking lot is now.

During World War Two, soldiers from Fort Casey would occasionally stand watch at the park's beaches.

Pioneers

At the end of the Civil War the Western Union Russian Extension Company built a telegraph line from the mainland to Victoria, coming across Fidalgo Island before dropping into the sea. Some of the poles for this line crossed north of Pass Lake. They built a log cabin telegraph station on the north shore of the lake. The line

A fisherman stands by his boat on the shore of Ben Ure Island, looking west toward Deception Pass, sometime around the turn of the century, long before a bridge spanned the water. Image courtesy of Washington State Archives.

was abandoned in 1880 due to the cost of maintaining the cable between the islands.

In 1876, the same time as the Battle of Little Bighorn further east, Thomas Sharpe homesteaded the land northeast of Rosario, where Sharpe Road is today. The Ginnett family arrived at about this same time, living eastward of Sharpe.

In 1884, a homesteader by the name of Halpin started a farm in the area, and noted that there was an old log cabin telegraph office still on the farm. Doug Allmond acquired this property in the Pass Lake area a short while later. The original telegraph office became the living room of a larger house that he built around it.

A town named Deception sprung up along the beach east of the Pass in the 1880s. The name changed to Fidalgo City in 1889, with its own post office. At the turn of the century, this was changed again, this time to Dewey.

In the 1890s, several homesteaders had established farms and mills in the area, and small towns arose at Oak Harbor, Dewey Beach, March Point, and Anacortes.

Although the military owned the core of the Deception Pass area, the fringe areas were being used and abused.

Loggers took out many of the trees in the Rosario area, and used Sharpe Cove, south of Rosario at the entrance to Bowman Bay, as a loading yard to ship logs to nearby mills. Only the forests protected from loggers by the military reserve remained untouched, allowing us to enjoy the old growth forests throughout key areas of the park.

Families camped along the beaches during the summer, not for fun as much as for a low cost place to live.

Dunnell Bowman built a store and printing press (publishing a socialist paper called "The Sound") in the Rosario area at this time, and his brother Amos built a cabin at Reservation Bay where the large parking lot is now. Amos was the one who named the growing town north of here after his wife, Anna Curtis. He changed the letters a little to come up with Anacortes, pronounced "Anna Cortis" if you want to sound local.

The bay became known as Bowman Bay after the family living there, but soon changed to Reservation Bay because of the adjoining military land. After the military left the Bowman name again took precedence.

The Rosario settlers were optimistic of a town starting there, and even had a post office. They built a dock in Sharpe's Cove, where the dock is now just south of the Maiden story pole. Steamers from Seattle would dock here three times a week with freight or passengers.

The main land route from Dewey Beach to the Sharpe and Ginnett road areas went along the north shore of Pass Lake and through Heilman Valley in those days. The Livingston family also lived here, on the north shore of Pass Lake, living in the Storm or Storme family house at the south end of what is now Heilman Valley. In 1908 Mr. Livingston went to work for the survey crew planning a prison camp on the north shore of the Pass. Construction began in 1909, and he kept employed for a couple years there. Family circumstances moved the family elsewhere a few years later.

Picnickers enjoy the afternoon at Rosario Beach. Image courtesy of Washington State Archives.

In 1918, Mr. Ginnett found copper on his land, and dug mines, finding three 5-gallon oil can loads of pure copper nuggets in one of them. The mining stopped for World War I, then in 1940 he started mining for manganese. This stopped when World War II began. The mine shafts are still on Ginnett Hill.

In the Thirties, Mr. Allmond wanted to sell his property surrounding Pass Lake to Washington State Parks, but the Governor at that time vetoed the purchase as being too extravagant. Allmond was asking ten thousand dollars.

Prison Camp

It's not a likely place for a prison, that's for sure. In 1909 to 1910, prison officials built a prison dormitory, power plant, and other related buildings in the woods west of Dewey Beach, at the east end of Deception Pass on the north shore.

As a joint effort, the State Highway Department and State Board of Control developed the first of five quarries at Deception Pass as the Fidalgo Rock Quarry. Incarcerated male workers came from the State Penitentiary at Walla Walla and the State Reformatory at Monroe, but only labored at the Deception Pass quarry from 1909-1914.

From 25 to 40 prisoners stayed here for various crimes, and built all the facilities.

The mine building sits high on the cliff north of Deception Pass. Rock was sent down the chute to the rock crushing plant at the water's edge, where barges were loaded and the gravel hauled elsewhere. The prison camp itself was a quarter mile east, to the right in this picture, close to the shore where it is not as steep. Image courtesy of Washington State Archives.

Nearby, they built a rock crushing plant on the steep talus slopes along the rock walls north of Canoe Pass, and then expanded part of a natural cave in that cliff-face into a twelve foot wide by ten foot high mine.

Prisoners were marched from the dormitory to the top of the cliff, where they descended a 150 foot ladder to get to the cave. Guards stood at the quarry as the prisoners cut the rock into gravel.

Prisoners cut rock out of that mine, sent it by gravity to the crushing plant, which created gravel. They dropped this down to a landing at the water's edge, where barges would load up with the gravel and take it to roadways and waterfronts under construction in the nearby areas. They produced 600 tons of gravel a day.

It doesn't make much sense to me, as gravel is not that difficult to create in much, much easier locations. But it did keep prisoners from wanting to escape as they looked at the sheer cliff above the mine and the quick drop to the waters of Deception Pass below.

One prisoner escaped, swam the Pass and was never found.

The prisoners were happy to be here, even though it was hard work in a challenging location; it far surpassed being inside the concrete walls of the penitentiary.

The camp was dismantled in 1924. Although abandoned as a quarry, the remains of the camp can still be found. Today, the prison buildings are gone except for rough outlines of their foundations. The mine remains, but the cave has been gated off to keep people away from this highly hazardous area that has led to several deaths over the years.

Ben Ure

Ben Ure, a Scot who is said to have started the chain of events that gave Cornet Bay its early reputation, homesteaded on what was to become "his island," and then set out to trade among the islands, using rum, opium, and woolens as his trade.

Ben Ure Island, also called Barnes Island for awhile, is a small rocky mound at the north end of Cornet Bay, just inside Deception Pass. In the 1890s Ben Ure had made enough money to invest in the Anacortes "boom days," only to have his investments in real estate swept away by the panic of 1893. He then packed his gear in his sailing sloop and headed back toward his island where he maintained a small lighthouse.

Ben Ure's life was a rocky one, and exciting. On Ben Ure's Island a dance hall and saloon sprang up where loggers and tugboat men spent their leisure hours under the watchful eyes of Revenue cutters. It was suspected that smugglers used Ure's setup on the Island. While the patrol boats were helpless, the rowdy partying in the saloon went on and the variety of boats tied up at the small dock were usually gone by morning.

Ben Ure Island, once called Barnes Island, as it looked in 1935 from Goose Rock, before trees grew to block this view. Image courtesy of Washington State Archives.

The Chinese importation took on a new phase of smuggling from the mid-1880s to 1900 and there were many harrowing stories of cargoes of Chinese dumped overboard when the Coast Guard approached the smuggling vessel. Deception Pass was a favored lookout for government vessels.

Then a small news item in a Seattle newspaper of May 29, 1902 carried this item: "White-haired Benje Ure, accused of harboring smugglers and pirates, is now under arrest, formally charged with receiving stolen goods."

So finally Ben Ure, whose Island will commemorate his name longer than his questionable activities of that period, was arrested, and charged with the possession of stolen goods. Several cases of contraband cigars, whiskey, and opium were found on his island. And when his trial came up, Ben Ure told of his exploits.

He had assisted smugglers such as "The Flying Dutchman" and "Pirate Kelly," the king of all Puget Sound smugglers. When asked why his Indian wife spent so much time on Strawberry Island he said, "She sits behind the fire when the patrol boats are around, and in front of the fire when it is safe for the fellows to come though the Pass."

Ben Ure spent only five days in jail, but it apparently changed his thinking and his ways. He was 72 years old and made a will disposing of his property, but made no mention of the island. The little island still retains the name of the old-time settler who died Nov. 15, 1908.

The island's reputation changed over the years as it was platted for residences and homes began to dot the shorelines. Most of the homes were for vacationing, but a couple had year-round residents.

Recognizing the value of the island to the Deception Pass viewshed, Washington State Parks began buying property on the island from owners willing to sell. By the turn of the new millennium, two thirds of the island was protected from development and secure in the ownership as state park land.

In 2005, State Parks acquired a parcel that had a small but comfortable cabin. With the consent of the other land owners on the island, we began to rent out the cabin to those who could get there in a kayak or canoe. It has proven to be very popular, beloved by our guests.

A few years ago we purchased another parcel on the island, on the southwest corner, the home of a former astronaut. Only three private homes remain on the island. Out of respect for these home-owners, only registered cabin guests are allowed on the island, and then only on the south side of the island, protecting the privacy of the land owners on the north side of the island.

Fish Traps at West Beach

Fish traps occupied all of West Beach from about 1900 to 1926. The traps, wire, pilings, and netting were all removed every fall, and re-assembled each spring for the fishing season.

Little shacks were built on the pilings, and watchmen stayed there to discourage thieves. The salmon they caught there were canned in an Anacortes cannery.

Ferry Days

Before there was a bridge connecting the north end of Whidbey Island with Fidalgo Island and the mainland, there was a ferry.

In 1911, Fred Finsen owned and operated a post office and store at Cornet Bay. A soldier from Fort Casey paid Finsen to row the soldier and his motorcycle across to Fidalgo Island. Finsen did, and the idea of a ferry service took root.

The first ferry across the Pass started where the county dock is now located at the west end of Cornet Bay. Ben Ure Island can be see over the top of the car. Photo courtesy of the Scott Harrison collection.

Official ferry service began in 1913 when Finsen constructed a barge-like ferry that he towed from Cornet Bay to Yokeko on Fidalgo Island. In those days, the Cornet Bay Road ended where the private residences are now.

"Ferry boat" may be a stretch. Imagine a raft with two logs on each side, propelled by a small gasoline engine. The autos rested on two-by-twelve planks, with nothing between them.

Finsen published these ferry rates in 1913:

7-passenger auto and driver	$2.50
5-passenger auto and driver	$2.00
Small auto and driver	$1.50
1 horse, buggy and driver	$1.50
Passengers	25 cents each
Sunday excursion rates 1 1/2 fare for round trip	
Horses, 1-4 in number	$2.00
Horses, 5 or more	50 cents each
Cattle, 1-4	$2.00
Animals, 5 or more	50 cents each

Paul Lang operated the ferry in 1918. He convinced the county to build the road out to Hoypus Point and build a landing there, as this route was a much shorter distance to Yokeko.

His barge could carry six cars, not just four. It ran on irregular hours at best. To notify the operator that you wanted to cross, you would raise a white flag at your side of the crossing, and the ferrymaster would come across to get you. However, imagine your concern if the operator was busy with other chores for awhile, or unable to see it in the fog, or rain, or in the dark. Patience had to accompany every trip on and off the island.

The trip itself took thirty to sixty minutes to cross in good weather. Imagine how this system served the needs of the island's residents and businesses.

In 1920 Berte Olson won the bid for the line. A long-time Whidbey Island resident, Berte Olson has the distinction of being the first woman ferry boat captain on Puget Sound. Olson began her maritime career going on commercial fishing trips with her brothers. On one such trip she met a man named Agaton Olson (no relation), and they eventually married.

During the early 1920s, she and her husband used Agaton's fishing boat towing a scow as their first ferry.

In 1922 they obtained a ferry big enough to carry twelve Model T Fords. It was 64' long with a 24' beam. They charged 50 cents for a car and 10 cents for passengers. The Olson's ferry was a lifeline to the Whidbey Island community, particularly in times of medical emergency.

Insider: A Ferry Different Era

Hike out to Hoypus Point and you can still see the concrete pier built by Paul Lang that served as part of the ferry landing for many years.

The dock on the Fidalgo Island side was at the west end of Dewey Beach, just east of Yokeko Point across the water and a little west of here.

Picture driving out this road to get to this landing area for the only vehicle access to the mainland from this end of the island. At least the Olsens offered scheduled service, a breakthrough idea.

Berte Olson was not your typical woman from a hundred years ago. Her nickname, "Little but oh my!" conjures up images of this tiny capable woman piloting the Pass, hauling rope, fixing engines, directing traffic, and running the business of operating several ferries.

The Olsons also vehemently opposed the construction of the Deception Pass Bridge, often personally lobbying with legislators in Olympia. Olson maintained that her family had all they owned invested in the ferry and stood to lose the entire amount of $30,000 if the bridge were built.

"I'm not anti-bridge, I'm just trying to fight for the preservation of the savings of a lifetime," she said.

According to the Olson's son, Gil, his parents "received only token payment for the loss of their livelihood." After the bridge's construction Berte Olson moved to Hood Canal and operated a ferry run there.

DECEPTION PASS FERRY

Summer Schedule

Leave Mainland (Fidalgo) side, 7:30 a. m. and hourly to 8:30 p. m. Special late trip Saturday night at 11:00 p. m. Running time, 5 minutes crossing.

Leave Whidby Island side, 7:45 a. m. and hourly to 8:45 p. m., then at 11:15 p. m. Saturday only.

Saturday, Sunday and Holidays every half hour with the exception of 12 noon and 12:15 p. m.

Newspaper clipping of the ferry schedule for the Mainland/Whidbey run, printed some time in the 1920s. Image courtesy of Washington State Parks.

The Years Before the Park

Although much of the park was still in the military reservation in the early part of the twentieth century, the forests and beaches around the reservation became very popular. These lands offered many of the same recreational opportunities we enjoy today, and some commercial activity too.

The photograph below shows Sharpe's Cove, south of the Rosario tombolo, and looking east into Bowman Bay. Bowman Hill rises above the bay. The dock at Sharpe's Cove has a structure or two on it for working with the many commercial and recreational boats that visited the area, some on a schedule to bring mail and passengers three times a week.

This is the only quality photograph that I have found so far that shows the southern shoreline of Bowman Bay before the rock rip-rap and pier were built there. From this photograph we can see that the beach is one continuous half-moon shape, with a forested wetland behind the beach where we now have a playfield.

On the following page, the photograph shows the Rosario uplands as seen from Rosario Head, the photo taken by moving just a little to the right of where the photo below was taken, and looking further left.

Notice the cars parked in the lawn where we now have the grass field at Rosario, and a restroom type building behind. Notice also the posts in the ground keeping cars from driving onto the tombolo leading to Rosario Head, and what looks like a ticket booth at that gateway area.

The CCC would eventually build a shelter to the left of that restroom, and a bathhouse just beyond the parking area on the right, which is now the Rosario Field Classroom.

The United States flag on the pole probably has 48 stars, as Arizona and New Mexico joined the Union in 1912.

Photos courtesy of Whatcom Museum

State Park Dedication

The concept of coastal forts guarding the entrances to Puget Sound ended with the advent of war planes. As a result, the War Department intended to sell their Deception Pass military reserve to private developers in 1921.

J. Grant Hinkle, secretary of the newly-formed Washington State Parks Committee, wired a protest to Congress. In his letter he suggested that the Committee

> *"...dedicated to the uses and pleasures of the people forever."*
> — from the 1922 park dedication

would prefer to have the property turned over to them for care rather than to see it leased to private individuals.

The Anacortes Chamber of Commerce and the Island County Farm Bureau agreed. They put into action a plan to have the federal government give the land to the state as a new state park. The Washington State Park system had begun in 1913, and had already received two parks in 1915. This seemed like a natural and desirable addition to the system.

Through various negotiations and agreements, the House agreed in February of 1922, the Senate on March 16, and on **March 23, 1922**, President Warren G. Harding signed and transferred the deed of the nearly 1800 acre reserve to the State of Washington for state park purposes.

The agreement stated that the land was *"dedicated to the uses and pleasures of the people forever."*

The State Parks Committee accepted the tract as a state park on April 17, 1922, and formal proceedings and speeches made it a reality on July 20, 1922, when the Anacortes Chamber and Island County Farm Bureau held an inter-island picnic at "the picnic grounds of the park". (Some say this was Cornet Bay, but East Cranberry seems more likely.)

Thousands attended the picnic, according to the newspaper report, joining with representatives of the federal and state governments to hold a celebration for the official opening of Deception Pass State Park to the public. State Treasurer Clifford Babcock accepted the transfer, and named the recreation grounds "Deception Pass State Park".

According to Park Superintendent Rutherford, 26,000 visitors came to Deception Pass in 1924, making it the most visited park in the state, an honor it has rarely relinquished. (In 2015, the park had 2.6 million visitors, again higher than any other state park in Washington.)

Civilian Conservation Corps

The Thirties brought the Great Depression. The nation elected a new president, Franklin D. Roosevelt, to change the economic directions we were heading. Within six weeks of his inauguration, Roosevelt had presented a plan to create the Civilian Conservation Corps as one of his forward-thinking strategies for rebuilding the nation.

President Roosevelt's program had several goals, including putting young men back to work, building families around the nation, and serving our parks and natural resources with focused efforts.

The CCC program succeeded beyond all expectations.

Enrollees aged 18 - 25, in need of work and training, came from around the nation to camps such as these. They were paid $30 a month, $25 of which went back home to their families, enough to survive on.

At Deception Pass, two camps were established, one on each side of the bridge. The Whidbey Island camp was at Cornet Bay, the site of the present-day Cornet Bay Retreat Center. The CCC crews built base camp structures, then moved out into the park to build shelters and a restroom at East Cranberry Lake, the residence and garage near the old park entrance, the North Beach facilities, the tunnel under Highway 20, and the highway approach to the bridge then under construction.

On the other side, the Rosario camp, stationed just outside the park boundary at Cougar Gap, built the Rosario and Bowman Bay shelters, bathhouses, and roadways and trails throughout the area. They also blasted out the route for the new highway along Pass Lake and up to the north end of the new bridge.

The camps lasted most of the nine years that the CCC program was in existence. They built the park's recreational features to create a landscape that was attractive and thoughtfully planned. And they improved the lives of thousands of young men and local residents too.

For a comprehensive story about the CCC at Deception Pass State Park, read **Two Hands and a Shovel**, available at the park, local bookstores, or through online outlets. The book has hundreds of photos of the CCC at Deception Pass and provides detailed descriptions of the work that they did and the lives that they lived here.

The Civilian Conservation Corps Camp at Cornet Bay, looking northeast toward Goose Rock. This camp developed facilities on the south side of the Pass. All CCC Images this page and next courtesy of Washington State Archives.

The CCC built the bathhouse visible on the far left, and created this beautiful swim beach at the east end of Cranberry Lake. Wouldn't it be grand to see this area restored to look like this again?

The Civilian Conservation Corps men building the residence on the south side of the park. Local experienced men taught the enrollees how to build quality structures that could stand the test of time.

CCC enrollees setting logs onto the pillars they had made for the new railing along the new highway leading to the bridge. You can still see much of the original railing today. In 2005, the Department of Transportation found some funding to replace the original log and pillar railing with an engineered railing. We insisted that it resemble the CCC style, and after extensive testing, they found a system that could stop dump trucks yet still look similar to the original.

Insider:
Enrollee John Tursi

John was born on July 24, 1917 in Brooklyn, New York, the son of Vito and Rosina (Caraciano) Torcia, who emigrated from Italy in 1910.

Raised on the streets of New York as a child with little family support, John attended school through the 8th grade, then did what he could to survive.

In 1933 the Civilian Conservation Corps advertised for members to work on a project to build a park near Anacortes, Washington. John was then 16 and applied at a local police station where his age was "adjusted" to 18 so he could qualify. He boarded a military troop train and headed west, ending up in a town called Anacortes on the other side of the country.

A ferry took him to Cornet Bay, and according to John, he knew he had come home.

His job was to help build Deception Pass State Park. His first day on the job, a wet rainy day, his new boss taught him to chew snoose and to light powder to blast out trees and roadways. He was all of 16 years old.

John Tursi on the left, cutting lumber in 1934 for the tunnel visible over his shoulder.

Over the course of the next year or so, he became a part of helping raise several of the buildings, creating some of the detail metal work on the buildings, blasting out a road with dynamite to the future bridge, and building the structure that became the underpass under Highway 20. He spent two terms of service here, staying on because he loved the work, loved the park, and had nowhere else to go.

He also met the love of his life, Doris Anderson, and they were wed here.

Johnny enlisted in the Army in 1944. He was sent to France as an Army Engineer Tech Sergeant, where he cleared hedgerows with a dozer and helped to construct bridges. Much of his three-year tour was spent in combat conditions.

Returning to Anacortes in 1945, John went to work in the salmon industry and later with Shell Oil. He was a recognized expert in hydraulic pumps and eventually retired as a supervisor in the Maintenance Department.

After retirement, he and Doris decided to do what they could to support forest lands and parks, projects that would "live on". John was on the boards of the Anacortes and Skagit Valley Museums and was a volunteer and supporter of the Anacortes Soroptimist Club.

John stayed involved at Deception Pass State Park, joining our newly formed Advisory Board in 2004, and assisting with the new Deception Pass Park Foundation financially and with great ideas. His funding helped support many of the interpretive projects throughout the park in the ensuing years.

In 2010, the Foundation created a special commemorative plaque in his honor, telling the story of his work in the CCC and throughout the Anacortes community. It was placed at the underpass to continue the legacy of his story.

I loved John's kind and gentle ways. He loved

John Tursi standing beside the plaque that describes his work in the CCC, and thanks him for his support of the park since that time. The underpass he helped build in 1934 stands behind.

this park, and he always had a word of encouragement for me in helping to care for this park. He also always had a story about an experience he had here, something that helped me see the history behind the scenery.

One story in particular has to be shared. He and another enrollee got into a scuffle of some kind in the dining hall. As punishment, the camp director had John plant a row of trees along the highway just east of the underpass. Today, those trees are over eighty years old, right next to the highway, in a straight row where he planted them. I think of John every time I drive past those trees.

In 2015, John was honored by the Skagit County Commissioners for his participation in the Skagit Land Trust when they designated the trail connecting the Anacortes Forest Lands with Deception Pass State Park as the "Tursi Trail" on South Fidalgo Island.

John Tursi passed away on Friday, April 8, 2016 at the age of 98. He is forever in our hearts, and his life is reflected throughout this park.

Liz Merriman, former president of the Deception Pass Park Foundation and one of John's dear friends, wrote these additional words in a message to our Foundation:

> "Please understand how much Deception Pass meant to John. He said it saved his life in so many ways. Three squares a day, a roof over his head, and learning trades like blacksmithing (which can be seen at the CCC Interpretive Center at Bowman Bay) and explosives (he "blew-up" the rock to create the south parking lot at the bridge).
>
> "He learned the work ethic and discipline that became the essence of who he was. Many a time on our drives throughout the park he would stop talking in mid sentence... he was, almost physically, back in the time and place when life really began for him.
>
> "John gave back to the park both monetarily and spiritually. I have never met a character of this capacity, and I suspect I never will."

To help guide the extensive development work that the CCC would accomplish, the National Park Service created a park master plan in the mid-Thirties. This plan envisioned a campground near Cranberry Lake, and a foot trail out to West Beach. They intended North Beach to have a visitor center overlooking the water and bridge. East Cranberry would be the center of recreation activity, with swimming beaches, docks for strolling over the lake, a bathhouse for changing, and a large parking lot.

Development followed the master plan of the park fairly closely, sensitive to the environment and heritage of the area, while encouraging recreational uses that were appropriate for the locations.

In the few short years that they were here, the CCC built over two dozen classic structures, nearly all of which are still in use. They built several miles of roads and trails, laid out miles of pipelines and sewer lines, all hand dug, and established Deception Pass State Park as a major destination for park goers, all while also protecting and truly enhancing the natural values of the park.

"In all, the whole development program is based on the most convenient and enjoyable use of the park by the general public with as little change in the original nature of the park as possible.

"Every step has been taken to preserve the natural flora and virgin settings. It is hoped that the beauty of the park and comfort and convenience of the park facilities made available by the present administration will be enjoyed by many for years to come."

— Max Luft, Project Superintendent
Cornet Bay CCC Camp, 1935

Mr. Luft's words can be my mantra as well, eighty years later. Our goal is to protect the natural and cultural values of the park, while allowing visitors to enjoy them for centuries to come.

Those National Park Service plans guided the CCC work, but the influx of visitors brought by the bridge changed the focus of the plans a decade later.

Insider: Deception Pass NATIONAL Park?

Although dedicated as a Washington State park in 1922, the park was administered by the National Park Service in the CCC era for management oversight by a federal agency.

It is an interesting mind game to ponder what would have been different had the NPS continued to manage Deception Pass, with their sizeable budget and tradition of grand interpretive efforts. Indeed, many visitors think that they are in a national park when they see the grandeur of the forests, the vastness of the landscapes, and the rustic nature of the CCC structures.

The character of the park is worthy of national attention and interest, and its popularity proves that. At the same time, the protection of the resources comes as our highest priority.

Perhaps it isn't the name of the agency that manages the park but the heart and character of the management priorities that makes the difference in the end.

I think this park is in good hands.

The Bridge

In 1907, a local mariner and legislator named Captain George Morse pushed a bill through the state assembly that called for building bridges over Deception and Canoe passes, linking Whidbey Island with Fidalgo Island and the mainland. A year later, site studies were completed and Morse secured $20,000 from the legislature for building bridge approaches. His dreams faded as the state established different spending priorities and spent the money on other projects.

The primitive ferry service at the north end was totally inadequate for the growing civilian and military traffic. Locals continued to lobby for the spans. In 1921 they attempted to convince the legislators that it was of military necessity to bridge the passes to give Fort Casey a road to the mainland. This effort also failed.

The local American Legion began to push for a bridge, and organized an annual Deception Pass Inter-Island Picnic to bring the communities together and to call attention to the need for the bridge. These picnics at Cranberry Lake's eastern shore created quite a gathering, as residents of Anacortes and Mount Vernon joined Whidbey Island residents for food, games, and speeches by local leaders.

The picnics continued for many years and became one of the highlights of the summer for local residents.

Of course, having dignitaries and off-island visitors experience the challenge of getting to Whidbey Island created a clear picture of the need for a bridge.

The Deception Pass Bridge Association formed in 1928 to promote the construction of the bridges. Local Island County and Skagit County representatives Pearl Wanamaker and William McCracken jointly sponsored legislation in 1929 that state lawmakers passed.

Nevertheless, fearing a loss of her livelihood, Berte Olson used her clout in Olympia to change opinions, and Governor Roland Hartley vetoed the bill.

The Bridge Association reorganized and again pushed for a bridge in 1930. By 1933 a Wanamaker-sponsored bill passed, granting the Washington State Parks Committee permission to build the bridges as toll structures if alternative funding through state bond sales failed to materialize!

President Roosevelt's "New Deal" economic recovery program eventually paid for the bridges' construction.

In December 1933 funding arrived in a package of $245,000 from the Washington Emergency Relief Administration and $150,000 from Island and Skagit counties. The Public Works Administration contributed $87,000 to reimburse the state. The Highways Department awarded $304,755 to the Puget Sound Construction Company of Seattle in June of 1934.

Work started on the north end first. Although this work was dangerous, no one lost their life. Image courtesy of Washington State Archives.

Local out-of-work farmers performed much of the labor to build the approaches and concrete work, along with the men of the CCC.

Construction of the concrete pier footings started in August and was completed in January of 1935. The contractor built a concrete mixing plant on the Whidbey Island side for the south cantilever piers, using a 6000-foot pipeline from Cranberry Lake for water. A second plant north of Canoe Pass created the concrete for the north piers, getting water from Pass Lake over a quarter mile away. A cableway connected Fidalgo Island with Pass Island to transport materials to the middle.

With Canoe Pass nearing completion, the main span began, this photo being taken in February of 1935 from North Beach. Image courtesy of Washington State Archives.

Meanwhile the Wallace Bridge and Structural Steel Company fabricated the steel members and transported them to the site from Seattle. They used liberal amounts of silicon steel instead of carbon steel because its stress capability was higher.

The steel work at the Pass began in January of 1935. They started with the north arch over Canoe Pass, then built the south arch, finishing that side in March. Then the north cantilever section grew out from Pass Island toward

The main span under construction as seen from Pass Island looking toward Whidbey Island. Image courtesy of Washington State Archives.

Whidbey, and then the south cantilever section from Whidbey. By early June they were ready to place the 200-foot suspended span to join the other two together.

It was a hot day in June when the crane operator lowered the final section into place. It was three inches too long.

The main span nearly complete in June of 1935. Image courtesy of Washington State Archives.

Paul Jarvis, founder of the Puget Construction Company, pulled out his pad and pencil and worked out the coefficient for expansion for the center span. He calculated that a temperature drop of 30 degrees would shrink the section to allow it to fit. At 4 a.m. the next morning, workers turned on floodlights, and they lowered the span into place, where it fit perfectly. They put the locking pins into place by hand.

The official dedication took place on July 31, 1935. Five thousand people attended the noon event, with Pearl Wanamaker christening the bridge with a bottle of sea water, and cutting a ribbon stretched across the structure. The crowds then retired to Cranberry Lake where the CCC had just completed an improved recreational area along the lake's shoreline.

Insider: Bridge Statistics

The Deception Pass Bridge is actually two bridges, one covering Deception Pass and the other spanning Canoe Pass. The longer span, over Deception Pass, is 976 feet long. The shorter span, over Canoe Pass, measures 511 feet in length. The bridge is 180 feet above the water, more or less, depending on the height of the tide.

The deck is 11 feet for each lane, and the sidewalk is three feet more on each side. The cable barrier alongside the lanes and the sidewalk were added many years ago for the safety of walkers.

<u>Quick facts:</u>
- Date Opened to the Public: July 31, 1935
  (For comparison, the George Washington Aurora Bridge in Seattle opened in 1931; the Golden Gate Bridge opened in 1937.)

- Total length: 1487 feet (more than a quarter mile)

<u>Canoe Pass Span:</u> Steel Arch design. One 350 foot arch and three concrete T-beam approach spans, total of 511 feet.

<u>Deception Pass Span:</u> Steel Cantilever design. Two 175 foot cantilever spans, one 200 foot suspended span, and four concrete T-beam approach spans. Total of 976 feet.

Above: the bridges as seen in 1936, looking north. Note the lack of trees blocking the view. The trail down to North Beach can be seen in the foreground. Image courtesy of Washington State Archives.

Below: Canoe Pass in the foreground, the main span in the background, as the bridge looks today on a typical busy afternoon.

It is difficult to exaggerate the bridge's impacts on the local environments, economies, cultures, and lives.

Whidbey's population exploded from 3000 in 1935 to 6000 five years later to 34,000 in 1977 to around 80,000 today. An average of over 15,000 vehicles now cross the bridge every day.

A year before the bridge was built, local writer George Albert Kellogg had this to say about the possible effects of a future bridge:

> "What will become, I wonder, of the mystery, the shaded quiet, and age-old charm of those deep swirling waters and the shores that confine them? The lone ferry, chugging in occasional passage; that sense of detachment from a prosaic world when once you've gotten across to the island?
>
> "Do you suppose the island roads, congested with traffic, will invite the outdoor advertising companies to erect their billboards? Will these winding highways of dignified rural beauty end in a sacrifice to the brazenly flaunted values of clothing, cigarettes, and gasoline?"

Food for thought.

In 1982, the bridge was listed in the National Register of Historic Places.

Heilman Family

E. C. Heilman was a landscape architect in Seattle. In the Thirties he didn't have much work, so he joined the CCC as a foreman. One of his assignments took him to Deception Pass State Park. He loved the area. Eventually he returned to his Seattle business, which began to do very well.

In the early Forties he wanted a change of pace. He remembered that parcel of land on Pass Lake that the Allmond family had for sale. He bought it from them for $15,000, closed his offices in Seattle, and moved here for the rest of his life.

The house they first lived in south of the highway burned down, so they moved into the Allmond house on the north shore of Pass Lake. This house had no electricity, no indoor toilet, and no phone. He set up business as a logger, building a sawmill on the south shore of Pass Lake.

The Heilman family raised cattle in Heilman Valley. Mt. Erie rises in the distance. Photo courtesy of the Heilman family.

Claire Heilman working in his sawmill, cutting lumber harvested around Pass Lake. Photo courtesy of the Heilman family.

He harvested trees from the surrounding area to make lumber. The Pass Lake trail follows the logging road he used to skid logs off the northwest shore to his sawmill on the south side.

He left several old growth trees standing in the area because he thought it good to let them grow. Mr. Heilman was a conservationist, and helped start Evergreen Islands, an environmental advocacy group on Fidalgo Island.

The Heilmans also raised 80 cattle on the land, using the pasture that can still be seen from the highway today. As part of that cattle operation, they built a large hay barn on the ridge above their house. That barn still exists. The Heilmans then moved out of the house by the lake and in the early Sixties built a modern house near the new barn.

In the late Sixties and early Seventies, local land taxes were raised to what the highest use of the land could be, not what it was being used for. As such, the Pass Lake property taxes were exorbitant for the potential home sites.

The Heilmans could not afford to keep paying those taxes. In 1969 a real estate developer offered them over a million dollars to sell their land, to be developed into numerous residences and other modern amenities. They did not feel good about the concept, but they considered the offer.

Neighbors formed the Save Pass Lake Committee, and encouraged Washington State Parks to buy the land and preserve it as a state park. The state agreed, but only purchased the land on the north side of the highway, leaving the wonderful ridge south of the highway to become a housing development visible from the pass. The Heilmans remained at their house until they passed away, and the remaining homestead acreage then became part of the park as well. Their daughter Kathleen, her husband Matt Brown, and their family continue to be advocates for the protection and wise use of the area.

Claire Heilman working on a fence at the Pass Lake barn. Photo courtesy of the Heilman family.

Because of the Heilman's work with the CCC in the Thirties, their long-time care of the Pass Lake area as residents, their support of conservationist causes, and their willingness to sell their land to become part of Deception Pass State Park, I feel it appropriate to honor their life here by naming the valley on the north end of their farm as "Heilman Valley". The valley currently carries the accidental name of Naked Man Valley after a story recently brought to light from the Seventies, but the Heilmans truly lived here, invested their lives and love here, and made sure that their investment and legacy continues to this day. They are deserving of having their name and heritage honored.

Pass Lake Changes

Pass Lake was the first lake in Washington to be designated for fly fishing only when on January 9, 1940 the Washington Game Commission adopted a resolution from the newly created Washington Fly Fishing Club of Seattle.

The Game Department did a rotenone treatment of Pass Lake in 1946. After the treatment Cutthroat trout were planted. Their growth over the next few years created a trophy fishery for fly fishers.

In 1947 Russ Willis and his partner Duane Genung bought 20 cedar rowboats and set up a rental on the the Heilman property. The Heilmans gave them a three year lease. They were allowed to use the pump house to store oars and to build a dock for the boats. Russ also used the pump house to tie flies which were sold to the fishers.

The dock built onto Pass Lake in the Forties from the Heilman property on the north shore. Photo courtesy of the Heilman family.

Russ and Duane ran the "resort" from late April to late September, charging two hours of boat rental for $1 and all day for $2.

Fresh water for the small hatchery associated with the experimental station at Bowman Bay came from Pass Lake. The large block of concrete you now see by the picnic table at the Pass Lake launch site was the base for the pump. A log framework extended into Pass Lake which supported the pipes. This framework and pipe were not removed when the station closed and parts of it remain today under the water.

The fly fishing only regulation was rescinded in 1955 until 1965 when it was once again designated for fly fishing only.

During 1984 the fly fishing club members set about to develop a spawning channel across the hayfield to the east of the lake and adjacent to Highway 20. The intention was to tap into a small wetland on the east side of the driveway to the Ranger's house for stream water flow. State Parks granted permission and donated two tractors with backhoes and front loaders to dig the channel.

The anglers found that the water flow was not sufficient during the dry months to maintain the fry if the eggs were to hatch. Decades later you can now see a line of alders extending diagonally across the field from the driveway to the lake across the meadow, following the path of the abandoned channel.

Fish Hatchery

In the late 1940s, the Washington State Department of Fisheries developed a fish hatchery at the south end of Bowman Bay. They buried the former wetland with 70,000 yards of gravel to create level ground. They plowed through the remaining wetland south of there to create a series of channels for getting clean fresh water for the tanks out of the creek coming from Pass Lake.

The new dock at Bowman Bay in the late Forties, with the brick duplex for the hatchery manager in the background. Photo courtesy of Washington State Parks.

They built the pier into the bay for bringing supplies in and out and also to support a pumphouse to pump salt water to the marine tanks. The hole in the pier for this pumphouse still remains at the end of the dock. To protect the tanks and pier, they buried the upland side of the beach with boulders for a rip rap wall.

They also built a duplex residence in the wetland behind to house the hatchery manager and workers.

Some of the fish tanks at the Bowman Bay hatchery. The pier is off to the right; the brick duplex off to the left. The operations manager worked in the building seen in the background. Photo courtesy of Washington State Parks.

The hatchery was intended to conduct experiments with salmon and other marine life to increase the yield of various species.

The station was a long, low building situated north of the dock along and parallel to the small creek. Some circular and rectangular concrete ponds with circulating salt water were on the field side of the shoreline. These small ponds were for salt water shore creatures and were a favorite for visiting families.

The hatchery was gone by 1967, with the U. S. Bureau of Commercial Fisheries taking over until 1969.

In the early 1970s, State Parks took over the land, crushing the tanks and burying the pieces in the field. All that remains of the experimental station and hatchery are the dock that extends into Bowman Bay and the brick duplex residence located on the north side of the field.

The residence is now occupied by park ranger families, and the pier is popular for crabbing, fishing, boating, and sunsets. The damage to the wetlands remains, but we hope to restore them in the near future. Time itself is working on that already.

Road to West Beach

Once upon a time, shortly after the glaciers receded, West Beach had a gap in its long stretch of sand, making Cranberry Lake a brackish marsh. Over the centuries, gravel eroded from the bluffs south of here and drifted along to fill in the opening, cutting Cranberry Lake off from the sea, eventually creating a freshwater lake separated only by wild sandy dunes from the waters of the Salish Sea.

Tribes used the open fields for temporary lodging at various times during the year, landing canoes at North Beach as well as West Beach.

When the CCC worked in the park, they built a trail here from the developments on the east side of the lake.

Then park manager Johannes Christensen building the road from the park entrance to West Beach. Photo courtesy of Gayle Glass and the Christensen family.

They gathered driftwood here, but otherwise let it remain as a wild and natural resource.

In the Fifties, park staff bulldozed a road from the administrative maintenance areas near the entrance down the hill to the Cranberry Lake shore, along the lake's north side, and out to the wild beach. It was certainly a popular change, as now cars could drive right to the water's edge. Throughout the next few decades, the parking expanded and formalized, covering the dunes and foreshore with pavement and picnic tables.

The West Beach parking lot had minimal paving in the Seventies when this picture was taken. The new concession building had just been built at the swim beach. Photo courtesy of Washington State Parks.

The western shore of Cranberry Lake became the new focus for swimming in the park, although the east end continued to host swimming lessons for many years after that. A concession building was built between the lake and the saltwater for food sales and changing rooms.

By the Eighties, West Beach was the center of activity in the park, attracting parties, drinking, family picnics, and swimming. Lifeguards sat in towers, and buoys in the lake marked the swim area which became very popular.

It took many years of effort by park rangers, but the partying was arrested and West Beach became an ideal location for families to gather, swim, picnic, walk the beach, watch sunsets, and hang out.

The parking lot became fully paved before the turn of the new century.

Park staff replaced an old closet at the concession building in 2006 with a beautiful pine-paneled meeting space, creating a delightful gathering place for events and celebrations.

West Beach is still the center of busy-ness at the park, but it now has a pleasant family-oriented atmosphere in the summer, and a beach-centered feeling year round.

Cornet Bay Retreat Center

The CCC program ended with our entry into World War II and the restoration of the country's economy. The CCC camp facilites at Cornet Bay remained in place, and groups began to use them as a convenient location for youth camps such as 4-H.

One now-elderly man reminisced about spending a week there in the Forties as a youth, eating in the same cookhouse that the CCC used, sleeping on the same bunkbeds, and playing in the parade field that the CCC had created for work and play.

According to the 1949 manual for Cornet Bay Camp, it was *"open to use by all organized groups whose purpose and practice is character building through an educational and recreational program in the out of doors. Youth groups are given first priority."*

The earliest campers to the Cornet Bay area camp continued to use the kitchens and shelters built by the CCC. Photo courtesy of Whatcom Museum

In the Fifties and Sixties, the cabins and cookhouse were upgraded slightly with newer cabins and bunks and cooking facilities, and over the years the camp has continued to evolve, slowly but certainly.

It still remains as a rustic facility, with the same basic layout as the CCC would recognize, but becoming more comfortable and useful with improved facilities thanks to the hard work of park staff and volunteers and the funding of various legislative grant monies.

The camp association at Cornet Bay helped provide a swimming pool for camp use around 1963. Sitting right outside the dining hall, the pool added a memorable experience for those days when it was warm enough to use it. Unfortunately, the cost of maintaining the pool exceeded the value of having it for those few days of use. Staff filled the pool in the Eighties and covered the area with a slab of concrete, now used as a patio area.

With the cost of providing a safe camp experience skyrocketing, along with the cost of transporting young campers to Cornet Bay, the camp saw a decline in youth groups after the turn of the century. Outdoor education became more incorporated into school curriculum, with less of a need, or perhaps less of an interest, in week-long camp experiences.

At the same time, people of all ages began to value opportunities to spend quality time with family or friends or other organized gatherings in places where they could live together, self contained, and free of distractions for a weekend or so. Retreat centers became highly sought after.

Cornet Bay fit the needs of many of these groups, with large gathering areas, professional cooking facilities, diverse recreational opportunities, and a variety of rustic, low cost but secluded overnight accommodations. The term Environmental Learning Center, which focused on school groups primarily, gave way to the Retreat Center label, attracting a more diversified clientele that appreciates the seclusion of the camp with its ample amenities.

Amphitheater

In 1961, volunteers constructed an amphitheater just east of West Point, at the west end of North Beach, facing toward the bridge. The area had a natural slope, perfect for a gathering of people to look down on a central stage area, and to enjoy the view of the forests, waters, and bridge beyond.

Volunteers rebuilt it through the years at various times, improving the seats, and built a parking lot behind the presentation area.

Then more changes eliminated the parking lot on the beach, added a screen for visual presentations, and again improved the seating.

The view from the back of the amphitheater, taken in the late Sixties, with the parking lot right on the beach. Photo courtesy of Washington State Parks.

Groups use it for church services, wedding ceremonies, award gatherings, and of course music and other performing arts.

```
Deception Pass State Park Snapshot:
                1957

Campsites: 175
Group camp capacity: 125
42,918 total annual campers
491,124 total annual park attendance
3 permanent staff
3 assistant summer staff
```

New Boat Launches Built

Cornet Bay and Bowman Bay had rough boat launches in the Sixties. Cornet Bay had a one-lane hole in the retaining wall; Bowman Bay had a gap in the driftwood for visitors to drive onto the beach.

In the Seventies, boat launches received major uplifts.

Cornet Bay transformed into a major destination for boaters. A long creosote wall built on the beach allowed a large paved parking lot to be built above, along with a spacious lawn area and a restroom.

The work was appreciated, but sometimes today's solution is tomorrow's problem. Two problems became evident.

First, the boat launch that was built had concrete lanes but the design called for large rocks to separate the launch lanes from the floats. Boaters could not get their vehicles close to the floats, causing all kinds of problems.

The 'improved' launches at Bowman Bay had four lanes of ramps, but ten feet of rock between the ramps and the floats. Photo courtesy of Washington State Parks.

The new bulkhead being built at Cornet Bay, destroying the upper end of the beach. I just want to shout out "Stop! Don't do it!" Photo courtesy of Washington State Parks.

Secondly, and more importantly for the environment, the bulkhead destroyed the upper levels of the beach, eliminating forage fish spawning habitat.

The first problem was resolved in 2005 when the launch was totally renovated. It now had six lanes of traffic and three floats, with the launch lanes paved right up to the floats. The improvement was obvious and appreciated.

The second problem would not be solved until 2012. That story will be shared later.

Bowman's boat launch improvements were limited by the western exposure of the bay. Whatever was built here had to be simple and able to withstand crashing waves. And the bay is shallow, making the launch useless at low tides. But the single lane launch was an improvement.

CHANGES IN THE EIGHTIES AND NINETIES

The Story of the Story Pole

In June of 1981, Anacortes artist Bill Mitchell contacted Ken Hansen, Samish Tribal chairman, about the possibility of sponsoring a totem pole in the Deception Pass area. Totem poles are an art form of tribes further to the north, so Ken proposed a Coast Salish style story pole instead. The tribe wanted to honor Kokwalalwoot, a guardian who still lives in the waters near the Pass. The concept soon turned into a sketch of a two-sided pole which portrayed the change of the Maiden into a sea spirit.

The Skagit County Centennial Committee, led by Dick Fallis, accepted the idea as a partnership project. Wood carver Tracy Powell of Anacortes created a two-foot sculpture of the sketch. Mr. Fallis carried this model from meeting to meeting, and was amazed to watch people who had been opposed, skeptical, or half asleep at meetings suddenly becoming delighted and enthusiastic when they saw the carved cedar model of the Maiden.

Terry Doran, manager of the Northwest region of Washington State Parks, became an early champion of the project, at a time when park funds were being cut back. State Parks Interpretive Chief Dick Clifton from Olympia soon joined the ranks of advocates.

Dick Fallis even tells the story of "a dour lady who came in army boots and field clothes from some archaeological dig to tell us that there was no way we would be allowed to dig or disturb the grounds at Rosario Beach. She became enchanted by the carving and the story of the Maiden, and arranged to get a group of trained students to do the digging and survey work at Rosario in preparation for the placement of the completed carving."

The U. S. Forest Service found a suitable tree growing near Baker Lake. The 25-foot pole arrived at Tracy Powell's workshop in March of 1983. Tracy, a non-Indian, spent a month in tribal spiritual preparation. Following the teachings of old Samish craftsmen, Tracy went to the mountains to bathe and grow strong so that the unseen could become visible through his carving. When he was clean and clear in his relationship to the cedar, it was time to cut into the huge log.

As the carving progressed, hundreds of visitors followed along. The Maiden became known and beloved by the Skagit community and beyond. She was no longer a mythical personage, but a member of the community, as she had been to the Samish all along.

Much credit for the smooth progression must be given to Tribal Chair Ken Hansen, who was prepared for every step that needed to be taken. Ken also gave credit to carver Tracy Powell.

"I have never seen a carver bring out more spirit or more life from a piece of wood," he said about Powell. *"We believe there is a spirit within that wood that is going through a transformation, just like she did."*

The last detail to be resolved was the exact spot where the carving would be located. A siting committee included tribal elders, the Skagit Centennial Committee, State Parks, and other interested people. "Grandma" Laura Edwards, about 85 years of age on that summer day, had been born before the turn of the previous century, at a time when young Indian girls were urged to turn away from the ways of their people to take up modern culture.

Laura's lineage was from several tribes affiliated with the Samish and Swinomish Indian communities. She married Alfred Edwards, whose father had been Charlie Edwards, one of the last, great Samish carvers. He had carved an earlier story pole, which depicted Kokwalalwoot at its base.

By the summer of 1983, Laura was thin, small, and seemingly frail, but with eyes and spirit bright and alive, she joined the search for the right place for the Maiden.

When she arrived at the narrow spit of land that leads up to Rosario Head, she sat down on the earth. Someone started to chat amiably as they had been all day, when "Grandma" raised her hand for silence.

The background calling of gulls nearby greatly increased as people sat there, and soon a great raucous mass of birds converged into a line that swooped down over the outer bay, flew directly over those sitting or squatting on the ground, then flew noisily off toward the Pass itself.

Laura looked up with a face that was all joy and laughter. "Here," she said. "This is the place for the Maiden."

And that is where the story pole of Kokwalalwoot was placed.

The story pole was unveiled in a colorful, spirit-filled ceremony at Rosario Beach on September 24, 1983.

CCC Interpretive Center Opened

In the mid-Eighties, Vic Olsen, a former CCC enrollee, and his wife Mae asked other CCC alumni living near them in Everett to share CCC memorabilia they may have with the hope of starting a viewable collection. Members brought in so many pictures and mementos that they knew they should get them displayed in a museum somewhere.

After years of searching, they met with then-director of Washington State Parks Jan Tvetan, and the head of interpretive services for State Parks, Dick Clifton. State Parks offered the unused bathhouse at Bowman Bay as a possible interpretive center.

It took more than three years of group work parties to renovate the building, which had been unused since World War II. More than 50 alumni took part on various weekends, gathering appropriate materials, cleaning the building inside and out, and preparing it for the exhibits being constructed by State Parks staff.

The prepared exhibits tell the story of the CCC throughout the state of Washington, with memorabilia, photos, diaries, life size displays, and personal stories shared by these alumni and others throughout the state. Alumni, park staff, and a crowd of visitors dedicated the center on July 16, 1988.

The Maiden is revealed in a ceremony at Rosario in September of 1983. Image courtesy of Washington State Parks.

The original Bowman Bay CCC Interpretive Center organizers, shown here at a work party in 1988. Front row: Walt Bailey, Jiggs Hudson, and Floyd Olson. Back row: Del Sells, Taffy Sells, Verla Bailey, Russ Bean, Mae Olson, and Vic Olson. Photo courtesy of Washington State Parks.

Park maintenance staff Mark Lunz, Marvin Wold, and Dan Dillard built a base to support the statue, using CCC-inspired methods for the rock work.

On September 18, 2004, the statue was unveiled to a crowd of over 200 gathered at Bowman Bay, the 28th statue to be installed in the United States, and the only one for the state of Washington.

In a speech held in the upper CCC shelter at Bowman Bay, State Parks Director Rex Derr congratulated the CCC alumni for their stewardship in building parks and for their dedication in preserving and sharing the story of the CCC.

Vic and Mae stayed at the Bowman Bay campground as campground hosts for many years, and volunteered their time at the interpretive center to tell stories of the CCC.

More than a decade later, CCC alumni from around the nation wanted to install a life-size statue of a CCC member in each state of the union that had a CCC camp. In 2004 several alumni came to me for permission to have one installed here. With Deception Pass as the iconic home of CCC interpretation for the state of Washington, it made sense.

We agreed in principle that Bowman Bay would be an ideal location. And we knew that raising the funds would not be easy. However, we did not realize the persistence and effectiveness of the alumni. Bob Robeson, Walter Bailey, John Hamilton, Jiggs Hudson, Albert Roundtree, and alumni spouse Berniece Phelps, along with many others, came through. They raised enough money to have the statue built. State Parks and a variety of charitable sources found enough money to have the statue shipped to the park.

The CCC worker statue in place overlooking Bowman Bay.

Hoypus Hill Added

To make sure communities had room for schools, two sections of land out of every 36 sections were set aside in the early days of our nation for school property. (A section equals one square mile.) These sections can be found all across the State of Washington. Our state government decided decades ago to have the Department of Natural Resources (DNR) manage these lands for timber, and the profits from those timber sales to go into the funding for our state's schools.

However, not all of these sections are appropriate for schools, or for timber. So the DNR has actively transferred some of them to other appropriate ownership to best manage the lands they can use.

One of these sections includes the Hoypus Hill area.

In the Nineties, the Department of Natural Resources transferred the Hoypus Hill area to State Parks, adding hundreds of acres to the park. The timber values were not enough for them to keep managing the area, and recreational opportunities were seen as the best use of the state land.

Some of this land had been logged as recently as the Eighties and replanted as a site to be harvested again in the future.

Dugualla Acquired

The Department of Natural Resources also owned the land that is now Dugualla State Park as part of the School Lands Trust. In 1992 Washington State Parks acquired the 586 acre property to prevent it from being logged. The site remains largely undeveloped and thus beautifully natural, or close to natural.

The area had been logged a few decades earlier. But on the eastern end, where the land drops quickly to the waters of Skagit Bay, old growth trees still dominate the landscape.

Local volunteers and the Island County Health Department in partnership with Washington State Parks added trail signage to the Dugualla area about 2008.

In 2013-14, the Skagit Whatcom Island Trail Maintaining Organization (SWITMO) built new trail routes, connecting together what used to be dead end trails to create a popular long loop route through the park, connecting at the Big Tree just above the beach.

New Entrance and Sewer Developed

Highway 20 is a busy roadway. When the park began in 1922, the entrance off the roadway was perfectly adequate. By the 1990s, with three or four million people coming to the park each year, many in large RVs, the accident potential for that many people trying to exit and enter the park on Highway 20 was extreme.

The Department of Transportation and State Parks planned a new entrance at the Cornet Bay Road intersection that would be controlled with signal lights and turn lanes for safe traffic flow. Work began in 1996, and the entrance opened in 1997 with a new entrance station.

Unfortunately, the entrance had only one lane while the exit had two lanes, which meant vehicles and RVs entering the park often backed up well out onto the highway. With a grant from the parking fees that began in 2003 (and which ended a couple years later) we converted an exit lane into an entrance lane in 2004, easing congestion and making the introduction to the park more welcoming. A year later we added what we now affectionately call the "baby booth", a small additional building to collect fees from drivers in the far right lane to help keep traffic flowing quickly into the park.

Not as exciting, but perhaps more importantly, nearly all of the restrooms on the south half of the park became connected in 1997 to one central sewer collection point near the park entrance. This allowed the park to stop using old septic drainfields for taking care of sewer. The Cranberry campground, all the beach day use areas south of the bridge, and the Cornet Bay Retreat Center now pumped effluent to this one tank in the park. From here, it is pumped to the Navy base, where it is treated with tertiary sewer treatment, good enough to be put back into the Salish Sea.

We buried telephone lines with the new sewer lines to let us know by a central control panel if any of the pumps or wet wells are having problems.

In recent years, we have now added the Cornet Bay boat launch restroom and the Quarry Pond Campground restroom to the system as well, so that only one small septic system remains on the Whidbey Island side.

CAMP Process

Washington State Parks wanted to assure its citizens that State Parks were being managed for their best uses. toward that end, they developed a Classification and Management Plan, or CAMP, that involved public dialogue to create zones in a park that determine the long term use of each park area, and a strategic plan for each area as to how to best manage the specific areas for the good of the park, the agency, the public, and the future.

The public meetings for Deception Pass were very well attended. Through several meetings and planning sessions, an overall plan came out that highlighted how

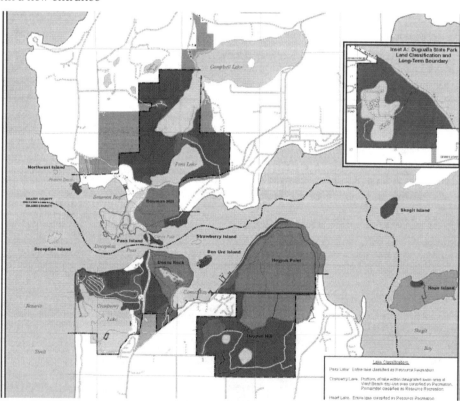

The CAMP zoning map is published in color, so black and white does not do it justice. These zones give us publicly-approved guidance for future land use decisions in the park. Map created by Washington State Parks.

each section of the park should be managed, and what the next steps should be to achieve that plan.

The CAMP plan zones the park into natural areas and natural forest areas for resource protection and minimal recreation; heritage areas for historical landscape maintenance with some recreation; resource recreation areas for a balance of resource protection and use; recreation areas for intensive recreation; and one natural area preserve, most of Hope Island, for the highest level of protection for natural resources.

At the same time, attendees agreed on a long term boundary that helped decide what future properties should or should not be considered were they to become available for acquisition as part of the park. The Commission approved the plan in 1999.

And finally, the plan triggered the development of several other guiding documents, such as a facilities and use plan that gave us specific ways to improve the park for long term use. Some of the ideas in that plan have been accomplished. Some have been postponed, and a couple discarded as untenable for today.

CHANGES IN THE 21ST CENTURY, So Far

Heart Lake Transferred

Washington State saved Heart Lake from development by acquiring it as a state park. State Parks then eventually transferred the land to the city of Anacortes in 2002, with stipulations that the area be managed according to the zoning guidelines of the 1999 Deception Pass State Park CAMP plan.

Bowman Expanded

The Bowman Bay campground had a curious arrangement of campsites. There were three on the right side as you entered the camp area, then a gap of a hundred yards or so with a fir and maple forest, then campsites on the right side again as you approached the water.

That gap was in private ownership until 2002, when State Parks purchased a small piece of property that made everything below Rosario Road part of the park.

In 2005 park staff took advantage of the new land and built four additional campsites in this quiet wooded area, quality sites with ample privacy and spacing. The camp loop is now complete, and these new sites are popular, not far from the bay and yet hidden in the forest.

Rosario Tidepools Protected

In the Nineties, Rosario's tidepools were overrun with school groups, families, and individuals who loved seeing seastars and cucumbers and crabs, and who loved them to death by stepping on them or taking them home in buckets. By the turn of the new century, the Rosario tidepools were a moonscape of barnacles, limpets, and little else.

Tidepool visitors look closely at marine life while staying near the rope line that marks the trail through the tidepools.

Our first steps were to require reservations for school groups. With the reservation came a park interpreter encouraging appropriate behavior from students and parents. Ranger Rick Blank, Part-time interpreter Heather Leahy-Mack and dedicated volunteer Sammye Kempbell began to invest many hours and days at low tides educating school groups and visitors of all ages about the fragility and value of intertidal life.

This continued and expanded under the next interpreter, Adam Lorio, who helped us take the next step in restoring the tidepools: a trail system through the tidepools, so that visitors would step in the same places getting from the high tide line down to the water's edge, thus protecting every plant and animal not on the trail. The results were slow but dramatic, as seaweeds and seastars began to come back.

The Rosario tidepools are still just a shadow of their former glory, but the life is returning, and with continued protection, there is more to see from the trails each year. The nearby Urchin Rocks area is off limits for visitors, due to nesting birds and as a last refuge for this threatened environment.

In 2011, Sammye Kempbell started a volunteer Beach Naturalist program, multiplying her efforts with newly trained volunteers each year who are encouraging everyone to use the marked trail through the tidepools, teaching anyone interested about what they are seeing, and continuing the restoration of the environment.

For a scheduled tour or to become a Beach Naturalist, contact the park office. Classes are held once a week in March, with about eight hours of classroom time and a few hours in the tidepools for hands-on training.

So come enjoy the tidepools; immerse yourself in a fragile and beautiful world. Follow the rope trail to protect the life there; care for the critters as you would your own.

Quarry Pond Campground Added

Formerly owned by Sunrise Resorts, which has campsites in Alaska, Washington, and Arizona, State Parks purchased this private campground to meet the overwhelming demand for campsites in the summer, and to provide safer campsites in the winter.

As part of the negotiations over what to do with members who had expectations of camping there for several more years as part of their memberships, State Parks agreed to honor those memberships as part of the purchase agreement. The last of the memberships expired in 2008.

Over the next few years, State Parks upgraded the electrical and water connections, and reduced and reconfigured the campsites to add privacy for State Park users.

In 2016, they added five park-model cabins for rental in the campground. These cabins are becoming very popular for every month of the year.

New Administrative Office Opened

Park staff have always made do with what they had to administer the park. One shortcoming had always been office space. With one of the largest staff in the park system because of the size, complexity, and popularity of the park, the staff struggled to find a place to sit down to do paper work. Fifteen permanent staff squeezed into a room the size of most people's dining room, along with all the desks and office equipment.

In the 1990s, a surplus school portable was added to the mix, giving a little more room to spread out and effectively manage the park, but the room still lacked space and a place for visitor interaction. Both of these spaces had mice running through the desks when we turned out the lights.

The Jet Drive-In in 1970, with two VW Bugs parked outside. Photo courtesy of Washington State Parks.

In the 1950s a local businessman began a hamburger store along Highway 20. Over the years, the "Cookhouse" grew in popularity and size, and changed its name to the Jet Drive. By the 1990s it had become the modern "Island Grill Restaurant", a busy dining facility with room for thirty or more diners being served lunches and dinners.

New owners used that same building to create a larger, nicer restaurant, the Island Grill.

Unfortunately, although very successful, the family had to sell the restaurant for personal reasons.

Recognizing the ideal location of the building in the middle of the park, and its potential spaciousness, State Parks bought the building in 2005 with a grant. A couple years later, we had the money and plans to convert it to office space.

Park staff were able to lay out their desired flow of the building, which architect Steven Story put into the design. He incorporated the context of the CCC structures, with rock bases that tapered as they rose at the corners, cedar siding, and fine grain wood in the interior. Landscaping outside incorporates native vegetation and a rain garden entrance.

The building opened with a special dedication by several local and state elected officials in October of 2008.

Park staff now have room to run the business of the park, greet visitors as part of that business, and have meetings for staff or the general public.

Oak Harbor Mayor Jim Slowik, Representative Barbara Bailey, Senator Margaret Haugen, me, Representative Norma Smith, County Commissioner John Dean, and State Parks stewardship manager John Krambrink cut the ribbon to dedicate the new park office in 2008, adapting the old restaurant to new service. Photo by Adam Lorio.

Deception Pass Park Foundation Begins

In September of 2005, I held the second annual park open house meeting. We gathered in the newly acquired Island Grill Restaurant, still looking like a restaurant as we sat in the dining room. I mentioned at the end of the meeting that the park would benefit from having a "Friends" group or a foundation to allow donors to have a qualified 501c3 organization to give money to, and to organize volunteer efforts beyond the scope of park resources.

Two couples responded to the idea, the Wallace family, who no longer live in the area, and the Harringtons, who live near the park.

Together they began the work of helping me develop Articles of Incorporation and By-Laws, which the state and federal governments accepted a short time later.

From this initial interest, the Foundation started very slowly, with a few minor hiccups, but steadily grew and improved until today it is an active and productive Deception Pass Park Foundation that contributes thousands of dollars and hundreds of volunteer hours annually to the park.

Their mission is to support education and resource protection at Deception Pass State Park. All their resources are focused on these two areas.

Consider joining the Foundation as a member to lend your support to the educational efforts at the park. All the funds raised by the Foundation go into the educational programming.

And consider lending your expertise to the Foundation Board, lending your hands with an event or project, or at least lending your special gift in any way that you can.

Hoypus Gate Closed

Ever since there was a ferry from Hoypus to Fidalgo Island, there was a road servicing Hoypus from Cornet Bay. The Road closely followed the shoreline, and ended in a very narrow turnaround that was jammed with a handful of cars that got there early enough to find a place to park. Late night parties and vandalism added to the troubled nature of the area.

In 2005 storms washed out a portion of the roadway. The park plans called for the road to be a walking trail with no vehicle access. Now was the time to make that a reality. The change was announced ahead of time, but changing habits can be a hardship for many. As it turned out, we had hundreds of positive comments and only a handful of complaints when we closed the road to vehicles.

The mile-long walk to Hoypus Point is now a popular place for finding a flat hike alongside the water without worries of traffic or congestion. The gate is still opened for the days when the parking lots fill up at Cornet Bay, to allow for overflow parking on major fishing weekends such as the opening of ling cod or crabbing.

Cornet Bay Boat Launch Improved

In the Seventies, four boat launch lanes were built at Cornet Bay for boaters to access the Pass and the San Juans beyond. The parking lot was expanded many years later to accommodate the popularity of the launch.

But the launch was an odd design. Up against the docks, where boaters normally want to be able to tie up and prepare their boats for embarking or trailering, a designer placed large rocks. It was weird and awkward. Finally, in 2005, we received a grant to expand the boat launch to six lanes and remove the piles of rocks.

It is now even more popular, as the modern design enables launching under almost any condition and tide, in protected water close to the Pass.

Highway Guardrails Changed

In my first year at the park, the Department of Transportation had money to replace some of the aging CCC railings along the highway. The historical railings could not be trusted to stop a car from going over the edge. DOT proposed a new railing, quite industrial in appearance. I was shocked to imagine how it would change the appearance of this scenic and iconic route through the park. When I suggested that they could come up with a more historical design, the lead engineer became incensed that I would suggest such a thing at this late hour of the planning process, just because I was new.

Our entire agency stood with me on this one, however, and we insisted. DOT came back to us with a design that from a quick glance appears similar to how the CCC built the railings. Look closer and you see that the logs are continuous, instead of stopping every twenty feet for a rock pillar. Now the pillars are behind the logs. Hiding behind the logs, iron bars give them strength. The entire system is then anchored in concrete with interlaced rebar, a design suggested by our maintenance chief Mark Lunz, allowing all of the pillars to work together as one unit to stop a wayward vehicle.

The new railings were installed during the wet winter of 2005-2006, using some of the original rock for the new pillars.

A wayward dumptruck tested the new railing system a couple years later when it careened out of control and struck the guardrail almost head on north of the bridge. The truck bounced off the new guard rail, then plowed into the old railing, which didn't even slow it down as it went off the cliff, fortunately being stopped by a large tree before the truck went over the edge.

Ginnett Property Acquisition

For decades Louis Hall, related to the Ginnett family by marriage, lived in a mobile home on a cliff overlooking Heilman Valley. Behind the mobile home he had a barn-like shed sitting on a large concrete slab.

In the Seventies, he and his wife sold their land to State Parks as part of a living trust, allowing them to continue to live there until they passed away.

After Mr. Hall's passing in 2007, the mobile home and shed were removed and the area became part of the park.

To reduce impact on the neighbors living at the end of a narrow, winding country road, the roadway turn-around area is designated as no parking. The Pass Lake trail serves as the only vehicle parking for trailhead access to Ginnett.

For some reason, many people struggle pronouncing this name Ginnett. In the English language, the letter g followed by an e or an i is almost always pronounced as a soft g, like the sound of the letter j. It is not a hard g sound. (Think gentle, or ginger, or giraffe, or giant.)

West Beach Shelter Developed

Built in the early 1970s, the long building sitting between Cranberry Lake and the salt water served as a restroom and concession building, serving up sodas, hot dogs, and ice cream treats. The south end of the building became a storage closet for wet life jackets for the boat rentals nearby.

Around 2005, we were able to put some money and energy into renovating that south end into something better. Park staff, particularly Mark Lunz and Marv Wold, took it down to ground level and rebuilt a shelter that now serves as a gorgeous meeting space, with warm pine on the inside and picture windows looking out in three directions to the beauty all around. It is popular with race events for runner orientations, and for various family gatherings and weddings.

Hoypus Hill Extended

The Old Hoypus Logging Road led hikers to a dead end for a couple of decades, forcing hikers to turn around and retrace their steps.

Neighboring landowners in the vicinity of Hoypus Hill offered to sell some of their land to enable the trail to continue and connect with the other trails of Hoypus Hill and Hoypus Point.

Thanks to the cooperative efforts of the landowners, and the funding of the Washington Wildlife and Recreation Program, the Whidbey Camano Land Trust, and Island County's Conservation Futures, three different parcels totaling 52 acres were acquired in 2007.

This provides more trail opportunities for equestrians and mountain bikers, and provides a buffer between the old growth forest and developed residential areas. The dead end trail is now a loop joining several of the trails throughout the Hoypus area. Our thanks to the Sandvik and Foster families for their willingness to make this acquisition possible.

Ben Ure Cabins Available

Over the past three decades, several Ben Ure parcels have been acquired by State Parks to protect the viewshed from Cornet Bay and the bridge. Of the seventeen parcels

The view from the living room of the Ben Ure Cabin, available for rent if you have a kayak or canoe to get onto the island.

on the island, twelve belong to Deception Pass, with five still remaining in private ownership.

We acquired the Christensen place in 2005, allowing us to offer the cabin to kayakers for overnight rentals ever since. This has been one of the most popular places to stay in the park. The cabin accommodates only two people in a snug and cozy room with a deck overlooking the waters of the Pass and Mount Baker.

We acquired the cabin of a former astronaut, Chuck Brady, in 2010, giving us the premier island parcel on the southwest side of the island.

The island still has three private residences, and is off limits to all except those who have rented the cabin. The dock is off limits as well, as it belongs to the private homeowner's association.

Kiket Island Co-acquired

Added to Deception Pass in 2010 and opened to the public in 2014, this island is accessible by foot or boat. It is fully within view of the bridge, yet a world apart from the hubbub of the bridge area.

The island was home to the Swinomish tribe for centuries. They harvested shellfish there, and also created cattail mats from cattails found in nearby Turner Bay.

Charles Wilkes, commander of the U. S. Exploring Expedition of 1841, mapped and named the island "Kiket", a random and totally unrelated word taken from the language of the far-away Nez Perce tribe.

When Governor Stevens arranged reservations for the tribes in 1855, the Swinomish retained the island as part of their land on Fidalgo. The Dawes Act of the 1880s allowed individual tribal members to sell parcels of the reservation for private gain. This happened at Kiket Island in the late 1920s when the tribal owners sold it to a consortium of private parties. The ownership group built a causeway from the island to the Fidalgo side so that vehicles could now drive onto the island at any time instead of having to wait for low tide.

Insider: As It Once Was

Kiket Island's history reads like the biography of a prodigal son, as the land was removed from the rightful tribal owners, then a road developed by a consortium of private parties, then a house erected across the most magnificent gathering point, then a nuclear power plant proposed, then the island acquired by a wealthy family and kept private for decades.

When Wally Opdycke proposed to sell it to Washington State Parks, who could not afford his asking price, he had an ex-son-in-law running a high-end dog sitting service on the island. With the sale pending, the dog business left.

I had the privilege of staying on the island the day before the ceremony celebrating the return of the island to Tribal ownership, shared with Washington State Parks. I could sense that the island was about to be set free again, free of heartaches and trouble for the land.

The pool was filled in shortly after acquisition, the tennis courts returned to soil over time after that. The house was removed in 2012-2013 as it was in need of too many repairs and becoming too costly to maintain.

With the completion of the small parking lot in 2014, the island opened again to the public and to the people of the Swinomish tribe who had longed to return for many, many years.

The restoration of the island as a gathering place of peace is nearly complete.

In 1943, sole title passed to a successful local business person named Gene Dunlap, who built a rambling rambler of a house with picture windows featuring the south and west views from the island. Many influential people enjoyed the retreat that Mr. Dunlap created, which included a swimming pool and tennis courts.

Seattle City Light bought the island in the late Sixties with the intention of building a nuclear power plant at the west end of the island. They planned to use the tidal movements of Deception Pass to cool the water from the cooling towers. Scientists studied the environment in great detail to see if the project was feasible. With the results, environmentalists challenged the proposal, citing the facts that the tidal waters did not flow past the island adequately, as well as the fact that having a nuclear power plant in such a magnificent setting just didn't make sense.

[For further details on the battle for a nuclear power plant on Kiket Island, visit this website: http://www.samishisland.net/documents/historicdocuments/NuclearPowerSkagitValley.html]

The proposal was defeated. Seattle City Light sold the island in 1982 to an affluent couple who then lived there sporadically for many years. They wanted to sell it to Washington State Parks in 2007 but State Parks did not have that kind of money. We partnered with the Trust for Public Land to find grants and donations that could raise the money. In a very short time they had raised enough funds, particularly because the island represented an intact Salish Sea environment virtually untouched by human development, and especially because of a pocket estuary on the east end of the island that offered forage fish and juvenile salmon habitat.

The only hang-up was that the Swinomish still owned the tidelands that surrounded the island, and the tribe was reluctant to give a long term access easement across their tidelands, and State Parks was reluctant to spend that much money with only a short term easement for access with no guarantees for the future.

It took a kindergarten idea of sharing that solved the problem. The Swinomish and State Parks became co-owners of the property, allowing co-management agreements to be set up that benefit both the tribe and our park visitors. The island and associated uplands now make up the Kukutali Preserve.

On July 30, 2010, the Swinomish Community and Washington State held a joint celebration on the grounds outside the house, with blanketing ceremonies, speeches by Governor Gregoire, Tribal Chairman Brian Cladoosby, State Parks Director Rex Derr and others, and a feast of epic proportions.

After four years of planning and preparation, the island opened for anyone to visit in May of 2014. For many tribal members, this was a chance to return to the island they last visited decades ago.

The name Kukutali comes from the tribal name for "place of the cattail mats" or "the place where cattails mats are made". And because the source of the funding and the purpose of setting aside the land is to protect and preserve its rare lowland and marine environments, it is designated a Preserve.

Kukutali may be the first park land owned by two different governments, the Swinomish tribe and Washington State Parks, in the entire United States.

Group Camp Moves

In the Nineties, park staff built three group camps along the road to North Beach. Each had an Adirondack shelter and vault toilets, and there were also two picnic shelters. For two decades, scouts and large families used the camps to be together but separate from the crowds in the other campgrounds.

Unfortunately, the trees around and above the camps are old, very old, and diseased. They could fail at any time, and drop widow-making branches or entire trunks at any time with no warning.

The three group camps were closed and consolidated into one group camp along the shores of East Cranberry Lake as a temporary solution. The large forested lawn works well for groups of up to fifty. The area has large lawn areas for tents and play, flushable toilets nearby, and easy access to the lakeshore. But the noises of the highway and main park entrance intrude a little on the experience.

A future group camp might be built in the Quarry Pond area when funding is found.

Bowman Shelter Restored

Chocolate brown paint may look like it belongs on a log building, but it sure doesn't belong on a Civilian Conservation Corps shelter at Deception Pass.

At some time in the past, all the CCC buildings at the park were painted chocolate brown, covering the original bright honey-colored logs into a dark woods feeling.

In 2012, thanks to the efforts of AmeriCorps volunteer Sam Wotipka, that all changed for the upper shelter at Bowman Bay.

Sam worked with the State Park historical preservation expert Alex McMurry to discover that the original log shelters here were never painted. The CCC oiled the logs

Governor Christine Gregoire and Swinomish Chairman Brian Cladoosby share the joy with two younger folks after the Kukutali dedication celebration on July 30, 2010.

Volunteer Lex Palmer retrofits a new old-style window into the Bowman shelter as part of its renewal.

Below: the Bowman upper shelter as it now looks.

inside and out with a preservative that not only protected the wood but also preserved the wood's natural bright sheen.

Sam also wanted to restore the windows to their original single pane glass and wood frames, and have the shingled roofs replaced with authentic shakes.

Alex found grant funding for most of the project, and Sam found the final amounts through the generous donation of the Deception Pass Park Foundation.

Park staff, led by Mark Lunz, and park region staff went to work on the roof, removing the shingles and replacing them with 36" long split shakes.

At the same time, volunteers from the Foundation, assisted by volunteers from the Navy Base, stripped all the chocolate paint off the logs, inside and out, getting down to the original bare wood.

Then they waited for the logs to dry enough to be soaked with the special oil mixture that brings out the grain and natural beauty of the wood while still protecting it from moisture and insects.

To finish the restoration, volunteers from HDR, an engineering firm in Seattle, took on the task of replacing all the windows and frames to have the original style of those as well, several of the group spending days of time at the project.

Visitors who saw the makeover marveled at the magnificence of the building with its new roof and oiled body.

We have now remodeled the interior lighting so that the classical appearance of this log structure can be used and enjoyed during the evening hours as well.

New Trails, New Railings

Since the turn of the century, many new connecting trails have been built in the park, expanding the opportunities to explore the furthest reaches of the park.

The Pass Lake trail was added in 2004 and 2005, connecting the bridge area with the Pass Lake parking lot, and then going from Pass Lake up to the Ginnett area.

Another connector trail was built from near the Highway 20 underpass to North Beach so visitors don't have to walk along a quarter mile of road.

Many of the park trails are near the edges of some of the steep bluffs in the park. The trails that are close to busy and popular areas attract many people who are not familiar with hiking or with the dangers of getting off a trail in an area they do not know well.

The entire park cannot be fenced off to keep people from experiencing the park. However, in those areas where inexperience and a lack of understanding about obvious dangers could get many people in trouble seemed like reasonable choices for adding some protection.

SWITMO members adding a fence near a steep drop-off on the Bowman trail.

That concern led us to partner with SWITMO to build some railings along some of the most heavily visited trails where the trail led quite near the edge.

We added a long set of railings on the busiest trail of all, from the South Bridge parking area to North Beach down below. With assistance from the Deception Pass Park Foundation, we also added railings along the Bowman Trail leading to Lottie Bay. A couple other fence railings were added in the Pass Island area.

With the acquisition of the Sandvik/Foster property, a new trail joined the Hoypus Hill area with the Hoypus Point trails, making a grand loop trail opportunity.

SWITMO also connected the new Hoypus Hill acquisitions to the existing trails, creating loop routes and connectors so hikers can get to Hoypus Point from the hill area.

For his high school senior project, Charlie Hartt laid out and developed the beginning of the Pass Lake Loop trail.

In 2008 Charlie Hartt planned and started construction on a Pass Lake loop trail as a senior project, and SWITMO finished it a month later. The new half mile section allows hikers to explore the area without having to retrace steps after making three-quarters of a circle.

In 2013 the Dugualla area received increased attention to create loop trails there as well, allowing hikers to enter from one direction and exit an entirely different direction, expanding the experience many fold for this quiet forest land.

In 2015 a short trail that took years of legal preparation was dedicated, allowing hikers to go from Goose Rock to the Cornet Bay Road without intruding on campers at Quarry Pond or the Retreat Center.

In 2016 the John Tursi trail connected the Pass Lake area with the northern park boundary and then on to Donnell Road to allow hiking all the way to Mt. Erie and beyond from the park.

Rosario Facilities Remodeled

The Civilian Conservation Corps built a small but functional bathhouse and restroom at Rosario Beach for swimmers in Sharpe's Cove to the south. Someone must have thought that people would want to swim in this cold salt water.

A Nautilus Construction worker sands down the interior logs of the new Rosario Field Classroom.

No one did, and as a restroom the building was a considerable distance from the parking lot, and tucked around a corner, so it wasn't getting much use in that regard either.

A new restroom was built near the parking lot many years later, and the CCC facility became mothballed and lifeless.

Until 2010, when it was given new life. The parking lot area was rebuilt to modern standards at that time, and we added the restroom into the project to restore it to a useful condition.

Nautilus Construction removed everything inside -- old toilets, toilet partitions, and decades of cobwebs -- and then took to restoring the original beauty of the CCC construction. They ground and polished the concrete floor, and sanded and oiled the log walls, creating a work of art enjoyable just to behold.

We had hoped to use it as a classroom for the many school classes that come here in spring for tidepool studies. This potential never reached the reality we hoped to see.

But the Foundation is breathing new life into the structure once again as they create a natural history classroom, complete with examples of local trees and plants, wildlife specimens, and more.

Long-term dreams also envisage an interpretive center at Rosario, to tell the story of the tribal use of the area and intertidal life. In 2013 the first step toward this goal grew into reality with the replacement of the old restroom with a new one, using a footprint that gives room for a future interpretive center.

The new restroom blends in well with the park environment, reflecting the CCC heritage of the area and the tribal heritage. The restroom was turned to face away from the parking lot so that it would face toward the future interpretive center. In the meantime, the Rosario Field Classroom is serving as our park interpretive center.

More CCC Structures Restored

It takes a community to maintain a park.

Harrison Goodall met me after a small presentation I had given about State Parks. I soon learned of his passion and expertise for all things historic, especially for our CCC buildings at Deception Pass.

Our first project together restored the small CCC shelter at the north end of the East Cranberry picnic area. His research showed that the original roof line was different. With awesome volunteers from HDR Engineering in Seattle, led by Lex Palmer, the existing failed roof was removed and a new, authentic roof raised in its place.

Harrison also helped with the restoration of the Rosario facilities, and then added further expertise on every other project we have undertaken so far involving our CCC structures.

He has done all of this with his bigger than life smiles and the kindness of his heart, with the energetic spirit of volunteerism that is too rare these days.

Above: Mr. and Mrs. LaGreid inspect the new rock fireplace at Cranberry Lake, restored thanks to the generosity of their grant.

Above: Modern expert stonemasons removed, restored, and then rebuilt the rockwork on the fireplace at the small Cranberry shelter.

Out of the blue, another great man, Ted LaGreid, contacted me by phone to ask if I had any information about his father or grandfather, who he believed had worked as a mason in the construction of our CCC shelters.

After some research, we did indeed find that a Mr. LaGreid had built at least two of the rock stoves in our shelters at the park.

Ted LaGreid then donated many thousands of dollars to pay a modern stone mason to rebuild two of the stoves, and to also rebuild the rock amphitheater fireplace at the Cornet Bay Retreat Center, and the incinerator at the retreat center. With additional funding assistance from the Deception Pass Foundation, these significant CCC features were restored.

And we restored the heritage in stone of the LaGreid family as well for everyone to enjoy.

Amphitheater Rebuilt Again

Originally built a half century earlier, the amphitheater was rustic but dramatic in its location. The view over the stage area to the east, with the Pass and the bridge as a backdrop, competes strongly with any performance or talk going on in front.

It has seen at least four different configurations, including what was probably the original design with a parking lot behind the stage area that ended right at the water's edge. None of the designs have been as good as what happened in the year 2012.

In that year, Eagle Scout candidate Nathan Wagner organized a work project to create the new seats now in place at the amphitheater, allowing groups of over 250 to sit here comfortably and enjoy good views of the stage area.

The next step is to create a stage. The Deception Pass Park Foundation has set aside money for a new stage, and the plans have been drawn up. The stage design reflects the log structures found throughout the park. With a roofed performance area, events can take place even on misty evenings, and multi-media presentations are possible.

Hopefully this will be a reality by 2017.

Above: Cornet Bay beach with a bulkhead wall.

Below: the same beach, now looking very natural and healthy!

Above: the boulder beach at Bowman Bay as it looked from the late Forties until 2015.

Below: the beach as it looks in 2016, waiting for the upland beachside plants to grow!

Beach Restorations

The purpose of Washington State Parks is to protect the special resources of our state, and allow citizens to enjoy and experience those resources.

Sometimes in the past this was not clear, especially in regards to our precious beaches.

At Cornet Bay, State Parks installed a bulkhead in the Seventies to give a little extra picnic and parking space, thereby destroying much of the beach and eliminating access to the beach that was still there.

At Bowman Bay, the Department of Fisheries built a breakwater riprap that destroyed the upper elements of the beach while preventing all but the most nimble footed visitors from reaching the beach.

These actions would not have happened in today's world.

Restoring those beaches became one of my goals, a lingering desire from my college days, and the right thing to do for the benefit of our natural resources and our park visitors.

That restoration began at Cornet Bay in 2012 by removing two football fields of creosote wall and fill between the parking lot and the beach, and replacing the lawn with a naturally sloped and vegetated beach.

Removing the bulkhead allowed each tide to add and remove detritus, logs, sea wrack, and other natural components of a living beach. Volunteers planted native plant species above the tideline, and in a couple of years we had a fully functioning beach again!

With that success underway, we were able to get grants coordinated through the Northwest Straits Foundation again to remove the boulder rip-rap at Bowman Bay in 2015 and allow a real beach to grow there as well.

Many of the boulders ended up in various other areas of the park to protect vegetation from vehicle traffic. The beach was then shaped to almost match the shape of the natural beaches on either side. We added a proper sand and gravel mix to fill the shoreline, and then added large woody debris to complete the structural changes.

What a magnificent beach this created! Where once visitors had to climb down precariously angled rocks to get to the beach, they now could just saunter down a gravel slope, with drift logs and beach life all around.

Volunteers of all ages, but mostly children from various schools, planted thousands of plants at the top of the beach in 2015 and on Earth Day in 2016.

Nature will re-arrange the shape of the beach over the next few years – indeed, the very next day after the beach was first planted, a storm hammered the new shoreline – and left it looking even better!

It will continue to become the beach that nature intended, the one that used to be here and will be again.

Insider:
The Forty Year Plan

My senior thesis for my park administration degree focused on the beach management of Washington State Parks. I looked at nearly every park in the Puget Sound area, including Deception Pass.

I typed the manuscript on my parent's Underwood typewriter. The pictures were printed, copied, and pasted into place. By hand.

The photo to the right shows one page of the several I devoted to this park. There are embarrassing typos and mistakes, even calling Bowman Bay "Burrows Bay".

I took the photo shown above from the pier, looking north at a low tide.

I gave the park great marks for most of its beaches, but low scores for Bowman Bay, Cornet Bay, and West Beach because of their excessive development in the "shore process corridor".

I had no idea that one day, forty years later, I would be a part of seeing Bowman and Cornet transformed back into living beaches.

If I had known back then that I would see results in forty years, I wonder how I would have felt. Hopefully as ecstatic as I am now!

A Brief History of Time

- 10000 BCE Glaciers recede from Salish Sea for final time
- 5000-10000 BCE First peoples arrive in the area
- 1500s Sailor Juan de Fuca allegedly on a ship in the strait now bearing his name
- 1790-1791 Carrasco and Narvaez explore the area
- 1792 Captain George Vancouver explores Puget Sound, names Deception Pass
- 1841 Meares exploration of Puget Sound
- 1855 Point Elliott Treaty
- 1866 Land around Deception Pass reserved by U.S. Government as a military reservation
- 1887 Dawes Act allows tribal land to be owned and sold by individuals
- 1910-1914 Prison caves actively mined by prisoners staying at the camp
- 1922 Military reservation transferred to State of Washington to be Deception Pass State Park
- 1930s Harvesting and replanting of parts of forest at Hoypus Hill and Dugualla
- 1933-1941 CCC enrollees at Cornet Bay and Rosario camps build many of the park structures and features
- July 31, 1935 Deception Pass Bridge completed and dedicated
- 1940s Camp Cornet first used as youth camp
- 1947 Department of Fisheries builds fish hatchery at Bowman Bay
- 1951 West Beach roadway constructed
- 1961 Amphitheater built
- 1964 Northwest and Strawberry Islands acquired for $100
- 1970-72 Fish hatchery eliminated
- 1983 Kokwalalwoot comes to reside at Rosario Beach
- 1991 Heilman Property added to park
- 1997 New park entrance established at the Cornet Bay intersection
- 1999 CAMP plan finalized after extensive public input
- 2002 Heart Lake transferred to the city of Anacortes
- 2002 Bowman Bay property expanded, allowing campground to expand in 2005
- 2005 Quarry Pond campground acquired
- 2006 Ben Ure Cabin acquired, offered as overnight rental
- 2008 New park office open on Highway 20, at the site of the former Island Grill restaurant
- 2010 Kiket Island acquired with grants, dedicated and co-owned by Swinomish Tribe and State Parks
- 2011 Discover Pass required for access to all state parks
- 2012 Cornet Bay Beach restoration begins
- 2014 Kukutali Preserve opens to the public
- 2015 Renovated cabins added as lodging at the retreat center
- 2015 Bowman Bay beach restoration begins
- 2016 Five cabins opened for use at Quarry Pond; bunkhouse added at retreat center
- 2016 John Tursi Trail dedicated.
- 2017 Cornet Bay docks replaced with a new float and pier design to expand moorage space, connect the docks, and help the eel grass environment

Old Growth Forests and the People Underneath

Washington State Parks has made quantum leaps of progress and understanding in its management of the treasured resources it oversees. One event at Deception Pass instigated one of those leaps, a step far overdue and taken too late for some of this park's old growth.

As the agency in charge of some of our state's most precious places, protecting those places has not always been a given. You can see from some of the stories shared earlier how that has been clearly illustrated: walls built on top of beaches, roads built along lakeshores and also on top of beaches, insensitive structures built in sensitive environments, and more.

One sad and clearly negative chapter occurred here in the early Eighties. The damage to the environment was only part of the problem. The damage to the public's trust in Washington State Parks suffered almost irreparable damage because of it.

In 1981, when this state was strapped for cash (notice that this happens frequently), the legislature saw all those trees in State Parks and ordered the agency to prepare timber management plans for any park with "significant timber resources". That phrase does not sound like the trees are being considered for their aesthetic, recreational, or environmental values. Timber is a value word referring to the lumber inside a tree, not the health of the forest where the tree is growing.

In 1982, foresters drew up plans for Deception Pass to remove trees that were "dead, dying, or otherwise defective." Parse those words and you realize that just about any tree in the park can fit into one of those categories. Seriously, all of us have some minor defect, whether we are tree or fish or human.

In that year, a windstorm damaged many of the trees in the park, particularly in the North Beach area. Park planners labeled numerous trees in the park into those categories, trees that would be felled by loggers and taken to the mill for profit to the park system and the loggers. The oversight of the program fell on the loggers and the agency foresters.

Hundreds of trees were marked at the park. Some were indeed threatening park facilities or campers, so the choice was made to save the facilities and not move the campground. But the number and quality of trees cut expanded beyond that simple logic. The law encouraged removing trees for the sake of profit, using the euphemism of "salvage" logging, getting the timber value out of trees before they started losing value.

Nearly 100,000 board feet of trees had zeroes on them for harvesting. As more "defective" trees were found, they were added to the list. The plan ended up identifying over 230,000 board feet of standing old growth trees for harvest.

Hundreds of trees were cut here. Nearly all of them were not dead, and in no danger of dying soon, unless attacked with a chainsaw. The trees at North Beach were not threatening any facilities or causing any safety concerns. The loggers and forester saw dollar signs, and the gates were open.

> *"The trees could be left alone, but there's real cash value in them. They're sold as surplus property, just like old cars that the state has."*
>
> *– a senior agency official in 1983*

"Some people feel there shouldn't be logging in state parks, but that's not the policy or the state law," one park official stated in support of the logging operation. "The trees could be left alone, but there's real cash value in them. They're sold as surplus property, just like old cars that the state has."

My blood boiled when I first read that quote. That is bad on so many levels throughout each of the phrases.

In the end, the local mill turned over 400,000 board feet of trees into lumber. State Parks gained $31,000 out of the sale. We lost dozens of trees that had been standing when Vancouver anchored off shore. Pockets of the North Beach old-growth habitat became a stump forest.

After the devastation, people were shocked to see what had happened to Deception Pass State Park. Some were horrified enough to say something. They expressed concern to the park manager at the time, who judged the complaints to be 'real minor', and who described the operation as 'sanitation logging'.

Some of the outraged visitors took their umbrage to the highest levels. Hearing the complaints, one state park commissioner expressed concern that things may have gone too far. "I'm against it," Commissioner Durand Cox said. "Parks should be left as they are ... as natural as they can be."

The director of Washington State Parks, Jan Tveten, acknowledged that the agency may have been over-eager in harvesting trees unnecessarily. He created a task force to look at State Parks' forest management policies. After several months of bipartisan, multi-lateral review, State Parks had an entirely new and comprehensive approach to managing its forests.

This new policy recognized the need to occasionally remove hazards from parks, but it gave strict guidelines as to how that can happen, with numerous layers of oversight and approval required. In addition, parks were layered with the zoning modules described elsewhere, giving even far more stringent protections to communities of forests and other resources in Natural Areas and Natural Forest Areas.

The logging may have happened, in part, because of the loose definition of 'danger trees'. The definition of a danger tree and the people who could make that determination changed dramatically after the event. The director soon had the sole responsibility to approve the removal of any tree over 10 inches in diameter. And that won't happen without full agreement with the forest ecologist and stewardship leaders and other senior officials, not just one guy on the ground who wants a tree cut down as 'salvage' or for 'sanitation' or 'surplus property' or 'cash value'.

Unfortunately, this was not the first time this had occurred here. I am proud to say it is the last time.

Amazingly, the same problem, cutting old growth trees in the park that were not a threat to people or facilities, had also happened in 1962. The same senior official led that harvest as would lead it again in the Eighties.

Many complained then, too, and letters written to legislators and others. At that time, however, the language protecting the park environment stayed ambiguous, easily misconstrued to prioritize profit over protection, to see trees as commodities rather than community treasures for the future.

There is a challenge in protecting expensive park infrastructures and facilities, and of course in protecting park visitors, while still protecting the very values of why the park is here – its natural, cultural, and recreational values.

State Parks wanted to be trusted for the work it does with the resources entrusted to the agency. The only way to gain that trust was to demonstrate a true commitment to both resource protection and visitor safety.

I have seen that commitment in action, and I know that each tree cut in this park has been looked at by several eyes and fully vetted to comply with all laws and policies. And those laws and policies have been designed to prevent any future disaster such as what happened in the early Sixties and Eighties.

Our parks are now managed to protect our forest environment, as this agency actively demonstrates that Washington State Parks is managing its resources for their intrinsic value as natural wildland, and for the long-term future of these forests. We recognize the sacred values entrusted to our care for all generations.

The value of the trees standing in the park is not measured in dollars but by their legacy for the habitat and the future..

Our park forest health expert Marv Wold, left, and our agency natural resource specialist Dr. Robert Fimbel watch Dan and Amy, two DNR forest scientists, examining an old growth tree in the Forest Loop of Cranberry campground with state of the art tools.

So there I am,

playing God with the trees.

With over 300 campsites located under trees, one of our staff members, Marv Wold, must get to know each tree personally to assess each one for any changes in health and stability. We must see the trees for the forest.

One winter he brings to my attention a tree that has him very concerned. It is six feet wide -- 6 feet! -- right between two popular campsites. Obviously, it is an old growth tree. So we have others look at it too. We measure and analyze the tree with boring tools, and as best we can tell it has only two inches of solid wood around the perimeter of the trunk, just inside the bark. The tree looks great from the outside, but most of the center is mush, five and a half feet through the heart of the tree. The tree is basically a thin shell holding up nearly 200 feet of trunk and branches.

The decision is made at the highest levels that it must be removed.

No one on staff has ever cut a tree that large with that little amount of sound wood, so we call a park neighbor who has logged trees his whole life.

How much would you charge us to cut it down, we ask him.

Are you kidding, he replies, I'll do it just for the experience, he says. You don't get many chances to cut down a tree that size and that challenging, he says.

With permits and approvals in place, we gather around the tree and cordon off the area for safety. After a final goodbye and a thank you to the tree, I stand on the perimeter keeping visitors away. I look into the front window of a motorhome nearby, see a kangaroo sitting there, look to the adjacent -- wait, what?! I do the classic double-take.

There is a small kangaroo looking at me, sitting on the large dash of the motorhome, wearing a diaper. The family comes into their campsite and sees me looking at their motorhome. They laugh. I ask if that is a kangaroo, and they say no, it's a wallaby, and would I like to meet it?

These are not offers I get very often.

A young man walks into the motorhome and brings it out. He says it is still young and being potty trained. He is its caregiver; his parents give him the full responsibility. He gets a lot of attention, he says, because of his little friend. He chats at length about the requirements of caring for it, and seems to be a professional in his knowledge and handling skills.

Then a chain saw starts up. I had forgotten about the work at hand. Back to business. The sawyers do their work. They cut, they undercut, they wedge, they cut some more, they wedge some more, making sure the hinge point has enough strength, and then a little more wedging and the tree starts to tilt, then falls with a 'whuuuumpphh' sound that is felt as much as it is heard, and it is heard throughout the campground. The tree falls precisely between the two campsites into the forest beyond. We clean up the branches in the sites, then climb on top of the now-sideways trunk, not out of triumph or power but out of respect and curiosity.

The stump revealed that the shell was indeed just a couple inches thick. It would not have stood there much longer.

The tree is now linked and known by staff as the wallaby tree.

You can still see the stump in site 61, and the trunk of the tree nearby.

The wallaby lives not far from Seattle.

Hikers pause to admire an old-growth, fire-scarred centurion Douglas fir tree on the North Trail at Kiket Island. It's age: probably close to 500 years or more. It's width: about five feet.

Visiting

"You can't capture this on an iPad or a flat screen or even an oil painting. You've got to come here and breathe it in yourself."

– Barack Obama, President of the United States,
spoken while visiting one of our nation's parks.

Having an enjoyable visit may take a little more planning than just getting in a car and driving to the park. Here are some ideas and suggestions to help you plan ahead and have a more pleasant experience.

How to Get Here

Deception Pass is only an hour and a half from downtown Seattle, if it's not rush hour in Seattle. And once you leave the metropolitan areas, rush hour is just a memory. Driving north along the I-5 corridor into Skagit Valley, you drop into this idyllic tranquility. Cares are left behind and the beauty of this corner of the world takes over.

Turn left at exit 230 (turn right if you are coming from the north) onto Highway 20 and follow that westward to milepost 48, where you will turn left up a hill instead of going straight into Anacortes. In just over four miles you will then see the pastures surrounding Pass Lake, your first views of the diverse landscapes of Deception Pass State Park.

In another mile you will wind your way through a canyon of trees to emerge at the north side of the bridge, the Pass before you, the waters of the Pass flowing far below.

Cross the bridge onto Whidbey Island and drive one more mile to get to the main park entrance to your right. The park embraces six square miles on both sides of the bridge. You are just beginning your exploration.

There are other ways to get here, of course. Island Transit buses come from Mount Vernon to Whidbey Island. BellAir Charters and the Whidbey Sea-Tac Charters can get you here as well. Or cross on the ferry from Port Townsend or Mukilteo to wander up the island.

Insider: Alternate Routes

If you are coming from the south and I-5 is crowded and slow, or you want to take a slower-paced and scenic route that actually gets you to the park just as fast, turn at Conway and go west on Fir Island Road. This goes past the Snow Goose Produce stand, the Rexville Grocery, and Christianson's Nursery, and then connects with Highway 20 at Best Road.

Turn left onto Highway 20 and continue as before, having enjoyed fantastic rural views, a country snack or two, snow geese and trumpeter swans in the winter farmlands, and the flats filled with daffodils or tulips in March and April.

If it is April, however, there is no shortcut through the crowds that you will find throughout the Skagit Valley, especially on a sunny weekend day. Can't help you there.

The park is on the water, so boating here works well if you have a boat capable of handling weather and currents. We have facilities for sailboats, power boats, and human powered boats.

Bicycle travel works well if you avoid the morning and afternoon rush-hour traffic, or the weekend traffic pretty much all afternoon. The roads here have narrow stretches and high speed limits that can be frightening.

We even had a man ride here from Eastern Washington on his trusty horse. He rode out on Highway 20. With a pack horse beside him. And yes he looked the part.

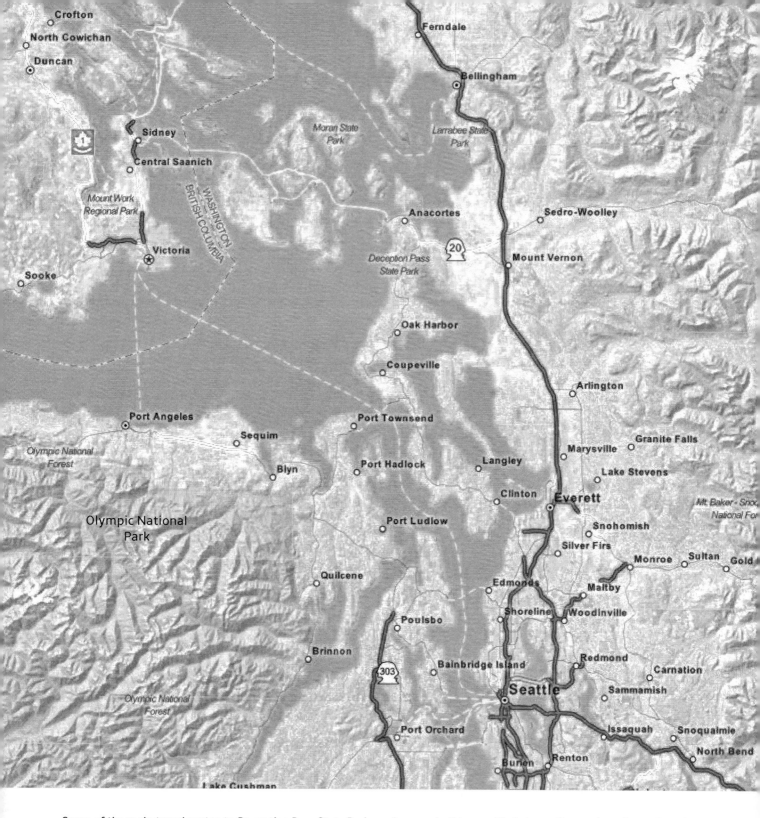

Some of the main travel routes to Deception Pass State Park can be seen in this map that shows the northern Puget Sound region up to the border with British Columbia, and the San Juan Islands and the southern tip of Vancouver Island. Deception Pass is in the center of the map, a little above the middle.

From Seattle or Vancouver B.C., take I-5 to Highway 20, which leads west to the park. An alternate route from Seattle offers a ferry to Clinton on the south end of Whidbey Island, and then up the island to the park. Map courtesy of the Washington State Department of Transportation.

Crowds

Yes, this is a popular park -- the busiest state park in Washington, actually, with an average of nearly three million visitors each year, and over 125,000 campers. So plan accordingly.

If you want solitude as you walk along a beach, don't come to West Beach on the Fourth of July. If you want to find a choice campsite, don't drop in without a reservation on a summer day, or a winter weekend for that matter.

But there are ways to find solitude on a beach, even in the heat of summer, and there are ways to get a great campsite at any time. I have gone hiking for miles to one of this park's beaches on a summer holiday weekend and not seen more than a handful of people. You just have to know the park, and this book will help.

The park is busiest from 1 p.m. to 4 p.m. We have to close the park maybe a dozen times a year because the parking lots are full, usually on holiday weekends when the sun is shining, but sometimes even on a Wednesday.

If West Beach is full, you can always park at East Cranberry and walk a mile to West Beach.

If Bowman is full, you may be able to park at Pass Lake and walk in from there. Rosario's parking lot may fill, but visitors can park outside the gate. Sometimes even those road shoulders get to be nearly full.

By the way, if our signs say we are full, we are full. At that point we allow cars in at the same rate that cars leave, so if you have patience -- it might be a half hour -- you will get in.

Please do not try to get creative with parking places, however. Putting your car on top of a planter island, or in the brush on the side of the road, or halfway on the road, earns you a sizeable ticket, not a free pass for creativity.

When Cornet Bay fills up, which it does on opening days of fishing or crabbing, or on a handful of weekends when a popular fish is biting, then we open Hoypus Road, with room for another 50 trucks with trailers or other vehicles. I have seen that fill up just a couple of times.

The bridge parking lot fills frequently, whenever the sun is out basically, but usually in the late morning to late afternoon timeframe. You can park along the west side of the highway south of the parking lot, or on either side north of the bridge. Be careful about parking at Pass Island; visibility in leaving that parking lot may be a challenge.

And just a note: don't leave anything of value visible in the car. We don't have many break-ins, but it does happen on occasion, unfortunately. Usually the victim had a purse or cell phone sitting on the backseat or front floor boards.

Seasonal Usage

There are many jokes about the seasons of the Pacific Northwest. One is that if the rain is warm, it's summer, and if it's cold, it's winter. In reality, the park gets less rain in summer than most of the rest of the nation, not only because of the typical summer drought, but also the rainshadow effect of the Olympic Mountains.

But there are seasons, and yes it does rain sometimes. And there are seasons of use as well.

The busiest season is from the Fourth of July through Labor Day. The campground can fill up all seven days of the week during this stretch, and if the sun is out and it's warm, the day use areas can fill up as well, usually reaching their peak business between 1 and 4 p.m.

But if there is an on-shore flow (wind out of the west from the water) and the land is warm, there is a strong likelihood of fog which will keep the air cool until it burns off, usually in the late morning, sometimes not at all. Day use crowds will then be much smaller.

From April through June, and from September until the rains come in October, the weekends will be very busy if the sun is out, or especially if it is an American or Canadian holiday weekend. Weekdays will be much

quieter. Parking at the bridge especially can be challenging on sunny weekends, again mostly between 1 and 4 p.m.

From mid October through early March, the crowds are diminished, unless -- yes, you know the theme now -- the sun is out or it is a holiday weekend.

Deception Pass has <u>always</u> been a popular place! This picture shows the East Cranberry parking lot in 1934, and yes it is full! Photo courtesy of the Washington State Archives, used by permission.

Reservations

That leads to your need to make a reservation if you choose to come to the park and stay in a campsite, picnic in a shelter, or overnight in a cabin.

I cannot stress enough the need for a reservation during the busy times of the year, and remember any promise of a sunny day may make it a busy time. All the major holidays fill up our campsites and cabins with reservations months in advance, and the shelters fill up months in advance for weddings and other family events. All of the campsites are reservable.

So, for campsites or cabins, call 1-888-226-7688, as of press time. [The reservation system may change in 2018 or so; check the State Park website to make sure you have the current number.] Reservations are accepted up to nine months in advance, and to reserve for summer holidays campers are online at midnight on the day that is exactly nine months ahead of the day they want to arrive, making a reservation. Plan accordingly.

Just go to the State Park website at:

http://parks.state.wa.us/223/Reservations Then follow the rabbit trail to Deception Pass to choose the type of site you want. [Remember, the reservation system may change in the near future.]

This system also works for all the shelters in the park (go to "Day Use Facilities" in the reservation system). There are two places you have to choose "Day Use Facilities" in the five step process on the left. This also works for the group camp (go to "Group camp").

Insider: Reserve early

I cannot stress enough the need to reserve your site early. Reserve exactly 9 months ahead, at midnight, if you MUST have a particular site on a particular day. Use the website, not a phone call. The web takes reservations 24/7.

You need to have an individual name for each campsite you reserve if you are reserving several sites. Remember that some sites may be reserved as multiple sites.

There are penalties for early cancellation, but you need to weigh the importance of the date you want versus the cost of getting it wrong, and not getting it at all.

This does not work for the Cornet Bay Retreat Center, yet. We hope it will with a new system in a couple years. To reserve a stay at the retreat center, you have to call one person in Olympia and leave a message. Call 360-902-8600. The retreat center has dedicated returning groups who reserve their space the day it is available to be reserved. [Again, the details of the reservation system may change in 2018. Check the state park website for reservation information when it does.]

Seasonal Closures

Operating a park the size of Deception Pass takes many people. Just properly cleaning each restroom once a day would take one person two days! And that is without having to wait while visitors use the facilities.

To give the limited park staff a chance to get other work done in the off season, such as building and equipment repairs, campsite improvements, and new construction, we close a handful of park facilities for a few winter months.

These closed areas are open for walking, but they also have their restrooms closed when the parking areas are closed, so plan accordingly. The months when park areas are OPEN for parking and with open restrooms:

<u>Day use areas:</u>
Rosario: March through October
North Beach: March through October
All other areas: open year round

<u>Cranberry Campground:</u>
Forest Loop: April through October
Lower Loop: March through October

Middle Loop: April through September
Back Loop: May through September

Bowman Campground:
April through October

Quarry Pond Campground:
Open year round

Cornet Bay Retreat Center:
Open year round

Ben Ure Cabin:
Open year round

Hope, Skagit Island Campsites:
Open year round

Kukutali Preserve:
Open year round

Water faucets in the campgrounds and day use areas are winterized before the weather freezes hard, usually in mid-November through about February.

The park hours change for the off season, with gates opening at 8 a.m. instead of 6:30 a.m. The gates close at dusk (about a half hour to forty five minutes after sunset) year round.

Fees

Did you know Washington State Parks are not supported by taxes, at least not very much? Many of our state's citizens do not realize this.

Most of the funding of parks comes from camping fees and other fees, and from the Discover Pass. Established by the legislature in 2011, the Discover Pass is a user fee to help keep parks open and functioning.

Fees change year to year, so make sure you check the web before counting on a certain fee or lack of a fee.

Each vehicle spending the night at the park has to pay a camping fee of some kind. The Discover Pass does not serve as an overnight pass.

Day use vehicles have to pay the Discover Pass fee. This is a $10 daily fee, or a $30 annual fee. Obviously, visit any park three times a year and it is cheaper to pay the annual fee for a Discover Pass, and it saves park staff a lot of time selling one annual pass instead of a bunch of daily passes. (Some will remember that it used to be $50 a year for each vehicle from 2003 to 2006, but that program did not last long.)

The pass is good for two vehicles, but not at the same time. I have left my pass in my wife's vehicle more than once, and ended up paying the daily fee that day. Frustrating.

You can buy the pass at hardware stores, online, at the park welcome station or ranger station, or at one of two credit card pay stations in the park. One credit card pay station is at the south end of the bridge, the other is at Cornet Bay. More pay stations may be added soon.

Another one-day alternative is to fill out an envelope in any of our parking lots, put $10 cash or a check into the envelope and rip off the top copy for your receipt. Make sure to put this top copy on your dash where it is visible!

Please do NOT try to use the Fish and Wildlife vehicle access pass that you get with your fishing license as a Discover Pass. They used to look almost identical for the first few years. Now the Discover Pass is a colorful green and white pass, very distinctive from the free fishing access pass, which is not valid in State Parks!

Boat launching costs $7 per launch. This is in addition to the Discover Pass, which every vehicle must have. So if you launch a boat and buy a day pass, it is $17 for the day.

A far better alternative to the Discover Pass if you also like to launch a boat is to buy a **Natural Investment Pass.** This pass grants free boat launching and works as a Discover Pass to cover all your day use parking anywhere in any state park. It costs $80 as of today, but if you launch your boat a handful of times, it will pay for itself.

The fine for not having a Discover Pass (or camp receipt for that day) is $99, and rangers issue hundreds of citations for violators each year, so make sure you take care of that.

People sometimes ask if the fees that they pay at this park help support this park. The answer is "no, but yes." The fees all go to the Washington State Park system as a whole, but from there the agency disburses them back to parks as needed. This park raises over $2 million a year, and receives about two-thirds of that back for staffing, utilities, and maintenance costs. So we make a significant profit for State Parks, which then goes to support parks that cannot generate as much revenue, such as historical parks or non-camping parks.

There are 320 campsites in Deception Pass State Park, and just about as many different fees. Camping fees are about $20 to $40 per night, plus $10 for each extra vehicle. Fees change from year to year, so check online. Camp fees are based on the quality and popularity of the sites and the time of year. Hook up sites cost about $5 more than nearby standard sites. There is a ten day maximum stay in the busy season, twenty in the off-season.

Remember, registered campers or extra vehicles do not need to pay the parking fee if they have a current receipt on their dash for this park. On the other hand, a Discover Pass (day use permit) does not cover overnight extra vehicle parking.

Showers require a token, costing 50 cents, giving 3 minutes of hot water, except at Cornet Bay where you use quarters, and at Bowman Bay which is currently free. This may change at any time. Get your tokens at the entrance station if someone is there, from camphosts, the campground store if it is open, or any ranger.

Cabins run about $50 to $90, again depending on the cabin, the day of the week, and the time of the year. They all require that you bring your own linen. The Ben Ure Cabin also requires you to bring your own beachable boat and your own drinking water! But the Ben Ure cabin does have a kitchen with pots, pans, and dishes, a bathroom, and other essentials. The Quarry Pond cabins only have furniture inside.

The retreat center has its own fees. Finding the fees is not easy. At the present time, you have to either call the reservation person in Olympia, or park staff. The retreat center runs about $12 a person per night, depending on the facilities you use. And don't forget to factor in the time and energy to clean the facilities when you leave.

Moorage

There is a fee for overnight moorage at Cornet Bay or the Bowman Bay docks, at seventy cents a foot right now, a minimum of $15, or five dollars a foot for an annual moorage pass, a minimum of $60.

Buoys are $15 per boat. Several are scattered around Hope and Skagit Islands. No commercial boats are allowed at the docks, boat launches, or buoys.

Dock and buoy space is first come first served, no reserving allowed, three night stay maximum. There is no power available, but this may change in 2017.

And at Cornet Bay, be aware that you will be sharing your dock during daylight hours with folks who are going after crabs, smelt, or other fish, unless you dock on the outer floats which have no pedestrian access without a dinghy. This too will hopefully change in 2017.

Groups and Special Activities

Deception Pass is a grand place to bring a class of students, or a large corporate gathering, or a wedding party or a race or other large group gathering.

To help a group meet its needs, and fit in with all the other activities going on throughout the park, we require a special activity permit. This makes sure that your time at the park does not conflict with other activities going on at the same time, and so that your expectations and desires can be met without damaging the park or interrupting other park guests.

Any group with more than 20 people should contact the park to see how we can help you schedule your event to give you the space and room that you need to meet your expectations. The permit asks the basic questions of when you will be here, how many people, what you will do for parking, food, shelter, music, sanitation, and other details. If you need extra canopies, bouncy toys, trailered barbecues, bands, or other features that make your event 'special', we will help site those where they don't interfere with our resources or visitors.

So call the staff. The permit is only required if your event will require some of this pre-event planning; and it isn't much money for the peace of mind it brings, knowing there won't be another wedding at the same place as yours at the same time.

School Group Tidepool Visits

We do require that all school class visits to the tidepools pre-register with us before your visit.

This is for your benefit. You do not want to bus 100 third-graders to Rosario, only to find that two other schools have done the same at the same time for that same low tide, and now you can't get to the tidepools before the tide comes in.

This is also for the benefit of the tidepools. We want to keep our human impact on this fragile area as minimal as possible. A couple decades ago, 1500 students arrived at the same day to look at the tidepools. The tidepools have not yet recovered from the impact of unrestricted numbers of people tromping everywhere for several hours across the struggling life forms there.

This is also for the benefit of your students' education. By pre-registering, we can send advance materials to help your students prepare for this experience, and we can also schedule our interpreters and volunteers to assist with teaching your students with hands-on experiential learning, as well as alternative simultaneous activities such as visiting the field classroom, interacting with the story pole lessons, and gaining a broader understanding of the natural world all around.

Park Rules

Of course there are park rules. The state has thousands of rules that cover what you and I can or can't do in State Parks.

Most of them are obvious. "Be thoughtful to others and to the park" would cover nearly all of them.

If you want the details, go to the State Park website, or search online for the Washington Administrative Codes, found in Title 352, Chapter 32.

Park Rangers are fully commissioned, trained, and equipped to enforce all laws of the state, including traffic and criminal laws, and make arrests if necessary.

Fortunately, this park's visitors are mellow and well behaved. Illegal parking is the most common violation we see, and we are doing all we can to make it obvious where to park and where not to park. If the parking lot is full, don't try to get creative to make a new parking stall.

However, there may be situations where you would not know the rule unless someone told you or you read it somewhere. Here are some of the common ones that may not be obvious:

- Keep your clothes on, or at least the essentials.
- Be quiet after 10. Sound carries.
- The park is closed to non-campers dusk to 6:30 a.m. in the summer, dusk to 8 in the off-season.
- Camp only in official sites. Official check in time is 2:30; you can come earlier and wait in the day use areas, or move in if the site is empty earlier.
- There is a 10 night stay limit during the summer, 20 during the off-season.
- Build fires only in the stoves provided.
- Do not use any wood you find in the park for a campfire. Bring your own, or buy ours.

Insider: Rangers and Law Enforcement

Rangers are law enforcement officers, but they are not cops.

Rangers receive the same training that a full-time deputy or city officer receives, which includes constitutional law, criminal law, laws of arrest, use of force, community policing, driving, firearms, search and seizure, defensive tactics, patrol procedures, evidence, traffic enforcement, and so much more.

But rangers have a different role than cops in that we also are called upon to clean restrooms, mow lawns, fix showers, plant trees, collect money, build trails, and give interpretive talks.

That can be a disadvantage, in that sometimes rangers don't have frequent experiences dealing with some criminal situations like a beat cop will have, who for example may have made three DUI arrests already today, whereas a ranger may only make that many in an entire year.

Still, you can rest assured that in the event a law enforcement officer is needed in the park, a ranger is trained and equipped to handle the situation, and they are in communication with other officers to get assistance if it is needed.

Deception Pass State Park is a safe park, with very few criminal incidents each year, so few that you may not need both hands to count them. We do have occasional minor problems, such as illegal parking, people drinking where they shouldn't, or a noisy campsite at night, but even these are not common.

Call if it happens. Rangers will take care of it.

They are public servants above all. They are here to help, in whatever way you may need.

- A maximum of one camping-equipped vehicle per site
- Up to 8 people per site. Extra vehicles cost extra.
- Please drive s l o w l y. Kids are everywhere.
- Keep your pets leashed at ALL times, and scoop their business.
- Drones are not allowed anywhere.
- Alcohol is okay but only at picnic tables or in campsites. And don't be intoxicated.
- Marijuana is legal in this state, but not in public places. State Parks are public places.

- Metal detectors are okay <u>only</u> at West Beach, the Cranberry Campground, the Quarry Pond Campground, and at Hoypus Point.
- No seaweed harvesting, and no harvesting of any intertidal animals that are not regulated in the Fish and Wildlife regulations book.
- No bikes in the Natural Forest Areas or Natural Areas, like Goose Rock, Hoypus Point (other than the road), or Kiket Island. Speaking of Kiket Island, it has further restrictions. See the Exploring section about that island for more details.

If you need help in an emergency or for any law enforcement need, don't hesitate to call 911. That is what they are there for, and they know how to contact park staff 24/7. We are here to help.

Safety

Mix high cliffs, steep and slippery rocks, big trees, deep, cold, and swift water, and three million people, and you have a recipe for potential danger.

Every year a handful of people suffer injuries at the park, most of them minor inconveniences, some of them far more serious.

One man was riding his bike through the campground while carrying his fishing pole and a large salmon in his hands. He lost his balance, fell, and put a brake handle into his thigh.

Another man jumped up and grabbed a branch to swing on, but then the branch broke. He fell on his back across a rock, opening a large gash on his back.

A woman hiking on Goose Rock stepped on a root, twisted her ankle, and had to be carried out by stretcher to a waiting boat to get her to safety.

A teenager on Pass Island stepped from one rock to another along a way trail, but both rocks were slippery for his tennis shoes, and he fell down the adjacent twelve foot slope, breaking a leg.

One toddler was playing in a campsite when he tripped on a piece of firewood and landed in the fireplace, burning his hand.

These are the kind of typical injuries that happen every year, some from carelessness, some from unplanned surprises, some from errors of judgment.

Park staff do their best to warn visitors of the potential for problems that are obvious: trails near high cliffs, beaches next to deep water, the dangers of cold water immersion, etc. But with so many people doing so many things in so many places over such a large area, the potential becomes reality in a new way several times every year.

Sometimes accidents just happen. But you can reduce your potential of being another story and statistic by having a basic awareness of safety habits and practicing that awareness as you travel through the park.

Here are some of the concerns that may or may not be obvious:

- Rocks are not always solid. They can crumble under your feet or in your hands if you are scrambling across them. They are also slippery when wet, and even when dry. Don't be in a place where this will cause a fall.
- Most of the cliffs do not have fences at the edges. Stay on established trails, and respect those edges.
- The salt water rarely gets much above fifty degrees Fahrenheit. Water this cold can numb the muscles very quickly.
- Tidepool rocks are covered with slippery algaes and slimy sponges. The barnacles will cut you if you slip on these rocks.
- Branches break. Trees fall.
- Trails have rocks, sticks, roots, and uneven places. They go up, they go down, they go sideways.
- Large logs on the beach can shift suddenly from waves or the weight of a person. They are also very slippery when wet.
- People are everywhere, bikes are everywhere, cars are almost everywhere. Sometimes they mix when they should not. Be aware.
- The bridge walkways are separated from a major highway by a half-inch cable railing.

Rangers and other rescue personnel carry the victim of a fall off of rocks along a remote beach to the park boat to take him to a waiting ambulance.

Insider: Marine rescue

The waters of Deception Pass are famous for their fast currents, whirlpools, standing waves, and constantly changing conditions. Boaters of all kinds can learn to navigate the waters safely if they recognize the dangers, the capacity and limitations of their vessel, and their personal boat handling skill.

Sometimes that means understanding that they should not be out in the Pass at certain times, especially with boats that are smaller, have minimal freeboard, or inadequate power; or in conditions where an outgoing tide is meeting an incoming swell or other hazardous water.

We see experienced sea kayakers enjoying the challenges of eddylines and surf; and we see inexperienced people in rubber rafts or toy kayaks or canoes out in the Pass in water way over their heads, in more ways than one.

We get calls to help people in all kinds of circumstances, in all kinds of weather, for all kinds of reasons. Deception Pass has a boat in the water at Cornet Bay for much of the year, or nearby on a trailer ready to launch. This boat has helped us to quickly respond to marine emergencies in the vicinity of the Pass. It is a multi-purpose boat, useful for maintenance needs along with law enforcement and search and rescue services.

Unfortunately, one of the more common calls we receive is to help rescue someone who has fallen on the land but in a place that is easier to access from the water. This can test many of our skills in providing medical care, navigating near rocks in difficult sea conditions, and landing on unforgiving shorelines.

We are not as well equipped as the North Whidbey Fire and Rescue boats or the Island County or Skagit County Sheriff's Office boats, but because we are stationed at the park, we can contribute a basic response faster than any other agency, arriving on scene several minutes ahead of any other emergency responders. Those minutes can sometimes mean the difference between life and death, finding the person in trouble or not.

Park staff train with the other rescue agencies on occasion. Together, the goal of all of the responders is always to save lives and protect property to the best of our ability, within the limitations of our training and equipment.

Navy Jets

The biggest complaint that our visitors have about Deception Pass is the noise from the Navy jets. Many campers never hear the jets, because flights are sporadic and unpredictable. They may not fly for weeks at a time. But when they do, it can overwhelm your camping vacation for awhile.

The thunderous sounds cut deeply into the experiences of our visitors, raising stress levels as a natural response to loud noise, raising frustrations with the inability to stop the noise and the constant wonder if it will ever end before visitors go home, and raising questions as to why the most scenic and rich environments of our state park system have to be subjected to the onslaught of jet engines.

We have worked at length with the Navy to get some relief for the hours or locations that they fly, but there is not much about their training that can be compromised. We have asked if they could move their flight pattern, but they are locked in because of other federal aviation requirements and the nearby border with Canada. The pilots need practice in all weather, day or night, so they will fly at any time of the day any time of the year. Some days go by without any fly-overs. Some days it seems they fly all day and late into the night.

They are practicing carrier landings with the EA-18G Growlers. As you can imagine, landing a supersonic jet on an aircraft carrier is a precision skill that perishes quickly without frequent practice. This takes repetition, so they go around and around and around. That wouldn't be so bad, but there is often a second jet 30 seconds behind. And another one behind that.

The afterburners can keep some campers up all night long; others sleep right through it. Conversations stop when they fly over, and if they are in a 30 second rotation, it may be hard to complete a sentence. Our rangers try to keep camper noise down after 10 p.m., only to sadly laugh with visitors when their radio music has to be turned off but the jet noise goes on unabated until well after our "quiet hours". In the summer, when we have the most campers staying with us, the sky isn't dark until ten, so their flights can last until the wee hours.

The Navy people are nice people. The base has always been a strong supporter of this park, and we have a great working relationship. Bottom line: their mission carries more weight than ours, and the park and your park experience may suffer because of it.

Some very good news: The Navy is now giving us a few day's notice of when they will be flying. We share that information at our entrance station as we obtain it.

Some more good news: they only fly for a handful of days a year after midnight. Unfortunately, those days are around the time of the summer solstice, the latter half of June, just as school is getting out and campers start filling our campground all week long. This is when the nights are the shortest and they need the hours for training.

The value of national protection and defense is unquestioned. The economic value of the base to the local economy is significant. Our nation's security is prioritized over family camping trips.

However, my assignment as park manager has been to protect the park and the experience of its visitors, so it is my calling to do what we can to at least mitigate if not eliminate the conflict. Some locals have bumper stickers that say "I heart jet noise". I want one that says "I heart peace and quiet".

The value of peace and quiet is vastly under-rated. And the value of treasured lands such as these to be free of overwhelming intrusions remains as a goal for the future. Perhaps in the future we can even do away with war, finding peaceful solutions to disagreements.

Comments, including noise complaints, can be directed to NAS Whidbey Island's comment line at 360-257-6665 or via email to comments.NASWI@navy.mil. All other questions can be directed to the NAS Whidbey Island Public Affairs Office at 360-257-2286.

Lake Quality

The lakes of the park are wonderful attractions for swimming, fishing, and boating, unless they are closed for health precautions. That sad reality can affect your visit, so read on, understand what can happen, and stay informed as your visit day approaches.

When I first came here, we would occasionally see Canada geese, but in small numbers. Something changed around 2010, when their numbers started jumping at the park. By the year 2012, we had over 80 Canada geese living at Cranberry Lake.

Island County tests our water quality during the busy summer season to make sure it is healthy for swimming. Their technicians reported to me on July 30 of that year that the lake quality was unsafe due to fecal coliform. I had the lake closed before the weekend, spoiling thousands of vacations but saving those same thousands from serious illness.

It turns out that a Canada goose drops a pound of poop a day. We realized that the goose droppings around the

The sign I hate to put up, warning visitors that the lake has toxic algae, and asking people to not let the water get into their mouth or onto their pet's fur where they may lick it. This was at Pass Lake.

lake from 80 full-size geese were enough to create hazardous and unhealthy water.

Cranberry stayed closed through that summer, fall, winter, and into early spring before the lake finally tested clean again.

At the same time, Pass Lake was changing. In November of 2012, I found a green pea soup scum lying on top of the water, almost as if someone had spilled green paint into the lake. I called health authorities in Skagit County, who tested it and found it was a cyanobacteria, toxic to animals and potentially to people. We closed the lake for a few weeks until that cleared up.

Although cyanobacteria have been around us all the time, it wasn't until the Eighties that the issue of "toxic algae" became a reality to State Parks when two dogs died from that at Anderson Lake, near Port Townsend.

In 2013, with geese not a problem at Cranberry -- they went elsewhere that year -- the lake was great for swimming and boating again. But then we started seeing cyanobacteria in the lake. The lake was closed in 2014 and again in 2015, for much of the use season, because of the toxins.

In simple generalities, there are two toxins produced by cyanobacteria. One is mycrocystins, which can cause liver disease if ingested over a long period of time. The toxin builds up in the liver and causes problems sometime in the future.

The other common toxin is anatoxin-a, an acute toxin that can affect the nervous system immediately. This is what caused the death of the two dogs at Anderson Lake when they licked their fur after swimming there.

Cranberry had anatoxin-a in 2014 and 2015, and we closed the lake completely. Pass Lake has mostly had microcystins, leading to warning and caution level advisories, and a closure for a few weeks when the levels were off the charts.

Cyanobacteria are not well known. We do not know why they are becoming such a nuisance and danger, but it seems to be related to the temperature of the water, which is increasing with climate change, and the abundance of nutrients, a problem in these shallow lakes with thousands of fish being added yearly and dozens of geese and other waterfowl also contributing their wastes.

So, what this means for you: call before you come if you are counting on spending time on or in either of the lakes, or check the website. Closures are posted on the web as soon as we post signs at the lake.

Connectivity

Yes, cell service is spotty around the park. Each carrier has its highs and its lows. Sprint is good south of the bridge, but spotty north of the bridge except around Pass Lake. The nearest Sprint tower is south of the park, which explains their good coverage on the south half of the park.

AT&T seems to have the poorest reception; Verizon does pretty well in places that Sprint does not. We are working on getting a Verizon cell tower strategically located in the park. It may be a reality by the time you read this. Other companies may then co-locate repeaters onto that tower, improving service for everyone.

Nothing works great at the south end of the bridge yet, which is sad because of how busy that area is. We are hoping the new tower will resolve this for at least the one carrier.

We are also working on getting Wifi into the park somehow. The many, many trees make this a difficult (read "expensive") proposition, as we will need several boosters to make it work for any coverage.

There is password protected Wifi at the park office, and also at the Cornet Bay Retreat Center, near the administrative building and Recreation Hall.

The park office, the welcome station, and the entrance to Quarry Pond have cable thanks to a cooperative venture with a cable company to lay a commercial line along one of our park roads.

Diversity

Parks do not always reflect the mix of cultures that make our society diverse and strong. Remote national parks tend to be white and affluent away from the parking lots, and white and elderly closer to the cars. City parks tend to reflect the neighborhood cultures immediately around them.

State parks tend to be a broad spectrum of diversity, depending on the locality of the park.

Deception Pass is a wonderful mixture of many cultures, partly because it offers so many diverse experiences, and partly because the park is so attractive to all people for various reasons, and partly because of its relative proximity to the major urban centers of Seattle and Vancouver.

Consequently, you will hear a smorgasbord of languages here, especially at the bridge and at West Beach. On a Sunday afternoon, I have heard German, French, Punjab, Hindi, Arabic, Japanese, Chinese, Korean, Russian, Tagalog, Farsi, Spanish, and English in the space of a half hour. I love it!

Our visitors come from all over the world, as reflected in the languages heard here. Island and Skagit County residents ("locals") are about a quarter of our day use visitors, Canadians another quarter, especially on Canadian weekends, and the Puget Sound area filling out the majority of the rest of our visitation.

And economically, our users are from all strata, some driving a Lexus or Tesla, some a family van, some whatever car is working today.

Families predominate at the gathering places such as West Beach, North Beach, the bridge, and Bowman Bay and Rosario.

Many of our campers answer a survey after they return home. The surveys show that our campers are also a mixture of cultures, ages, education levels, and economic brackets, tending toward higher than average education and income levels, but with a complex variety.

This eclectic gathering brings us a great synergy of human involvement and excitement as people enjoy the park together, the human family, a microcosm of our world at peace for the day.

It saddens me that some people in our communities have to think about not only the mix of people at the park, but also the mix of people along the way to the park, or in the nearby communities, in case they want to visit a restaurant, go to a store, or fill up with gas.

I believe I can honestly say that both the Oak Harbor and Anacortes communities are tolerant compared to many other rural cities in the Northwest, even if they lack some of the diversity that most cities of the country enjoy. It helps that we have a strong Hispanic population in Skagit County, a Navy base with a diverse population, and a variety of First Americans sharing this land.

E pluribus unum.

ADA Accessibility

Deception Pass State Park has been in operation for nearly a century as a state park, longer as a wildland recreation area.

Society's awareness of accessibility issues has only begun to catch up in places like parks, where historic structures and rough terrain can be a challenge.

However, for the past twenty years or so, great strides have been made to improve access to basic park facilities and features, and expanding those opportunities as time and funding allow.

If you wish to reserve an ADA campsite, call the reservation line and tell the operator that you qualify for the ADA site. Otherwise it is not reservable.

Here is a list of improved-access facilities and opportunities in the park:

Cranberry Campground ADA Campsites:
- 31, 32, 89, 209, 218

South side Restrooms and facilities:
- Forest Loop – both restrooms accessible
- Lower Loop – both restrooms accessible
- Middle Loop – the one restroom is accessible
- Back Loop – minimal accessibility
- West Beach – Hilltop: some minor limitations
- West Beach – Swim beach area: accessible
- East Cranberry restroom: minimal accessibility
- East Cranberry shelter: minimal accessibility
- Entrance station: accessible
- North Beach: minimal accessibility
- North Beach shelter: some accessibility
- Quarry Pond Campground: some accessibility
- Cornet Bay: accessible
- Park office: accessible
- South Bridge: accessible

Quarry Pond Campground ADA Campsites:
- 338

South side trails:
- Dunes Trail: mostly accessible
- Hoypus Point Trail: mostly accessible

Cornet Bay Retreat Center
- cabins: minimal accessibility
- Duplex: accessible;
- Bunkhouse: accessible;
- recreation hall: accessible;
- dining lodge: mostly accessible

North side trails:
- Bowman Bay: mostly accessible along south side of bay; pier is mostly accessible
- Rosario Head trail: some accessibility

North side Restrooms and facilities:
- Pass Lake vault toilet: some accessibility
- Bowman south side restroom: some accessibility
- Bowman north side restroom: some accessibility
- Bowman Bay shelters: beach side has limited accessibility; forest side is mostly accessible
- Bowman Bay Interpretive Center: minimal accessibility
- Rosario restroom: accessible
- Rosario shelter: some accessibility
- Rosario Field Classroom: some accessiblity

Friends and family members push a wheelchair along the Sand Dunes Trail at West Beach.

It's early in the morning on April 20. One of our maintenance people notifies the ranger opening the gates of the park that he sees a banner hanging from the bridge, but tied on well below the deck level, unreachable from the top. The ranger comes and looks at it and realizes it cannot be pulled up without someone climbing down with special gear. He notifies our Department of Transportation, and then looks down at Lottie Point and sees four males standing in the meadow closest to the bridge, looking up at the bridge.

So there I am,

waking up to a phone call. My ranger notifies me that there is a banner hanging from the bridge, and he sees four young men down on Lottie Point. He also says he saw a vehicle parked outside the Rosario gate before the park officially opened. I'll meet you at the bridge, I say.

We look down off the bridge, and see the four young men still standing on Lottie Point, looking up at the bridge. Hmmm, we say to each other, at this hour of the morning, it seems odd for four young men to be sightseeing out there.

I wonder what sight they may be looking for, my ranger says sarcastically. Something on the bridge maybe, he says. We realize that they are probably the owners of the vehicle parked outside the locked gate at Rosario. By parking outside the gate at Rosario, they are outside the park, so the car cannot be cited for being in the park before it opens. Or more likely they just didn't want their car to be seen in the vicinity of the bridge.

My ranger and I hike down from the north side of the bridge on one of those trails we don't advertise but which gives a great shortcut down to the Lottie area. We scramble over the backside of the point and drop right down on the meadow where the four young men are still sitting, looking up at the bridge.

We greet them kindly and ask them what they are doing. Just looking at the view, they say. What are you seeing, we ask. Someone put a banner up on the bridge, they say. Oh really, we say, what does it say? Something about smoking weed, they say. Hmm, I can't read that from here, I say. How do you know what it says? Oh we saw it closer earlier in the morning, they say. I ask if they put it there, and they all say oh no, not us. We know nothing about it, they assert. I ask if that is their car over at Rosario, and they say it is. I ask if they camped here during the night, and they say no, they came out early this morning to go hiking through the park.

I explain that they are in the park before the park is open, which is illegal, and would they please show us their identification. They do. Their initials are JW, MF, VB, and MM. I run the names through our State Patrol dispatch, and one comes back with a warrant for his arrest. I call him away from the others, explain what I have discovered, and ask him to turn around. I cuff him without incident. Our dispatch then informs me that the jail will not take the young man with the warrant as the jail is full. I tell the young man it is his lucky day, I uncuff him, and we say goodbye to them all.

The next day, our Department of Transportation spends several thousand dollars in time and equipment using a boom truck to safely remove the banner from the railing. They set it on the side of the highway for a few minutes when they bring it back to the roadway, and two young men walk up to look at it.

A newspaper photographer snaps a picture of the banner and the two young men, who give the photographer their names – their initials are MM and JW.

I arrive a few minutes later, after the young men and photographer leave, to take possession of the banner since no one wants to claim ownership. On the banner I see three initials: JW, MF, and VB . The banner also has a swastika, a four letter word in front of the name Obama, a marijuana leaf, a picture of a house with the letters BIG around it, the numerals 420, and statements such as "smoke weed".

The picture that graces the front page of the newspaper the next day shows the young man I had handcuffed and his friend, smiling with Cheshire cat grins at the photographer.

We end up using the banner as a tarp to cover loads of garbage in our truck going to the dump until the tarp also becomes part of the garbage.

Exploring

"We shall not cease from exploration, and the end of all our exploring will be to arrive where we started and know the place for the first time."

— T. S. Eliot

Park Entrance

Welcome!

Drive west from Highway 20 at the signal at Cornet Bay Road, and you enter the main entrance to Deception Pass State Park. A large entrance sign welcomes you to the park, as do two little buildings ("welcome stations") to help you buy a pass, register for a campsite, or get a park map or souvenir.

This area gets busy in the summer, especially on a Friday evening or weekend afternoon, with traffic backing up onto the highway at times. The gates open at 6:30 in the morning in summer, or at 8 in the winter. They close at dusk; previously registered campers or campers with reservations may enter at any time.

If you don't need to buy a pass or register for a campsite or say hello, use the right hand lane to bypass the congestion.

We are glad you are here!

East Cranberry Lake

The large lake on your left as you drive into the main entrance is Cranberry Lake, a large but shallow freshwater lake. At its east end, near the entrance, you will find a large grassy but forested field sloping down to the lakeshore, with parking for over 150 cars, a large kitchen shelter, and two small kitchen shelters.

A footpath leads down to the lakeshore where there is a long dock parallel to the shore, commonly used for fishing and wedding photos.

To the south we have a group camp for up to fifty people, with a small kitchen shelter, picnic tables, barbecues, and a large fire ring near the lakeshore.

A CCC restroom with flushing toilets sits in the middle of all this, near the parking lot.

East Cranberry used to be the hub of the park. Now it is quiet and almost forgotten.

This is the only shelter in the park where we allow amplified music, by the way.

Maintenance area

The main park entrance used to be a half mile north of today's entrance. The CCC built a residence near this historical entrance. The ranger used to greet campers as they entered the park, using his home as the park office. Behind his residence he had a garage, which served all the maintenance needs of the park.

Wasn't that a quaint era?

Fast forward a few decades and a few million visitors a year, and this did not work. State Parks kept adding maintenance buildings to try to keep up with the needs of operating such a popular park with such complex infrastructure, and it kind of worked for awhile. The staff offices moved into one of the garages for awhile, then staff brought in a school portable for additional office space, but it was always a mix of old and almost old, almost effective and not effective, duct tape and bandages. We made it work.

The school portable became a wood shop when the new park office opened in 2008. Still, this area is the hub of park services for keeping the facilities humming.

This maintenance complex is at the four-way intersection at the top of the hill after you leave the East Cranberry area. Just before you get to the four-way, you pass the **trailer dump station** on your right. There are two lanes for campers to use here to empty their waste tanks and to fill up with potable water nearby.

Cranberry Lake

This large freshwater lake is separated from saltwater by a short dune of sand, but it is a world apart from the saltwater environment, with trout swimming within and beaver and ducks paddling the surface.

Cranberry Lake Road follows the north shore of the lake all the way to West Beach, and makes for a great early morning hike or jog.

The lake is uniformly shallow, except for the northern shore near the campground entrance, where it drops to over 25 feet.

The south end is mostly wetlands and marshes, with dense vegetation. Cranberries used to grow here, hence the name of the lake. Eventually the entire lake may fill with vegetation and become a marshy wetland. This process is called eutrophication, where nutrients and warm shallow waters allow vegetation to keep filling in a lake to the point where it loses open water.

But for now, it is a delightful place to paddle, swim, or just enjoy the constantly changing views from the shoreline.

If you get out on the lake, explore the southern reaches of the lake as well. In fact, get out onto the marshland southwest of the East Cranberry pier. You will find yourself standing on ground that is actually floating over the lake!

Cranberry Campground

The largest of the three campgrounds at Deception Pass, Cranberry has four distinct loops. The Forest Loop is in old growth away from the water; the Lower Loop is near the lake; the Back Loop is close to North Beach; and of course the Middle Loop is in the middle between the lower and back loops.

The Forest Loop is mostly hookup sites; the others are mostly non-hookups. There are several restrooms, all with showers.

Check out the Camping section in the Activities chapter for my favorite sites in each loop.

West Beach

West Beach is the busiest beach in the park. You can drive your car right up to the beach's edge and look out at the Strait of Juan de Fuca and Rosario Strait. Stretching a mile from West Point south to the southern park boundary, the beach is a mixture of sand and cobbles framed by a natural backdrop of driftwood and beach vegetation.

The north end has an outcrop of rocks that you can walk onto at low tide; just be aware of what the tide is doing so that you don't have to swim back to shore.

The north end is great for dramatic photographs of waves crashing on rocks when a wind is out of the west. The rest of West Beach is a long expanse of sand and

gravel, great for walks along the beach with expansive views of the Olympics, the Strait, and Rosario to the north.

The concrete "bench" at the tip of West Point at West Beach was the foundation of a search light used by the military to watch for enemy ships approaching the Pass. Now it is popular as a seat for watching the blazing and glorious light of sunsets.

Go around the corner to the north to get a dramatic view of the bridge and North Beach.

South of the parking lot is the swimming beach at Cranberry Lake, and the West Beach Shelter. Future use may include weekend breakfasts here or other special opportunities.

Swim Beach

Children splashing, parents relaxing, sunshine bathing everyone on a warm afternoon at the park.

This Norman Rockwell moment has been brought to you by the swim beach at Deception Pass State Park on a pretty summer day.

The swim beach has a cacophony of joyous sounds as families play in the shallow water or on the sandy beach and enjoy a picnic on the tables or on blankets around the beach area.

It's a short walk from the parking lot to all of this.

There are two tiers of swim floats out in the water. The first section has shallow water, up to my waist usually. The second can get over my head, and has vegetation growing on the bottom that is tangly if you get your feet into it. But boats stay out of here so your swimming time is for you and other swimmers only.

We have no lifeguards due to limited budgets; please swim safely.

Nearby we may have canoe and rowboat rentals. The earlier concession has ended, and we are looking for new solutions to meet this need.

Insider: Your Own Swim Beach

The crowds around the designated swim beach may not be your thing, and the salt water is twenty degrees too cold for you. I get it.

For your own private swim beach, wander down the east side, the Cranberry Lake side, of the Dunes trail, and then turn off the trail towards the lake just before the trail enters the tall trees of the forest.

You will find your own sandy beach, a great place for a blanket and a beckoning entrance into the warm waters of the lake.

Unless someone else reads this note too.

Dunes

South of the swim beach you can find a rare feature for the Salish Sea shoreline – sand dunes.

A paved and flat trail leads from the concession building south through a valley between the fore dunes and the back dunes, then turns inland and comes back along Cranberry Lake and the back dunes with much denser vegetation in an area protected from the direct winds of storms from the west.

Interpretive signs along the entire trail tell the story of the plants and wildlife that make this dune area their home. The land is fragile here; please stay on the trail.

A wooden platform near the end of the trail gives a great overlook of the lake's marshland, unseen and unknown by most park visitors. The trail to the overlook is easy to miss. Look for it on your right as you walk north on the inland side. The side trail to the overlook takes off quite a ways before you get out of the trees and back into the dune grass approaching the swim beach.

Amphitheater

Located at the west end of North Beach, just east of West Point, the amphitheater has been a gathering place in the park almost ever since West Beach Road was created in the Fifties.

I remember sitting in the amphitheater in about 1962, and watching the evening become nighttime with the bridge in the background.

Interpretive programs of various kinds and subjects have been held here throughout the years, along with Easter sunrise services, weddings, memorials, and music concerts. We try to present programs every Saturday evening in the summer season, and maybe more.

The amphitheater can be rented at other times for special events. With its natural incline facing out over the Pass and the bridge, it is a popular location for gatherings of large groups.

North Beach

There are many special places in the park. One of my top favorites is the sweep of the sea strand at North Beach, stretching nearly a mile from near the bridge's south end to West Point near West Beach.

The natural crescent shape of the beach makes inviting photographs. The wildness of the beach creates memorable walks. And the chance to catch pink salmon from its shores makes this place popular in August and September in odd-numbered years.

This mile-long crescent-shaped beach is popular but still has wildness to it, with a gravelly and sandy beach backed by driftwood and forest. Two small headlands jut out into the beach at the west end; you can walk around both of them at low tide. A bigger headland separates the North Beach area from Little North Beach, a short but attractive beach right at the base of the bridge.

A parking area at the east end of North Beach gives quick access to North Beach and Little North Beach.

This beach is popular in odd-numbered years for fishing for pink salmon right from the shore. People line up almost shoulder to shoulder for half the length of the beach.

It is reported that tribal villagers once kept their canoes at North Beach when they were camped at West Beach, as it was easier to launch here with its smaller waves.

A trail parallels the beach up on the bluff above the seashore, with few access points back to the beach.

Underpass

When I ask visitors and even locals if they know where the tunnel is under Highway 20, I usually get blank stares. You will now know that it exists because you read it here and then hopefully hiked up to it.

When the CCC built the park, they wanted park users to avoid highway traffic to get from the Cornet Bay side to the North Beach side. So as the roadway to the bridge was being built, they also built a tunnel under the roadway to allow cars to avoid the highway traffic above.

Traffic patterns have changed, so what used to be a road is now a foot trail, but the highway tunnel remains as a way for hikers to get from the North Beach side to Cornet Bay and Goose Rock.

Think about this story of a young man who came from the East Coast to Cornet Bay back in the early years of the CCC, to start a new life as an enrollee. That young man spent two years at Cornet Bay, from 1934 to 1936, building the highway to the bridge, using dynamite to blow up rocks, building this underpass beneath, and working throughout the south side of the park.

That under-aged enrollee went on to serve his country in World War II, become a successful manager at the Anacortes Shell refinery, and also become a beloved CCC alumni, cherished for his generosity in supporting the virtues of the CCC. He helped people and helped fund the preservation of parks and our natural resources.

The Deception Pass Park Foundation wanted to honor that young man, John Tursi, with an interpretive sign, now installed at the west end of the underpass, to illustrate the building of the underpass, and to honor the work that he accomplished back then and continued to offer.

Mr. Tursi contributed grandly with his stories, his time, and his money for so many projects in the area. His kindness and care for this land and its people will never be forgotten. The interpretive sign, dedicated in 2010, recognizes how Mr. Tursi has benefited us all.

To get to the tunnel, hike north from the Cornet Bay Retreat Center and stay west of Goose Rock, or climb up from North Beach and turn east where the road or trail stops climbing steeply. Cars driving on the highway will never see you. Few people know it's even there.

Goose Rock

Accessible from several different areas of the park, Goose Rock is the highest point in the park south of the Pass (Ginnett and Bowman Hills on the north side are higher), and one of the higher points on all of Whidbey Island.

The views from the top of Goose Rock are worth the half mile hike to get there. Rising over 400 feet above the water, it is a quick climb. From the top you can look out west to Deception Island, south over Cranberry Lake to much of Whidbey Island beyond, east over Cornet Bay to the Cascades, and find a peek-a-boo view north in a few places as well.

At the top you also find "balds", meadows filled with sensitive wildflowers in spring. Please stay on the trail and avoid stepping on the meadows. Flowers abound here in the spring time. Let them grow.

Goose Rock has two peaks. The highest peak is to the northwest. Be careful getting there from the end of the main trail, as there are a couple slick rocks to be negotiated or avoided by going around them. The southeast peak is slightly lower, but has great views out over Cornet Bay and eastward.

Both peaks are just a stroll away from each other, so take the time to enjoy them both.

Climb the rock by parking at the park office, or at South Bridge, or going from Quarry Pond, or from the Retreat Center, or from anywhere that feeds those areas.

Another route to consider is the perimeter trail that goes all the way around Goose Rock, sometimes near the water's edge, sometimes far from it. It makes a great alternative for your return trip.

I like to go up either the north or south trail, then descend by the opposite trail to get the distinct variations between deep forests on the north and the drier, more open side of the south. The best rhododendron gardens in the park are on this south side as well.

Quarry Pond Campground

Today this campground has 56 sites, 49 with power and water. Some of the power sites are extra long for long RVs.

Five additional sites have rustic cabins available for nightly rental. The cabins are 10 feet by 20 feet, with a porch on the back end, heating and air conditioning, 110-volt power outlets, and rustic furniture. They have no running water or cooking facilities other than the fire ring outside.

The campground is open year round, and offers sunnier and warmer sites than those closer to the water. However, getting to the beach involves hiking a mile or getting in your car to cross the highway and drive to the beach.

A small pond separates the campground from Highway 20. This was a large quarry in the Thirties for providing rockeries throughout the local area, and now gives the campground its name. When quarry work ended, the lower reaches filled with water. Teenagers loved to come here and jump off the higher rocks on the north and east sides. Unfortunately, some hit unseen rocks underneath, leading the owners to post it as closed to swimming.

Later owners developed a "Sunrise Resorts" campground nearby, which they operated for many years before selling it to State Parks in 2005.

Goose Rock rises to the north, with trails leading from the campground to the summit and out to the rest of the park.

Cornet Bay Retreat Center

The Cornet Bay Retreat Center, formerly called an Environmental Learning Center, is perhaps the least known feature at Deception Pass.

Part of that is due to its location, tucked between Goose Rock and Cornet Bay in a bowl-like refuge.

In this ideal retreat area, we have beds for 200 people, a full size and fully equipped kitchen and dining hall with dining space for 150, seventeen cabins with bunks, a recreation hall for an additional 70 people with its own kitchen that can comfortably prepare meals for several dozen, two full size restrooms, a large play field with basketball court, volleyball court, and an amphitheater and

fireplace for large group gatherings, all in a scenic setting facing Cornet Bay and Mount Baker.

Two of the cabins were just remodeled to offer quality accommodations, queen size and bunk beds, and modern kitchens and restroom facilities. One sleeps four, one sleeps five. These can be added to a camp for an additional charge.

A modern bunkhouse was also added to the mix, with bunk beds for twenty on each side, and modern restrooms with showers.

The retreat center is a rustic facility, requiring guests to bring their own linens for the beds, but the price is reasonable, and appeals to groups of all kinds, from schools to churches to weddings to family reunions to medieval reenactments to kayak clubs and many more.

Reservations are made through the Olympia office. The summer months are very popular, with the shoulder seasons being busy mostly on weekends.

Top: The Recreation Hall holds up to 70 people for meetings. It has a small kitchen as well.

Middle: The new bunkhouse sleeps 40.

Bottom: The dining lodge has a professional kitchen and seats 150, with views over Cornet Bay.

Cornet Bay

Cornet Bay is a busy place! There are six lanes of boat launching, parking for almost two hundred vehicles, a restroom, a small kitchen shelter, and moorage docks for dozens of boats of all sizes.

When it's boating season, crabbing season, salmon season, ling cod season, shrimp season, smelt and herring season, or anything else where a boat or dock access is needed, Cornet Bay can be busy.

Near the restroom area, State Parks built a base for the Marine Crew, a four-person crew that operates a 75-foot buoy tender called the Thunderbird. This crew builds all the docks for the entire state park system, and installs and maintains all the floats, mooring buoys, and other marine facilities. They are busy people! Their boat is moored at the dock now referred to as the Thunderbird dock, just west of the public moorage dock. The Navy once used this dock for military purposes.

Deception Pass State Park staff keep the park rescue and service boat here as well, ready to go at a moment's notice. The only marine pump-out station in the park is here for boats.

The moorage dock holds boats of all sizes, with large sailing vessels tying up here on occasion, as well as a plethora of recreational boats of all shapes and sizes. Moorage is limited to three nights in a row, and currently moorage cannot be reserved. (This may change in 2018.)

The docks are also popular for people to fish for smelt or drop crab pots into the water.

The nearby picnic shelter can be reserved; it is popular when people are busy at Cornet Bay. A handful of picnic tables line the beach. The restroom is brand new, with a design that fits the motif of the park.

The beach at the Cornet Bay moorage and boat launch area is changing. It used to be walled in by a creosote bulkhead, but with that removed, it is becoming a pleasant and inviting walkable beach, with sand and gravel as a substrate. Eventually the restoration work will remove the rocks under the maintenance dock, allowing currents to restore the entire beach to a healthy condition.

Hoypus Point

Hoypus Point lies east of the Cornet Bay boat launch. This mile long beach is what Salish Sea beaches used to look like, with cobbles and sand overshadowed by various trees and other vegetation.

Around the eastern corner of Hoypus the beach continues for another mile before ending in private property at the south end of the park.

Above the beach between the boat launch and the point is a mile-long trail, a gated-off roadway for the first three-quarters and then a true trail the last quarter mile. The roadway is open when overflow parking is needed for the boat launch, such as on opening day of ling cod season or crabbing season. A turnaround at the end of the paved section allows these vehicles, usually with trailers, to park alongside the road after launching a boat.

A short way down the road from the launch, near a memorial bench, the view opens up to see the bridge. At each of the equinoxes, dozens of people come here to photograph the sun setting underneath the bridge.

The turnaround area has a burn pile and gravel pit nearby, used by park staff for extra loads of vegetation.

Beyond this turnaround, the trail used to be a road, but the hillside slid enough toward the water to wipe out most of the roadway, leaving a nice trail to the point.

Hoypus Point used to be a ferry landing to get from Whidbey Island to Fidalgo Island. Closed after 1935 when the bridge opened, it is now a quiet destination for hikers and clammers, with views to the north to Mt. Erie and to the east to Skagit Island and the Cascades beyond. Eagles sometimes rest in the old growth forests behind the point.

The trails of Hoypus Point, other than the former roadway along the beach, are off-limits to horses and bikes.

Hoypus Hill

South of Hoypus Point, trails meander upwards through the old growth to a somewhat newer addition to the park, Hoypus Hill. This former DNR land, last harvested a few decades ago, is becoming a delightful route for hiking, biking, and horse traffic. The trails tend to be muddy in places, and nettles love the sides of the trails, but for getting away from the noisy crowds, this is a good choice.

One of the trails is the former logging road, which wends through the south section of the hill, then joins with the Fireside Trail at the north boundary of the area. This makes a good loop route.

One alternative trailhead to access these trails is at the east end of Ducken Road. Here there is room for several cars or combinations of trucks and horse trailers. The new additions of trails on the east side of the hill make loops intersecting with Hoypus Point and/or the Ducken Road trailhead full of possibilities. It is open to horses and bikes.

Ben Ure Island

Although most of this island is owned by State Parks, we wish to protect the homeowners who also live on the island. Access to the island is only for those who rent the State Park cabin on the east end.

And what a great place to rent for just two people: a nice all-electric kitchen, futon bed, outdoor shower, small bathroom, wood stove, and sliding glass doors leading onto a deck overlooking the waters east of the Pass and Mount Baker. A kayak is required to get here, and you need to bring your own bedding and drinking water.

It has pots and pans, dishes and other basic supplies for your use.

Because part of the island is privately owned, we ask that cabin renters stay on the south side of the island, which has a sunny trail leading to the cabin at the east end.

Strawberry Island

Another natural area island in the park, but inhabited by small forests and lots of nesting wildlife. Strawberry has one tiny landing area on the southwest corner. Let the wildlife enjoy this one; we can enjoy Strawberry from a distance and know that it is in good hands.

The Bridge

Some claim it is the most photographed bridge in the state. I'm not sure about the statistic, but I know it is fabulously scenic, in all seasons, in all weather, at all times of the day, but not all the time, unless it's the only time you can be here.

As local author Elizabeth Guss wrote, the Deception Pass Bridge began as a dream, became a convenience, and has now developed into an icon.

There are three main parking locations: the north side, Pass Island, and the so-called South Bridge parking lot. Each of these have an interpretive panel that tells a different element of the story of the bridge and the Pass.

View of the bridge from the north side parking area, near the interpretive panel behind the guard rail.

The north side has a couple hundred yards of parking on the water side of Highway 20, and a hundred yards or so on the cliff side as well. (Getting across the highway can be challenging on a sunny weekend.) This is where many of the iconic photo shots are taken from, with the arc of the bridge sweeping into the background of the picture, the foreground framed by trees and the waters below.

Pass Island is only legally accessible by car by northbound traffic, and has room for up to about ten cars. A short footpath leads east to a viewing platform that looks out over Strawberry Island and the waters to the east. A stairway goes under the highway leading to another stairway coming up the west side, meaning you don't have

Above: the view from the main span on a summer evening.

Left: looking at the main span from Pass Island on a foggy morning.

Left: view of the main span of the bridge from the west end of North Beach, not far from the amphitheater.

Below: the view from the Canoe Pass span of the bridge with a light ebb tide taking water away. The Lawson Reef buoy is visible just below the horizon near the left edge.

to dodge traffic to get from the east side of the bridge to the west side at Pass Island.

South Bridge has a restroom and designated parking stalls for about 25 cars, with extra parking further south on the south-bound side of the highway. The Discover Pass is required to park in this parking lot. From here you have access to the bridge, and a stairway here also goes under the bridge giving access to the other side, or to begin a hike to North Beach or up Goose Rock.

Insider: 2013 Bridge Inspection Report:

Status: Open, no restriction
Average daily traffic: 14,828 [as of 2010]
Truck traffic: 8% of total traffic

Deck condition: Satisfactory [6 out of 9]
Superstructure condition: Fair [5 out of 9]
Substructure condition: Good [7 out of 9]
Structural appraisal: Somewhat better than minimum adequacy to tolerate being left in place as is [5 out of 9]

Deck geometry appraisal: Basically intolerable requiring high priority of replacement [2 out of 9]

Roadway alignment appraisal: Equal to present desirable criteria [8 out of 9]

Channel protection: Banks are protected or well vegetated. River control devices such as spur dikes and embankment protection are not required or are in a stable condition. [8 out of 9]

Scour condition: Bridge foundations (including piles) on dry land well above flood water elevations. [9]

Operating rating: 46.5 tons [42.3 metric tons]
Inventory rating: 27.7 tons [25.2 metric tons]

Evaluation: Functionally obsolete

Sufficiency rating: 48.7

Recommended work: Bridge rehabilitation because of general structure deterioration or inadequate strength.

Estimated cost of work: $36,115,000

Pass Island

This is the most visited island in the park, simply because Highway 20 crosses it. Pass Island has a parking lot for about ten cars. Be careful parking here. There have been dozens of fender-benders as cars slow to enter the parking stalls or attempt to leave the parking area with limited visibility due to people crowds and the framework of the bridge hiding the traffic.

Next to the parking area is a short paved walkway leading eastward to an interpretive sign talking about the bridge area history. On the rocks nearby you will find a plaque that describes Vancouver's visit on June 10, 1792.

A stairway leads from the walkway under the bridge to another walkway on the west side of the bridge.

Various social trails lead east and west on the island. Please be careful. They are not maintained trails, and have many rocks, dips, climbs, and cliffs. Falling can be deadly, or at least hurt a lot.

At the far east end you can watch the ebb current pile up against the island, waiting for a chance to get out through the narrow openings of the Pass. This wall of water can be as much as five feet higher than the water going under the bridge.

From here you can see Strawberry Island immediately to the east, Ben Ure Island south of Strawberry, and Kiket Island several miles to the east, beyond Hoypus Point on the south.

You can also see the caves on the vertical rock face to the northeast, a part of Bowman Hill.

Bowman Hill

There are no trails on Bowman Hill, for a couple of reasons. The area has some extreme hazards, particularly the steep cliffs facing Deception Pass. Several people have lost their lives in this area. We ask that visitors not recreate here.

Secondly, the cliffs can be home to peregrine falcons. We like to let them enjoy their home. They don't have many undisturbed places left for them to be free.

Bowman Bay

Perhaps the second most popular part of the park after West Beach, Bowman Bay offers access to quiet beaches, open water, large playfields, the CCC Interpretive Center, a campground, two large shelters, and even a playground.

It has a half mile long sweep of beach, mostly sand and mud with gravel at the higher end of the beach. This beach is a great place to launch kayaks or small boats so long as the wind is not out of the west.

There are two halves to Bowman. The south side has most of the day use areas, including playfields, the playground, a boat launch, fishing pier, kayak rentals, and access to Lighthouse Point trails.

There is a large field south of the parking lot that is perfect for frisbee, soccer, or throwing a football. Picnic tables dot the shoreline. Exploring options abound, starting with the beach and pier and leading to the many trails in several directions.

The playground at Bowman Bay provides hours of alternative fun for wee ones who get tired of playing at the beach.

The boat launch here is okay at a medium to high tide for trailered boats. I would not recommend it for launching at any low tide however, as it shallows out and becomes almost unusable.

On the other hand, Bowman Bay is perhaps one of the busiest launches in the area for kayakers, with immediate access to the generally calm waters of the bay leading to the intense challenges of Deception Pass itself, or as a jumping off point for exploring the many bays and islands just offshore or all the way to the San Juans.

Taking advantage of all these opportunities, the Anacortes Kayak Tours kayak rentals operates out of Bowman Bay from about Memorial Day through Labor Day. Guided tours head north out of Bowman to the many coves and inlets along the shores of Sares Head. The owners and operators are great people. Give them a call at 800-992-1801.

The north side has the campground, the two picnic shelters, the interpretive center, the statue of the CCC worker, and the trailhead to get to Rosario by foot.

The shelters are popular for gatherings and celebrations. One is right on the beach, the other tucked in the woods but still close to the views and action of the area, as well as having ADA access.

The Civilian Conservation Corps interpretive center is open all day long during the busy season. It tells the story of CCC projects around the state. We are making the center come alive with a host and a new focus on the CCC history of Deception Pass.

The beach at Bowman Bay is in the process of being restored. The restoration work removed the rock riprap from the middle of the beach, allowing human access all along the beach again. Native plants are taking root, and the beach is beginning to look like a beach again!

Insider: The Bowman Pier

It attracts everyone who visits Bowman Bay. Extending 400 feet into the waters of Bowman Bay, the pier supports more than timber. It hosts crabbing ventures, model boat sailors, first time fisherfolks, boaters in dinghies from out in the bay, sunset watchers, engagement proposers, kayak watchers, dreamers and poets, to say nothing of the occasional river otter and abundant seagulls and swallows who sometimes call it home.

Built by the Department of Fisheries to bring in clean salt water for their hatchery and to receive supplies coming in by ship, the pier has remained from those days and become part of the scenery, part of the heritage, and part of the destination of any visit to Bowman Bay.

Count the boards going out if you wish. I have, since I had to nail each one down a couple of times. Check out the pilings underneath, supporting healthy marine life and not supporting the pier for many more years as they begin to fail with age.

Ride the waves in a storm at the floating dock at the end of the pier. Catch the sun setting over Rosario Head, and catch some rays and good feelings as you rest on the benches.

Time spent on the water clears the head and cleanses the soul.

Bowman Bay Campground

A young boy rides his bike along the quiet roads of the Bowman campground. The waters of Bowman Bay are just beyond the trees on the left.

It's the smallest of the campgrounds in the park, the quietest, and the busiest. Only twenty sites here, but they sit within a stone's throw of the water and all the amenities of Bowman Bay, yet off by themselves out of the busy traffic patterns.

Some of the sites are up in the woods a little, some are down close to the water. Only two are hookup sites, and one of those is for camp hosts. Reservations are almost essential for this campground on a weekend or at any time in the summer.

Lighthouse Point/ Reservation Head

Okay, there is no lighthouse on Lighthouse Point. It's a light bulb in an official Coast Guard beacon marker so mariners can find the north side of the entrance to Deception Pass as they head out to or return from the sea.

It sits on a rocky point that is an island at only the highest of tides. However, getting onto the point is dangerous and difficult, requiring a scrambling climb over slippery and steeply angled rocks. The light and surrounding area is owned by the Coast Guard. A ladder used to make the climb easier, but not safer. The Coast Guard removed the ladder in about 2008 for safety reasons.

Having said all that, I have to say that the Lighthouse Point area, formerly called Reservation Head, has to be my favorite place in the park. Yes, I say that about a couple other places as well.

Here you feel like you are in a world apart, a splendid mix of rocky trails, quiet coves, bold headlands, windy meadows and intimate hidden places.

The trail starts at Bowman Bay, rises quickly to the top of a headland then drops quickly back to the sandiest beach in all of the park, north of Lottie Bay. It's only a

A sweet toddler enjoys playing in the sand at the very sandy beach on the south side of Bowman Bay. The beach faces toward Rosario.

For the adventurous, go off-trail to the northwest and find precious meadows with views to the north and west over Rosario and the San Juans (see page 222). Travel lightly; respect the sensitive environment here.

Then return to Bowman Bay by the trail in the middle of the head.

[For a shortcut to Lighthouse Point, you can park in a pullout, with room for three cars, along the southbound lane of Highway 20 a quarter mile north of the bridge.]

hundred yards long, but the sand there is perfect for running on bare feet and making sand castles.

Cross this beach, then follow the trail on the west side of Lottie Bay to reach the Lighthouse Point headland.

The trail forks as you ascend Reservation Head. Notice the hollow cedar tree at the fork, then make a choice, left or right.

If you go left, you come to a small beach with views of the bridge and the Pass where it joins the Straits. This is one of my favorite beaches in the park (see lower photo on page 5). It is only about a hundred feet long, but it has a small grassy field above and rocks to explore all around, along with views of the Pass and the bridge.

The rocky cliffs at the west end of Reservation Head. Lighthouse Point is in the top center of the photo. North Beach stretches across the water in the background.

The south end of Reservation Head has magnificent views toward the bridge, and glorious windswept headlands and pocket beaches.

The west end of Reservation Head has a series of finger beaches separated by hundred foot high walls of rock. The little beaches are hazardous to get to, and I don't recommend it except by kayak. One of them has a small cave, exposed at all but the highest of tides. But the points of land offer incredibly wild and wonderful views.

Lottie Point

Closer to the bridge than Lighthouse Point, Lottie gives a close up view of Canoe Pass and a great angle to the main span for watching moon rises.

Lottie is a short spur trail hike from the Bowman to Lighthouse Point trail, or for the most direct access, drop down from the highway pullout at the west end of the north side of the bridge.

The point also offers great sunsets in the winter months as the sun descends into golden water over Lighthouse Point and West Point.

Nearby Lottie Bay is muddy at low tide but a pleasurable backwater from the bustle of the rest of the park. Wildlife loves this area.

Rosario

I have called Rosario the heart and soul of Deception Pass. I know that is hyperbole and quite misleading perhaps, especially since it is nowhere near the middle of the park, being tucked off in the northwest corner, and has limited parking, limited recreational opportunities, and a deeper, quieter experience for its visitors, separate from the pace of busy-ness at the center of the park's main features.

Maybe that is part of the attraction, as it speaks to our soul in ways that business and action cannot. The highway noise disappears as you drop down off Cougar Gap into Rosario. Far from the usual crowds, the landscape draws you down to the intimate cove, sometimes calm and sometimes wild with waves and wind.

Looking over Rosario and in the other direction toward Bowman and Deception Pass, Kokwalalwoot stands as a silent ancestor, a welcoming spirit to those who wander back from travels elsewhere.

This was home to the Samish for millennia. It is still their home, and they kindly share it with us.

This is home to the storied tidepools, slowly coming back from the devastation they endured in the Nineties when school children and adults removed bucket loads of marine life to wastefully expire in the parking lot nearby. The strong love of the intertidal life expressed in practical action by our volunteers and staff created opportunities for the life to return. Slowly it is.

The tidepools are at the south end of the sweep of the Rosario beach. The rocks are only an acre or two in size, and the marine life is very fragile. To protect this fragile community, staff and volunteers have laid out a trail through the tidepools, delineated by a rope in the summer season, to confine footsteps to one designated area. In this way, the rest of the life of the tidepools will not be trampled. PLEASE, stay on the designated trail. Do not go toward Urchin Rocks to the west, out of respect for the marine life here.

Rosario is also home to a CCC heritage with the beautiful shelter in the field area, and the former bathhouse restored now as a classroom and museum.

And at the end of the trail, Rosario Head beckons to me like a comfortable visit back home, where one can sit in the meadow and view the 360 degree scenery: Sares Head to the north, the San Juans, the Strait of Juan de Fuca, the Olympics, Whidbey Island, and Bowman Bay in a circle of beauty all around.

Sharpe's Cove is on the south side of Rosario, with a moorage pier and a short stretch of cobble and sand beach for exploration. I love the single tree on the grassy point at the east end of Sharpe's Cove.

Rosario Beach north of the tidepool rocks is all gravel, with some of the best skipping stones in the area. It is a steep beach, so be careful if you have kids who want to play in the water.

Sharpe's Cove south of Rosario on a quiet foggy morning.

Look for other special features here as well: twisted ropes of volcanic rock on the northwest corner of the Head area; wind-sculpted trees on top of the head for framing sunsets and marriages; eagles commonly seen hovering nearby.

Listen for the sound of waves shushing as they retreat down Rosario's cobble beach in a storm. Hear the sigh of the wind in the trees above. Feel the depth of moisture in the air on a foggy morning as sounds are muffled and thoughts are echoed all around.

Listen patiently for Kokwalalwoot to tell you a story.

For the adventurous, explore Potlatch Rock rising above Rosario (be safe; falling can be deadly), and know that there are other scenic treasures hiding between here and Bowman Bay.

Cars fill the parking lot at Pass Lake when the fish are biting or when the sun is shining.

Deception Island

Seen by thousands every day, visited by only a handful every year, the solitary island at the west entrance to Deception Pass is a refuge for wildlife and solitude.

Because it is a natural area, we do not encourage visitors, and because it is not user friendly, we really do not encourage visitors.

The only access is by a human-powered boat in a very small cove on the northeast corner, with a tough scramble up the crumbly cliff to the salal-covered ground above.

Truly, Deception Island is still a wild place of beauty. Let it stay that way.

Northwest Island

Another natural area, and even less friendly than Deception Island for landing any kind of watercraft. No trees grow on the small rocky outcropping. Native birds love the lack of human traffic as they use every nook and crevice they can find for nesting. The water is deep all around the island, dropping to well over 300 feet nearby.

Let this one be a distant background to your pictures; let the wildlife have it.

Pass Lake

The lake is a hundred acres of solitude if you can ignore the highway noise that is very prevalent at the west end. You can almost tune that out and forget about it at the east end.

Pass Lake used to have active hay and cattle farms and a wood mill on its shores. Current park management protects the scenic rural landscape by continuing to cut the meadowlands around the lake for hay.

A small drainage stream comes in at the southeast corner, and a pipeline at the west end of the lake allows water to drain out of the lake and down to Bowman Bay. Up until that pipe was installed, the natural drainage stream was lower, so the lake's shoreline was lower than it is now. The pipe was installed too high, putting what used to be very pleasant sandy beaches around the lake under water even in summer.

The parking lot at the west end fills up with cars in early spring when the flies hatch, as fly fishing folks from around the Northwest seek to ply their craft in this lake. It is a quality fishing lake, meaning fly fishing only, catch and release required, and no motors of any kind allowed on the water. This makes for a tranquil lake (other than the highway noise) with abundant and hefty trout.

Pass Lake is also the trailhead for the Ginnett and Tursi Trails, lengthy hikes well worth the effort. On the shores of the lake you may see bald eagles or osprey. Mt. Erie rises above the northern shore, outside this park but reflected in the lake on a calm day.

Heilman Valley (Naked Man Valley)

The alternate name gets your attention. And the landscape will hold your attention.

Back in the Seventies, the Love Israel family of Western Washington fame had parties in this neck of the woods from time to time.

One morning, Mr. Hall heard a knock at his door at the Ginnett area and found a naked man standing there, lost and in need of not only directions but clothing as well.

Someone shared this story at a park planning meeting in the Nineties. A park planner needed a name for the valley below Ginnett to frame discussions about how to manage the area, and he chose Naked Man Valley. When I came here a couple years later, I saw the name in the planning documents, so, thinking that was the official name, I put it on the map. And it stuck!

But the Heilman family that homesteaded here and eventually protected this area from development, selling it to State Parks instead, deserves the honor of their name for the valley.

Start at the Pass Lake trailhead to get here. Hike over a ridge a half mile from the lake, and notice what happens to the highway noise: in the space of twenty feet there is now no noise at all, just natural sounds. You have now entered Heilman Valley.

It takes a lot of kids to wrap arms around the Big Cedar! It also takes some extra effort to follow the side trail to get here, but the option provides a good alternative route back to Pass Lake. Photo source unknown.

The valley itself is now a tangle of salmonberry, rose, cedar, and alder in a wetland and marsh nearly a mile long. It is nearly impenetrable. The trail skirts the edge of the valley for ease of access and a stable trail base.

The trail drops down quickly into the forested ravine of alder and old growth. A side trail at the bottom takes one back up a short ways to the biggest cedar tree in the park. This cedar is big; huge even. It takes several full-size people to wrap arms around it. The tree has found a protected place at the head of the valley, free from the most severe winds, and nourished by the groundwater filtering through the earth into the valley.

From this tree, you can continue on the side trail to reach the Pass Lake Loop trail and take a different route back to Pass Lake, seeing new country.

Or come back down and continue north to the Ginnett overlook. The overlook is worth the price of the hike; so is the Big Cedar. So is the quiet of the valley.

Ginnett

Ginnett is not an access point for the park, as it has no parking for cars. However, it makes a great destination for a hike starting at Pass Lake. The views are well worth the hike, and you will remember the peace and quiet long after your feet have recovered from the three mile round trip hike.

At the overlook you can see Rodgers Hill on your left, to the east, Pass Lake beyond the forests of Heilman Valley below, and the unnamed hill to the southwest that you just hiked around.

From the overlook you can keep going north on the Tursi Trail toward Mt. Erie.

An alternative trail from Ginnett starts just east of the Ginnett gate, goes straight up Ginnett Hill, almost, then veers a little west to give peek-a-boo views of Trafton Lake outside the park. These are not park-maintained trails, so scrambling and a good sense of direction will be required in places. Respect private property.

Tursi Trail

Anacortes has a wealth of hiking trails in the Anacortes Community Forest Lands, the highlight of which is Mount Erie, rising 1273 feet above the countryside.

The northern boundary of Deception Pass is only one mile from Mt. Erie and the network of Anacortes trails. Connecting these two recreational and environmental giants has been a web of challenges to find a legal and accessible route. A short stretch of private property separates quiet county roads from the two areas.

The connection has long been called the "Cross Island Trail", not that by itself it crosses the island, but if the connection were to be made, several other existing connections would be whole, allowing a hiker to walk from one end of Fidalgo Island to the other, then go halfway down Whidbey Island. Indeed, it is also part of the Pacific Northwest Trail, the PNT, connecting the Continental Divide to the Pacific Ocean by trail.

Thanks to generous easements by private property owners, this connection became a reality in the fall of 2015 and spring of 2016 as Skagit County Parks, the Skagit County Land Trust, and Washington State Parks joined forces to create the John Tursi Trail. It connects the existing Pass Lake trail with the park's northern boundary on the north side of Ginnett Hill, then crosses the private properties of two park neighbors who gave generous easements to allow the trail to go to Donnell Road. This quiet country road then leads to Heart Lake Road and the Anacortes Community Forest Lands, with Mt. Erie rising above as a beckoning beacon.

From Ginnett, this trail traverses a somewhat roller-coaster route through meadowlands, past a defunct quarry, through quiet glades of fir and fern, past a log cabin from the late Eighteen hundreds or early Nineteen hundreds, past the opening of an old mining cave, then to the park boundary and beyond on the private easement lands.

Looking east from Flagstaff Point toward the bulk of Kiket Island. Please stay off Flagstaff Point to protect its fragile environment.

Dedicated park volunteer Rick Machin looks back out of the cave along the Tursi Trail. The cave was mined in the early 1900s for copper and other metals; it goes into the hillside about 60 feet.

Kiket Island/ Kukutali Preserve

Come discover the newest state park and celebrate the return of Swinomish land to the people who have always called it home.

To get there, take Highway 20 east from the park to Reservation Road. Turn south, then angle right onto Snee-Oosh road in a couple miles. Go another couple of miles and look for the parking lot on your right just off Snee-Oosh Road. The parking area is small by design to keep the visiting crowds small to protect the resources and the island experience.

There are three trails across the island. The main trail is the old roadway, which leads you directly to the old homestead (the house has been removed) at the west end. The north trail is more strenuous but also scenic, with views over the water and a stretch that goes through old growth woods. The south trail is more direct, with less elevation gain as it wanders through the maple forest on that side of the island.

My preference is to take the North Trail going out, as the grade climbs gently then drops dramatically to beautiful views before getting to the beach. Then I return by the South Trail, the easiest grade and the quickest route back home.

Unfortunately, then I miss the middle section, which has a beautiful yew tree near the intersection with the South and North trails, and a great feel to it, especially in autumn.

At the west end of Kiket you cross a second tombolo to Flagstaff Point. Flagstaff is presently closed to hiking to keep the natural meadows untrammeled. You can go around the point on the south side unless it is a very high tide. At the west end of the point you have awesome views west to Skagit Island and the Deception Pass bridge.

Kiket Island is open for daytime low-impact recreation, such as hiking and picnicking.

> **Special Restrictions at Kukutali:**
> - Pack out anything you bring in
> - Walking access only (no bicycles, horses, or motorized vehicles).
> - No pets, to protect the environment and habitat
> - The beach is open for walking, but not for harvesting of shellfish, as the beach is still owned exclusively by the Swinomish tribe.
> - The north side of the west tombolo is closed to all use August and September. These restrictions are to protect the eggs of spawning forage fish during these months.
> - No fires or overnight use
> - Please stay off the meadows of Flagstaff Point to protect rare wildflower environments and nesting habitat
> - Kayaks allowed *except* in August and September on the north bay to protect spawning grounds for forage fish
> - Open daily from dawn to dusk
> - Discover Pass required

By the way, to pronounce Swinomish, put the accent on the first syllable, not the second.

To pronounce Kukutali, put the accent on the third syllable, and say it like "kook-a-TALL-ee".

Skagit Island

A baby brother to Hope Island to the south and with Kiket just a stone's throw to the east, Skagit Island has its own charms and beauties.

It also has a lurid history. In 1901, the "Flying Dutchman" Henry Ferguson had a hideout here. Officers had a shootout with him on the island and captured him, sending him to jail. Today you would never suspect the violent history of a century ago.

What I like most about Skagit is the trail that goes all the way around, through various forests and meadows. It is not a large island, so you never feel like you are far from your boat, which is most likely beached at the north east corner, the only decent landing on the island.

The campsites here come in two flavors: big and bold, or small and hidden.

The big and bold campsite is on the very northeast tip of the island, with a grassy meadow for your tent and a fireplace and table. The site is open to anyone wishing to camp here, whether power-boater, kayaker, swimmer, whoever.

To the west, on the north shore, are a handful of small campsites built by and set aside exclusively for people who arrive by human-powered craft only. Between the two areas is a vault toilet, serving everyone.

> ### *Hanging Out at Skagit*
>
> *Come listen to the story of Henry Ferguson, the fast-hitting pirate-smuggler-thief whose wide-ranging exploits earned him the nickname, "The Flying Dutchman."*
>
> *Ferguson had once been a member of Butch Cassidy's notorious "Hole in the Wall" gang of Wyoming. When vigilantes and the U.S. Cavalry finally made things too hot for them there, Ferguson changed his name to Wagner and headed to the Pacific Northwest. He arrived in the late Nineties and promptly embarked on a career of highway and high sea robbery which terrorized island and seacoast dwellers from Vancouver Island to Olympia.*
>
> *Ferguson's trademark was the stolen boat. He used a succession of them, reworking and repainting each one so it would be unrecognizable overnight. In such craft he sped from place to place on the Sound, smuggling opium and Chinese workers, stealing from fish traps and logging booms, looting stores and warehouses, sometimes commandeering whole cargoes from small Sound freighters.*
>
> *Ferguson had several hide-outs, including a cabin on Skagit Island.*
>
> *It was here that sheriff's officers finally cornered him in October, 1901, and captured him after a prolonged shoot-out. He was prosecuted for a warehouse burglary committed at Stanwood the year before. So for the next several years his home was the State penitentiary at Walla Walla.*
>
> *He gained freedom a few years later on parole, but was caught again after a deadly shootout in Canada in which an officer was killed. The Canadian court sentenced him to death, and so his life ended in 1913.*

Hope Island

Hope Island was a homestead for someone once upon a time. Evidence can still be found at the southwest corner, indicated by some of the plants you find there.

Hope is a place of refuge for me.

It is also supposed to be a place of refuge for the natural environments on the island. Nearly all of Hope Island is designated as a "Natural Area Preserve", the highest level of protection that Washington State Parks provides for an area. People are not supposed to be changing the island by recreational or more destructive pursuits.

However, the northern bay, Lang Bay on some maps, is a boat-in campground, and in the waters of Lang Bay are five moorage buoys. Boaters camp and moor here all summer long and into the off-season.

The campsites are primitive, right on the waters of the bay. The area faces north, so it is cool in summer and cold in winter. But the sites are right on the water, and they are popular. The bay's waters are protected from typical southerly winds. You will find a vault toilet a few dozen yards beyond the campsites.

You will also find a monstrous horde of mosquitoes in this campground in summer, so plan accordingly.

The rest of the island is technically off limits. One unmaintained trail traverses the island from Lang Bay to the south bluff, and then gets even fainter as it splits east and west. Following the trail takes you from the dense woods of the north side, with old growth trees and overhanging big leaf maples, through a transition forest as you approach the south, and then into grassy fields ablaze with colors and delicacies of wildflowers.

The meadows on the south shore are fragile! Please do not trample these sensitive areas. We spend hundreds of people hours each year trying to remove invasive scotch broom from the meadows, and little by little the meadows are returning. Let them grow forth and multiply.

Growing among the flowers in the meadows are junipers, a long ways from their normal homes in the deserts of America's West, but happy to be here on sunny, well drained slopes. [See * note, next page]

Driftwood blankets the southern beach. The beach is fine for picnicking as you kayak by, but please do not camp here. Rangers may find and fine you if you do.

On a warm sunny morning, however, sitting on a rocky outcropping in the meadow, sensing spring in your heart and with all your senses, listening to the wild ways at peace, on your own island in the middle of the sea, it is hard to beat the enjoyment and refuge that Hope Island brings.

Dugualla State Park

Dugualla State Park is little known, even by locals. It is managed by the staff of Deception Pass, and it is a great place to enjoy a hike through a variety of forests types, from old growth to alder groves to marshes, and then to drop down to a wild and natural Puget Sound beach.

You can access the park from the east end of East Sleeper Road, where you can park along the side of the county road turnaround.

The trails can basically be described as forming a circular route through the park with a center trail bisecting the circle and continuing to the beach. All three trails connect on the ridge just above the beach at the "Big Tree", a large Douglas fir tree in a section of old growth timber.

The beach is difficult to hike at high tide, especially in the winter months, because of the many trees, some standing and some fallen, mostly overhanging the beach or lying as driftwood at the high tide line. This makes the beach healthy for our ecosystem but a challenge climbing over and under and through the many logs and branches.

Hiking the full circle, and taking the short side trail from the Big Tree to the beach and back up the hill again, will take well over an hour or two for most hikers. The many forest environments you traverse keep the hike interesting and challenging.

The trails are little used, but they are gaining adherents now that the trails form a loop. Mud can be a problem in the wet season, and mosquitoes are pesky when the air warms up.

"May your trails be crooked, winding, lonesome, dangerous, leading to the most amazing view."

- Edward Abbey

Stay on the trail

We've all seen the signs. "Please stay on the trail".

The park manager wants you to stay healthy by not getting off the trail and into trouble from steep cliffs, falling rocks, hot geysers, big waves, poisonous snakes, or whatever else lurks off the trail. Or she wants to keep the park healthy by not having a thousand careless boots crushing a wildflower meadow or introducing noxious weeds or disturbing nesting wildlife or threatening the life of a fragile tidepool or wetland.

I have shared that exact message in many places throughout this book and this park, in asking visitors to stay safe and to help keep our at-risk environments safe from overuse.

But I am a wanderer at heart. I believe our human nature is to wander at times. Seek and ye shall find. Not all who wander are lost. The still small voice can seldom be heard in a crowd or sensed while following the trail of others. The thought of boldly going where no one has ever gone before attracts something within. The road less traveled leads to places not commonly known.

Yes, there are times and places where we should stay on the trail. Our large numbers of visitors make this an essential pathway to guard the values of the park for every person, one person at a time. If we trample our wildlands they will no longer be wild.

And yes, several visitors have been injured permanently, and some have lost their lives, by venturing into places where they may fall.

But yes, there are times and places where we need to find our own way, to explore without the benefit of knowing where we are going or where we will end up. Sometimes we need to experience the wild heart of life, with the outcome undetermined. The venture can be a forest glade, or the exploration of a new line of thought, or meeting with people outside our normal networking, or the pursuit of a lifelong dream whose time has come.

It is those ventures, those explorations, those meetings or pursuits that may give us quantum leaps forward in the trajectory of our lives. Or not.

Let's find out.

---

* Note: Hope Island had a large wildfire burn most of its southern meadow in August of 2016. For the next few years we get to watch how the meadow will recover. Will the wildflowers return? Will scotch broom be wiped out for good, or will it come back with a vengeance? Will trees die and open up more meadow space? Will the firefighting actions change the meadow? How long will the changes take? Should more of the meadow, or the forest, been allowed to burn?

So there I am,

in May, and I get a call that there is a tent on Strawberry Island, a remote rocky natural area just east of the bridge. The island is a wildlife refuge, and no camping is allowed.

It's surrounded by strong currents that pass by both sides of the island because it is truly right in the throat of the eastside entrance to Deception Pass.

Rangers Rick and Jim and I motor out there. Rick and I climb onto the rocks while Jim stays in the boat since there is nowhere to land. We find a couple plastic tubs of books and snacks, a broken plastic paddle, a broken tent pole, and a sealed container about a half gallon in size. I open the container and find gray ashes with flecks of white pieces. They look like human ashes, I assume.

We hike pretty much the entire rest of the small island, finding lots of geese and a couple active goose nests among the wildflower meadows, but no tent. We see where the meadow has been matted down as if there may have been someone lying there, but no other evidence.

We haul the tubs and other stuff down the rocks to where Jim is waiting for us with the boat. We admire the intertidal life as we clamber on board, then head back to the office.

Two weeks later, I ask a wildlife friend to join me on the island to look at the goose nests, to assess if the island is a critical and successful nesting area or if it was just a couple outlier geese using the island.

Jim again drops us off at the east end at high tide. We start checking under every bush and tree, as well as in the wide open meadows. I see one or two nests; he sees one or two. Both are obvious nests but with broken egg shell pieces scattered around; the nests are also a mess. As we hike the island we find more. Two here, one there, two over there, down by the cliff edge, two more under that tree, one out in the open, all with broken shells and scattered nest material. My friend speculates that they have been targeted by a predator, perhaps an eagle, or ravens, or maybe a river otter.

We go all around the island, finding more and more nests. I am getting into it, plowing through sharp rose bushes and dense growth that is almost impenetrable, and finding more nests in each hiding place. Each nest has been dug up and shell pieces left behind.

We get back to the east end where Jim is a little concerned about the falling tide, as the current around the island is now making it hard to nose the boat against the rocks and not get turned sideways and out of control. We have found 27 nests already, all of them uprooted and empty. The handful of geese sitting on the island don't challenge us at all, as if they have nothing to hide or protect anymore.

I ask Jim for five more minutes to check one area that I had glossed over right at the start. My friend and I duck under some more thick tree branches low to the ground, and I find a pile of toilet paper. It is fairly fresh, if that is descriptive enough. That gets my attention and curiosity. It's too fresh.

I scramble deeper into this woodsy enclave, into a small depression in the rocks, and there it is -- hard to describe as a tent, but definitely a

The view from the west end of Strawberry Island, covered with meadows and scrub forest pockets.

shelter of some kind. I approach cautiously, seeing a couple of small plastic paddles nearby.

The shelter has old tent poles up to support a big tarp-like covering. I peek inside and find an old chair in front of a makeshift table; a battery-operated round clock tied to one of the tent poles, the clock ticking away; a battery powered light aimed at the table, and on the table–

Legos.

Four large cabinets with little drawers jam-packed with Legos surround the work area, which has a small Lego structure in progress. There are pieces scattered around, and more boxes of Lego pieces on the ground within arm's reach. I look around the inside of the shelter for anything else. Nothing but Legos.

I'm on an island in the middle of an eight knot river of water rushing past, and someone came out here in what must have been a rubber raft because nothing else has plastic paddles like this, bringing with them these cabinets of Legos and constructing this shelter to make Lego things. And they have someone's ashes with them, some light reading, and some snacks. I am bewildered. I am incredulous.

I find the hidden trail that this person used to get from this dense forest glen to the meadows just a few steps away without giving away this structure for building Lego things.

We pack up as much as we can, making over a half dozen trips each to carry all the material down to the rocks where Jim is still patiently waiting and keeping the boat ready. We struggle to get the Lego cabinets onto the boat, as they are not designed to be carried onto a moving boat in a racing tide.

If anyone is missing a lot of Legos, and some other unusual camping items, please contact me. I would love to hear the story.

Or maybe not.

Above: A dense thicket of ocean spray can make a forest pocket quite private.

Below: Pass Island in the foreground points right at Strawberry Island in the middle of the channel. Currents rush around it on both sides.

Doing

"Our parks and preserves are not merely picnicking places, they are rich storehouses of memories and reveries. They are bearers of wonderful tales to those who will listen, a solace to the aged and an inspiration to the young.

"A state park cannot be planned until it is found. Speaking for myself, I would not be at all interested in park work if the function of parks and recreation would merely be to provide shallow amusement for bored and boring people. Folks so disposed should be referred to bingo or any other of the abounding inanities."
-- Richard Lieber, *America's Natural Wealth*

Bicycling

Bicycling in Deception Pass has its highs and its lows. There are some spectacular rides, some good family rides, some adventurous challenges, some dangerous roads, and some places that are off limits entirely.

For families, the campgrounds are great places for the kids to ride, so long as you aren't near the steep hills of the Forest Loop. The traffic is mostly very slow and going in one direction. Quiet Quarry Pond is all gravel, so it is not as pleasant, but has some advantages for kids.

A young rider cruises down the camp loop roadway in the Lower Loop Campground near Cranberry Lake.

There are two special places that are great for young riders. One is the Dunes Trail at West Beach, a half-mile long paved loop with zero cars and very few hikers. The other is the Hoypus Point road, which no longer has any cars except on busy crabbing or fishing weekends in the spring and summer. Most summer weekends it remains as a quiet and flat paved area about a mile long, wide open to ride to the end and back.

For those looking for longer or more challenging routes, there are some available. Hoypus Hill (not Hoypus Point, where trails are closed to bikes and horses) has miles of routes you can get lost on, get muddy on, and get sweaty exploring. So too does the Pass Lake trail, which has far less mud to deal with, and some great views at the Ginnett area if you get that far.

Goose Rock is off limits as a Natural Forest Area, as is Hoypus Point other than the roadway. The North Beach trail is rough, busy, and not a lot of fun for bikes. Bowman Bay could be explored by bike, but the runs are short and the views and associated foot-trails too good to ride by; it's better explored on foot.

Dugualla may soon grow as a bicycling destination. The routes are of moderate length, but with some good challenges of terrain and minimal conflicts with hikers and horses at the present time.

Kiket Island is off limits to bicycles.

Highway 20? Good shoulders south of the underpass. Between the underpass and all the way to Pass Lake and beyond the shoulders are almost non-existent.

Boating

So many boating choices, so little time.

Large boat or small, sail or electric or gas or human powered, the options are nearly limitless.

Cranberry Lake is ideal for rowboats, kayaks, paddleboards, small sailboats, and electric powered motorboats.

Pass Lake is also a popular sailing area, with fairly steady winds year round. Pass Lake does not allow any motors of any kind, but it's great for canoes, kayaks, rowboats, innertube float boats, or other devices that let you get onto the mostly protected waters. Just use common sense and be safe as the lake is large, and if the wind is blowing out of the west and you go east, remember it will be quite a bit of work to paddle west back to the parking lot.

Motor boats of all sizes power through the waters of the Pass, so long as operators know the limits of their boat in the current and expected weather conditions.

Tied to a buoy at Hope Island, one of several along the north shore of the island.

Calm waters on Pass Lake, with Mt. Erie rising above the ridges to the north.

Larger sailboats know that the waters of the Pass can be hazardous when the tide is running, but motoring through the Pass works at slack tide. Beyond that, the waters of Rosario Strait to the West and Skagit Bay to the east offer great sailing waters.

Cornet Bay has six launches, and ample parking. When the parking lots fill up at Cornet, the road to Hoypus Point is open for additional parking. That is a lot of parking.

From there, you can simply tie up at the moorage docks in Cornet, and pay for up to three nights at the head of the dock. The depth at the docks is sufficient for large sailing craft.

Or you can head to the buoys at Hope Island (four) on the north shore, protected from southerlies, or the two buoys at Skagit Island, also on the north shore.

The dock at Sharpe Cove, south of Rosario.

Boating through the main Pass in a large motor cruiser with strong tides running and calm weather is fine. Just keep your power up.

Or head through the Pass and tie up to the floating island docks in Bowman Bay, 96 linear feet of docks on each side, or anchor in the bay, safe from all winds except westerlies.

Or tie up at the dock at Sharpe's Cove, on the south side of Rosario.

Or go anywhere else you wish in the Sound or San Juans.

The fine print: no commercial vessels allowed on State Park docks or buoys. Moorage space is first come first served, no reservations or holding of space (at the present time). Pay at the pay station at the head of the dock if you do not have an annual moorage pass. There is an annual moorage pass which costs the equivalent of seven nights of moorage. And there is a Natural Investment Pass which provides free boat launching AND no need for a Discover Pass for your day use in the park for one year.

Boat Rentals

The park used to have a concession-operated boat rental business on Cranberry Lake near the swim beach at West Beach. That may or may not be available again in the near future. Bowman Bay has kayak and paddleboard rentals.

Boat Tours

The Deception Pass Tours boat operates out of Cornet Bay during the spring and summer months. The tour of the Pass lasts one hour, and is definitely worth the price of a ticket, especially if you have never been on the water under the bridge. The tour guides are very nice, informative about the area, and provide a professional and memorable experience.

From the comfort of the large boat they view the Prison Caves, the bridge, Lawson Reef and any marine mammals swimming around out there, Deception Island, Northwest Island, and any other attractions on the water. It is well worth it.

Visit their website at www.deceptionpasstours.com

The Island Whaler takes a large group of visitors through the waters of the Pass. Their tour guides give a great background story to all they see.

Cabins

Want your own island get-away cabin?

The view from the Ben Ure cabin isn't bad. The interior, shown below, is comfortable and cozy.

Ben Ure Island has a cabin you can rent by the night. The cabin is for only one or two people. It is all electric, so it has heat, a stove and oven, refrigerator, flush toilet, semi-outdoor shower, dishes and pots and pans, a futon bed, table, wood stove, and peace and quiet.

It overlooks the waters of Skagit Bay and Mount Baker beyond.

You have to paddle or row a beachable boat to get there, and you have to bring your own water and linens. Otherwise, it's ready for your escape.

After getting your key from the park entrance station or park office, drive to Cornet Bay and park in the stall near the boat launch with the sign that says "Ben Ure Guests Only". Your destination is the island right in front of you, about a quarter mile of somewhat protected water. (Don't bring an inflatable raft, as one couple did, only to find themselves drifting east of the island as the wind and gentle current carried them away.)

Land your boat at the southwest end of the island, walk the south beach trail to the east end, and your cabin waits for you at the edge of the forest, just above the water's edge.

A large deck invites an outdoor picnic and a game of Sequence if it isn't raining. But if it is, get a fire going, snuggle up together, listen to the rain in the trees and on the roof, and drift off to sleep with dreams of contentment.

Make your reservation early -- summer days are locked in as soon as the nine-month window allows. Weekdays in winter are often the easiest to snag, of course.

The cabins at Quarry Pond will also be mentioned with the campground description, but they bear repeating here. There are five of them, rustic in nature, sleeping five people each – two on a futon, two on a full bed on the bottom of a bunk, and one on the top bunk.

Above, the exterior of one of the Quarry Pond cabins, and below, the interior.

They do not have plumbing of any kind, but the restroom building with showers is nearby. The pine wood interior of the cabin looks warm, and the quiet heat pump keeps the rooms warm in the winter and cool in the summer. Each cabin has a table and four chairs, and several outlets to keep your electronics powered up. No cooking is allowed inside the cabin, but the fire ring and picnic table outside give you options. The large porch offers an outdoor place to relax.

These have been well received in the short time that they have been here. Make reservations, as these will be popular year round. Imagine not having to dry out your tent. Imagine staying warm in the winter. Imagine not having to tow an RV and still have a comfortable bed in the park. This may revolutionize my camping.

Camping

Deception Pass State Park has three main campgrounds, and a handful of remote sites for those with boats. All of the campground restrooms have showers now.

Campsite fees change once in awhile, so visit Washington State Park's website for pricing. Basically, sites with power cost a few more dollars than sites without power; popular sites cost more than less popular sites; and sites cost more in the summer than they do in the winter. There is a fee for any vehicles you bring with you after the first vehicle. Fires are allowed in the fire rings in each site, unless the summer drought has created a burn ban. Dogs must be kept on a leash. Amplified music and loud talking needs to end at 10 p.m. There are other rules too, but basically just be considerate of your neighbor and the campers coming after you for the next few generations, and you will be much appreciated by all of us.

If you do encounter problems at any time, contact our entrance station, or the nearest camphost, or call 911. Seriously, our 911 dispatch folks love waking up a ranger at night to let the ranger know there is a problem in the campground. That is what 911 can do for you here, and that is what rangers are here for. Call, don't suffer.

And don't forget to make a reservation. It's no fun to show up at eight o'clock on Friday evening after driving here for four hours with hungry kids expecting a great vacation and your wife expecting relaxation and then have us tell you we are full and the nearest available campsite is in the Cascades. We have the dubious privilege of giving this message to people all summer long. Call 888-CAMPOUT or go to the State Park website and make your reservation nine months in advance.

Bowman Bay

on Fidalgo Island is a small campground with only 20 sites, and only two of those with power. The sites are close to the water and close to the woods, and in a cul-de-sac roadway which limits who drives by your site.

Some of the sites have some privacy by being in the woods on a shelf above the other sites. The other sites at Bowman are near the water, except for a couple which are in between and not as popular.

From this campground you have easy access to the beach at Bowman, and the trails to Lighthouse Point,

Sites 289, 288, 287, 286, 285 and 284 in the Bowman Bay campground. The bay is just to the left.

Lottie Point, and Rosario. The pier is popular for crabbing and sunsets. Moorage in the bay attracts many, and the campground provides an alternative place to spend the night. The restroom is older but pleasant, with few campers competing for the shower.

Bowman is closed October through March.

Cranberry Campground

on Whidbey Island is a sprawling conglomeration of 235 sites situated on a ridge between Cranberry Lake and North Beach. It has four main loops.

The Forest Loop, sites 1 - 78, lies in the shadows of old growth trees, and is furthest from the beaches, but has most of the powered sites in this campground. The Forest Loop closes in the five off-season months.

The Lower Loop is closest to Cranberry Lake and West Beach. This is a popular loop with some good sites scattered throughout, with second-growth trees providing wind music in a breeze and shade when the sun shines.

The Middle Loop, sites 146 to 169 and 197 to 225, has what are probably our least popular sites in the Cranberry Campground, but also the lowest priced sites. The ground here is close to wetlands or marshlands or muddy areas, depending on your preferred adjective.

The Back Loop, sites 170 through 196, are closest to North Beach. There are some private sites back here, with personal trails to the beach and some with sizeable acreage away from the roadway. This loop is also the quietest for traffic. It is only open May through September.

Quarry Pond Campground

The newest campground joined the camping options in 2005. We remodeled it a few years later, though still not quite to the standards of the other campgrounds. It's just a little less developed, but the sites are open and sunny, and nearly all of them have power. It is the only campground open year round. Although it is a mile or more to the beaches, being on the east side of Highway 20, it does provide easier access to Goose Rock and Cornet Bay.

We now have five cabins in this campground, rustic in nature, but a nice place to stay if you don't want to bring an RV or rough it in the winter, or at any time. The cabins have a futon that can sleep two, and a bunk bed that has a full-size mattress on the bottom and a twin on top. They also have a kitchen table, four chairs, and electric heat. Outside, a picnic table and fire ring complete the campsite arrangement.

Site 118 and vicinity in the lower loop campground of Cranberry. The lake is just to the right.

Each of the three campgrounds has its own character and attractions or detractions. Those who like smaller crowds, quieter roadways, and closer proximity to wildland hikes tend to prefer Bowman Bay's intimate setting. Those who look for action, for activities like swimming and trout fishing, congregate at the Cranberry Campground. And those who are just happy to get a site, any site, or prefer power sites without old growth trees nearby or to find smaller crowds in the shoulder seasons choose the Quarry Pond site.

Each to their own.

Which site is best? I get asked that question at least once a day or several times a day in the summer. And I never answer the question, because everyone has different preferences for what they think makes for the "best" site. Some people want to be close to their friends, and choose multiple sites. Some want to be close to the restroom, or the swim beach, or deep in the woods. I love it when someone calls on July 1 and asks to reserve a private site for the upcoming weekend, close to the water, not far from the restroom but not real close, in the trees but with lots of sunshine in the morning, and no traffic nearby or close neighbors. I laugh and suggest Alaska, then tell them that the campground probably filled for the July 4th weekend around January if not earlier. The caller doesn't usually laugh.

Insider: For Better or Worse

For me: I would choose Bowman Bay Campground of the three, and site 280 at Bowman Bay is my favorite, right on the water, the farthest from the crowds, and the closest to the Rosario Trail. But even that site is too close to the trail, and gets headlights from cars coming around the corner.

See? There is no "best" site.

Site 282 at Bowman is perhaps even better. I just changed my mind. Those who camp with other family groups really like 287 to 289, but 285 and 286 are more private. The new sites, 274, 276, 277, and 278 are on the hill away from the water but more private. 275 is in the middle of the fishbowl.

Some Cranberry Campground personal preferences: Sites 148, 170, 171, and 179 in the back loop, close to North Beach and off by themselves; sites 173 and 151 are back to back, a surprisingly good choice for two families to share; sites 183, 184, 186, 188, 190, 191, and 196 have nice privacy and proximity to North Beach; sites 115, 117, 118, 120, 122, or 124 are close to West Beach (but also close to traffic)

Try sites 318, 333, or 353 at Quarry Pond; these would work for me.

Many people love the Forest Loop, and there are some large sites in there that are nice. I suppose 15 and 19 deserve mention, and 26 is small but it has a nice view. The upper 30s and the 40s through the 50s are popular. The south side 40s are close to the Cranberry Road, though. The Fifties through mid-Sixties are in the truly immense old-growth trees.

There are some bad sites as well, sites that have little room, no privacy at all, no view, subject to headlights shining into the site, close to restroom foot traffic, or other detracting qualities. And sites 70, 10, 21 and 22 get very wet in the off season from groundwater, as do a handful of other sites.

The reservation system has photos of each campsite to give you a little idea of what the sites look like. The map in this book and on the website also give you ideas about how close the site is to others, or where it is in relation to a restroom or trail or traffic. Plan ahead.

Other alternatives: get a kayak and head out to Skagit Island, and get there before anyone else to get the site right on the northeast point. It's a heavenly spot.

Find your favorite. And reserve it early.

Make a note on your calendar or smart phone to make a reservation nine months in advance, not a day before (because you can't) and not a day after (because it may be taken by someone else by then). Go online at midnight. I'm serious, if you are serious about getting the site or sites you really want.

There is a chance you can find a site without a reservation during the busy season, but it probably won't be a quality site.

When is the campground busy? Spring weekends; every day of the week in July and the first three weeks of August; September and early October weekends; and any holiday weekend (including Canadian holidays) year round.

Island Camping:

One of the campsites at Hope Island, looking north across the little bay of the island to Skagit Island and Mt. Erie in the distance beyond.

For the more adventuresome, other campsites await off-shore. Skagit Island has half a dozen sites, most of which are for kayakers only, but one of which is for anyone able to get there by a boat of any kind, or by swimming, but then your sleeping bag may be wet.

The kayak sites on Skagit are a part of the Cascadia Marine Trail, a series of campsites available to paddlers of human powered craft and set aside exclusively for them as they don't have a lot of options to choose other parks nearby when it is late in the day. There is one vault toilet.

Kiket Island does not allow overnight use. Strawberry and Deception are off limits for all overnight use as well.

Hope Island has a handful of sites in the bay on the north side of the island, available to boaters of all kind.

And Bowman Bay also has a Cascadia Marine Trail site, located near the foot of the pier, again reserved for humans arriving in human-powered craft.

>
> ### Insider: Cascadia Marine Trail
>
> *Begun by Puget Sound paddlers striving to protect public access to our shorelines, the Cascadia Marine Trail gained power when the legislature passed a bill in 1993 to fund a water trail of campsites, a trail that would stretch from Olympia to our border with Canada.*
>
> *Their goal is to have a campsite for watercraft every eight miles along the Sound. At last count, I think there were 55 campsites so far, carrying on a tradition of travel on the Sound that is thousands of years old.*

Camp fires

Every campsite has a fire ring for building reasonably sized fires and building unreasonably sized s'mores.

Outside of the campgrounds, there are very few fire rings available for fires. There are dozens of braziers around nearly all the picnic grounds of the park.

Fires must be reasonable in size, and may be banned if we have a dry spell, which has been happening quite often the past few years. One year the fire ban began in late June and ran through all the summer months.

During a fire ban, charcoal fires may <u>or may not</u> be allowed, depending on the severity of the fire danger. Fire bans are posted prominently, and violators are fined a significant amount.

During summer weekends from 4 p.m. to 8 p.m. you can purchase firewood from the store at the entrance to the Cranberry Campground if we have hosts available to operate the store. Firewood is available at the main park entrance station when the entrance station is open, which is 9 a.m. to about 8 p.m. during the busiest season, and with limited hours during the off-season. (Hours are posted on the building.)

This is good firewood; our vendor has always provided dry wood at a reasonable price. A bundle of wood will last well over an hour, two hours if you keep it at a reasonable size where you can get close and comfortable.

Quarry Pond campers can purchase firewood at the park entrance station or at the privately operated store at the west end of the campground. Bowman Bay campers can also come to these two locations or drive to Harold's Market, on Highway 20 at milepost 45.

Just please be sure to clean up after your fire. Did you know aluminum cans do not burn? You would be surprised how many people throw aluminum cans in their fire ring, expecting some nameless volunteer or staff person to come along and pick it up for them the next day. Is that how they were raised?

>
> ### Insider: Some More, Please
>
> *Everyone knows how to make a s'more, right? I'm always surprised when people ask me what a s'more is. So, just to make sure your children don't miss out, or so they don't surprise you with the request, here is the recipe:*
>
> *Take a lot of patience and adventure, stir in laughter, remove any shell of expectation of cleanliness or propriety or even safety, and then put the following ingredients into a sandwich of graham crackers: one fire-melted (or burned) marshmallow, one half of a Hershey's chocolate bar, some grit from the ashes of the fire and some sand from where you laid down your burning stick or your cracker or your napkin, which is now stickier than the bag of marshmallows, which tells you how sticky your hands are. And now your pants and your kids' shirts look like you've been camping. And if all those messy faces are laughing or at least smiling – c'mon, it's sugar, sugar, and flour, what's not to like? – you've had a great s'more dessert.*

Insider: Alternatives to Fires

Really? What beats having a smoky fire that makes everything smell bad, throws soot and ashes all around, adds to CO2 gas problems, gives your spouse breathing problems, pushes dense smoke in circles so everyone gets it equally, makes cleaning up difficult, throws sparks that could lead to a forest fire, and adds toxic poisons to your lungs?

During a typical weekend evening at Deception Pass, I doubt our air would pass any air quality tests with all the dense smoke hovering at nose level throughout the campground.

Try a propane fireplace. Okay, it still creates CO2 gases. And I suppose there are some toxic poisons, and maybe breathing problems. But there are no soot particles and ashes to deal with, and no sparks to cause a forest fire. And no smoke to deal with.

During fire bans, we still allow campers to use propane stoves. Just plug them in, turn them on, have your fire, then turn it off and you are done.

They look and feel just like a wood fire. In fact, the picture on the preceding page is of a family having a campfire during a burn ban. They used a propane stove. The kids enjoyed it. Dad was happy too.

Or, move beyond campfires. Enjoy the freedom of a carbon-friendly experience.

Clamming

Although the park has miles of beaches, very few of the beaches have clams available for harvest.

The best places: southeast of Hoypus Point, and the south side of Hope Island. Both require extra work to get there, either by a long walk for Hoypus or a short boat ride to Hope.

Kiket Island is owned by the Swinomish tribe, and off-limits to non-native clamming.

Crabbing

Even without a boat, you can catch a limit in a short time if you have the right equipment.

The best and easiest place to go is the Cornet Bay moorage dock. When crab season opens, this dock is full of crabbers with pots, dropping baited traps off the dock and bringing up a crop of crabs, some legal, some not. Please make sure you know the current rules. We don't want to give you a fine for making a bad choice.

Many people also enjoy crabbing at Bowman Bay, dropping pots off the pier.

Of course, if you have a boat, you have access to miles of good crabbing water, from Cornet Bay to West Beach to Bowman Bay to Hoypus and Hope Island's shores and more.

If you want to learn how to crab, talk to those who know how. Find a successful crabber and ask for advice.

Dogs

On a leash at ALL times (and that means a physical leash attached to both the dog and the owner), dogs can be great companions on the trail or at the beach.

The problem with dogs is that the owners sometimes don't understand that other people do not like to have large animals jumping on them, sniffing them, snarling at them, or threatening their children or pets. And no one wants to get in a car and find out they stepped in some dog's forgotten mess. Responsible dog ownership is easy -- and unfortunately not universally understood.

Please don't wait for a ranger to see you with your dog off a leash before you reach down and put the dog on its leash. Be responsible even when no one is looking. Parks are for relaxation, and it is not relaxing to come around a corner in a trail and see a dog ready to jump on you.

Nor is it fair to our wildlife to be chased by Fido.

Okay, having gotten that off my chest after forty years of dealing with frequently-encountered inconsiderate dog owners, there are some great places for a dog to join you in exploring Deception Pass.

Dogs will enjoy most of the park with you; there are a few places that they are not going to enjoy. These include Rosario Beach, with sharp barnacles and loose gravel; Hoypus Hill with lots of mud; and Kiket Island, which is off limits to all pets.

And beware of any lake closures due to cyanobacteria toxins. Dogs like to lick their fur after swimming. If toxins are in the water, this can be a deadly mistake. We post the lake if it has toxins. Heed the warning.

Fishing in Freshwater

Fly fishing at Pass Lake

Deception Pass has two large freshwater lakes for wetting a line, offering two distinct fishing experiences.

Cranberry Lake, open year round, has mostly rainbow trout, planted every year, with residual bass and other species to catch too. One recently caught bass tipped the scales at five pounds!

Regulations for the lake are the standard variety, no special rules, so just look at the fishing booklet and you will have your limits and equipment spelled out for you.

The lake has a boat launch just before you get to West Beach. There is a small parking lot here as well. No gasoline powered engines are allowed on the lake; use electric motors only, or human power.

People fish in many places around the lake, with success based more on experience than location. Popular areas include off the rocks along the Cranberry Road area, either east of the campground entrance or off the large rock between the campground and the boat launch. The dock at East Cranberry is also popular. The lake is mostly shallow, with one deep spot of over 25 feet near the campground entrance. (See the map in the map section.)

Pass Lake on the north side of the bridge is a totally different kind of experience, with fly-fishing only requirements, catch and release only, and no motors of any kind allowed on the lake. It mostly has brown and rainbow trout, of very good size. Because of the selective fishery, these trout have grown very wary of any angler's offerings. The fishing here can be tough but the rewards are well worth it. Trophy sized fish roam its waters and anglers that hook into them have earned their catch.

Most people fish near the boat launch at the west end, along the southern shore, or near the ranger house on the northeast corner.

Because it is human-powered craft only, be careful about which direction the wind is blowing to plan your outing.

The bottom of the lake is fairly uniform, about 20 to 25 feet throughout most of the lake, shallower near the shore. Highway noise is pervasive on the south side, minimal at the northeast corner.

Does Quarry Pond have fish? Check it out. Some say they have caught fish there. It isn't planted, and the quality of the lake is questionable for fish, but have a go.

Fishing in Saltwater

Saltwater fishing in and around Deception Pass -- this is a subject far too big to even begin to wade into the details here. So I will stay with generalities, and ask the reader to find someone who fishes here regularly to learn more.

So many species abound in the waters around here: ling cod, perch, halibut, smelt, shrimp, several species of salmon, and all the others native to the Salish Sea.

The launch at Cornet Bay gets most people out onto the water the easiest, with safe and abundant launching at nearly all tides. Bowman's ramp is fine for small boats at a medium to high tide, but difficult at low tides.

Fish on! Salmon fishing at North Beach, the bridge in the background. Region Manager Eric Watilo brings in a pink salmon.

You can catch pink and silver salmon off the beach at North Beach, West Beach, and Hoypus Point when they are running. I have even seen silvers caught off the dock at Cornet Bay. If you want to catch a salmon off the beach and don't mind crowds, this is the place.

When the pinks are running, every odd numbered year, it becomes combat fishing under the bridge at North Beach, with enough boats to walk halfway across the Pass, and enough people on shore to cause traffic jams in the parking lot and elbow to elbow casting. But everyone seems to get fish and be happy with it all.

Speaking of the docks, Cornet Bay has smelt fishing taking place much of the year right off the docks. When the fishing is good, the docks can be nearly full with people filling their buckets.

Fishing for piling perch and other small critters is popular here as well, and at Bowman Bay with less success.

People fishing for smelt, perch, and other smaller fish line the dock at Cornet Bay's east end.

The busiest fishing times are when each season opens: ling cod in May, shrimp and halibut around that time too, and salmon whenever it may open. Be prepared for crowded boat launches and full parking lots, especially on opening day and on any weekends that aren't windy.

Geocaching

This relatively new activity gets people out into our parks and exploring many of the trails and vista points. Some caches even provide history or environmental lessons. All geocaches in State parks need prior approval to be installed, and can only be located in areas that are not protected natural or historical grounds.

Deception Pass has a handful scattered around the park and its islands, some being virtual caches and some physical.

Visit geocaching.com for all the locations of approved geocaches in the park and to learn about this popular activity.

Group camping

From about 1990 to 2011, Deception Pass had three group camps, all just off the road leading to North Beach. The first of these three camps held 64 campers, the other two each held 32. They had Adirondack cabins, picnic shelters, and pit toilets, so they were primitive but useful for groups like Boy Scouts and church retreats wanting a remote camping experience.

Alas, they were built in old-growth forests. Old trees around here have big branches that fall down and hit things, and people. They also get diseases, being old, and then the whole tree can come down without any warning. All three camps were closed in 2011 for the safety of our visitors because of the danger of falling branches and failing trees.

We established a temporary group camp at the east end of Cranberry Lake, near the main park entrance. This area has a large lawn area for tents and gatherings, a large fire-pit in a natural swale near the lake, and a pleasant setting, other than being near the noise of the highway and the bustle of the park entrance.

It holds up to 50 campers, and has access to flush toilets, a large parking area, and the dock at the lake. The large picnic shelter here is also available for rental, or for free if it has not been reserved by others.

Hiking

Grab a quality topo map published by the park for a handy and helpful guide to all the park's trails. It costs a whopping $2, and is worth so much more than that.

Each area has memorable trails to experience. Some of the trails are described in the "Exploring" sections earlier in this book. There are a handful of generic trail maps near the end of this book to give an idea of the shapes of the hills and the routes of some of the trails.

The park topo map is perfect for seeing where the trails go and what the route will be like.

Trails on the south side of the bridge:

- West Beach Dunes Trail: *1.2 miles round trip. No elevation gain. Paved.* 18 interpretive signs in a dune, forest, and wetland environment. Crowds: minimal

- Cranberry Rock Trail: *0.1 mile one way. Not on the map. Minimal elevation change.* Goes out onto the rock south of the Cranberry boat launch to a popular fishing location or scenic view of the lake. Crowds: busy when fish are biting, otherwise quiet.

- Blind Curve Bypass Trail: *0.1 mile one way. Elevation change: 20 feet up then down.* Cuts off the corner on the Cranberry Lake Road just before you get to the boat launch so you don't have to walk in the curve area where there is no shoulder and no visibility for vehicles to see you.

- Cranberry Road trail: *1 mile one way. Elevation change: 150 feet at the east end, otherwise minimal.* Connects the maintenance shop area with the West Beach area without having to walk on the road or through the campground. Crowds: can be busy when the campground is full.

- **Upland Interpretive Trail:** *0.25 miles loop. Elevation change: minimal.* Self-guided hike through typical forest environment of this area. Crowds: never

- **East Cranberry Trail:** *0.2 miles. Elevation change: minimal.* A side route that goes from the bottom of the Cranberry Road hill to the East Cranberry area, avoiding the hill to the maintenance shop. Beautiful views of marshes along Cranberry's eastern shore. Crowds: minimal to moderate.

- **Entrance area to Shops Connector Trail:** *0.2 miles. Elevation gain: 80 feet.* A bypass route for those heading toward the intersection near the maintenance shop area from the park entrance, or going the other direction. Nice woodland walk without having to deal with cars or the steep road. Crowds: minimal or none.

- **North Beach Trail:** *0.7 miles one way. Elevation change: minimal.* Route between amphitheater and North Beach parking lot. Crowds: some

- **Bridge to North Beach Trail:** *0.2 miles one way. Elevation change: 180 feet, from sea level to bridge (somewhat steep).* Popular route to get to the beach from the bridge. Crowds: moderate to heavy.

- **Discovery Trail:** *0.7 miles one way. Elevation change: 150 feet, up and then down.* Route: connects Cornet Bay Retreat Center with North Beach. Wide trail, moderate grades mostly, with the bonus of going through the underpass under Highway 20. Crowds: low to moderate at times.

- **Cornet Road to Goose Rock connector trail:** *0.3 miles. Elevation gain: 80 feet.* Connects Cornet Bay Road with the trails heading to Goose Rock, avoiding Quarry Pond campground and the Cornet Bay Retreat Center by going between them. Crowds: none.

- **Goose Rock Perimeter Trail:** *1.9 miles round trip. Elevation change: 180 feet, mostly near the bridge and on the south side of Goose Rock.* Great views from the side of Goose Rock, traversing the open southern area and the heavily forested north side. Crowds: moderate

- **Northwest Goose Rock Summit Trail:** *0.7 miles. Elevation gain: 250 feet.* Climb from the bridge to the top of Goose Rock in the most direct ascent route, going through thickly wooded forests. Well beaten path. Crowds: moderate.

- **South Goose Rock Trail:** *0.4 miles from the base of Goose Rock near the Retreat Center to the top. Elevation gain: 400 feet, very quickly.* This route has great views nearly all the way, starting in a rhododendron forest then climbing steeply through open grasslands to reach the summit. Crowds: minimal to moderate.

- **Lower Forest Trail:** *0.4 miles. Elevation gain: 150 feet.* Parallels the Discovery Trail, going through some rhododendron forests.

- **Office Connector Trail:** *0.3 miles. Elevation gain: 60 feet up and down.* Connects the park office on Highway 20 with the intersections of the Discovery Trail and Goose Rock trails. Crowds: none to minimal.

- **Hoypus Point Trail:** *1.0 miles. Elevation gain: minimal.* Follows the old ferry road out to Hoypus Point, paralleling the beach a few yards away. Paved for 0.75 miles, then a well hardened trail beyond that to the point. Great views at the end, peek-a-boo views of the bridge and water all the way. Ideal for an easy pedal with bicycles. Crowds: minimal to moderate.

- **CCC Crossing Trail:** *0.4 miles. Elevation gain: minimal.* Parallels the Hoypus Point trail but in the woods higher up. Used historically by the CCC. Crowds: minimal.

- **East Hoypus Trail:** *1.9 miles. Elevation gain: 100 feet.* Traverses the east side of the Hoypus Point natural forest through classic old growth. A spur trail leads down toward the water but not to the water. Popular connector route to access Hoypus Hill trails. Crowds: minimal to moderate.

The always-busy Bridge to North Beach trail. Easy going down, a little bit of work going back up.

- West Hoypus Trail: *0.6 miles. Elevation gain: 250 feet.* Connects the Hoypus Point trail with the Hoypus Hill trails. Crowds: minimal to moderate.

Hoypus Hill Trails:

Numerous trails traverse the Hoypus Hill area of Deception Pass State Park. Some of these are described in detail below. Not discussed: Little Alder, Forest Grove, North Fork Trail, Shady Way, Fern Gully, Hemlock Hideaway, Julie, Slug Slough, Short Trail (named for the neighbor, not the distance), and Big Marsh.

All have minimal to moderate crowds, and some issues with mud and nettles; the trails interconnect throughout the area. All are open to horses and bikes, but you don't see many bikes up here.

The Hoypus Logging Road trail is wide for multiple use.

- Fireside Trail: *0.9 miles. Elevation gain: moderate except at the east end, where it climbs over 180 feet then descends 100 feet, or visa versa.* Crowds: moderate.

- Old Hoypus Logging Road Trail: *1.7 miles. Elevation gain: 100 feet up and 100 feet down early on the trail at the west end, otherwise fairly moderate.* The wide logging road has become a trail connecting Ducken Trailhead with the East Hoypus Point Trail and from there to Hoypus Point. A short side connector trail goes to the Park Acres housing development off this trail as well. Crowds: minimal to moderate.

Trails on the north side of the bridge:

- Pass Island Trails: short social trails go west, south, and east of the parking area on Pass Island. These non-maintained trails are not well built, nor are they entirely safe, going near cliffs and swiftly moving water. The meadow at the east end is a delight to enjoy away from the thousands of cars just a quarter mile away. Crowds: moderate to heavy, but as you go farther east, the crowds fade to minimal at most. Stay safe.

- Bridge to Pass Lake Trail: *0.6 miles. Elevation gain: 100 feet up and down.* Parallels Highway 20 from the bridge to Pass Lake, but leaves the noise of the highway in the background. Interesting route through a variety of forests and terrain. From Pass Lake, pick up the trail across Rosario Road from the Pass Lake parking area, behind the long wide sign that points left to the bridge and right to Bowman and Rosario. From this direction, you will follow Pass Creek for a hundred yards, then turn south away from the creek and toward the bridge, going down and up a couple times. Crowds: minimal.

- Lighthouse Point Trail: *1.5 miles round trip. Elevation change: 200 feet total.* Go south from Bowman Bay, up over a headland, back down to a great beach near Lottie Bay, then a short trip to a fantastic meadow and beach facing the Pass, then around the corner to Lighthouse Point and bold and steep rocky points and inlets. Continue around to come back toward Lottie Bay. Crowds: minimal to moderate.

- Lottie Point Loop: *1.5 miles. Elevation gain: 200 feet.* At Lottie Bay, go southeast instead of southwest to get to Lottie Point, directly west of

Insider: Private meadow

To get a meadow all to yourself, hidden from the trail but with great views of the bridge, take a left into the salal just before you get to the south meadow and pocket beach on Reservation Head (heading toward Lighthouse Point). You will see a place where the salal has a a seldom used trail going east up a small hill.

In fifty feet you break out of the salal, go over the top of the hill in open woods, then eastward down toward the entrance to Lottie Bay. The bridges open up right in front of you in your small grassy meadow; the waters of the Pass a little to your right.

the Canoe Pass span of the bridge. This trail is more of a scramble than Lighthouse Point. Crowds: minimal to occasionally moderate.

- Bowman Bay to Rosario Trail: *0.5 miles one way. Elevation gain: 100 feet.* Follows the south facing slope of the north shore of Bowman Bay to Rosario. Start behind the CCC shelter near the beach at

Approaching Rosario from the Bowman trail.

Bowman Bay, go behind several campsites, and then pick up the trail heading west, steeply at first, then slowly descending to Rosario. Great views the entire route in a dry madrone - Douglas fir forest. Crowds: moderate to heavy.

- **Rosario Head Trail:** *0.4 miles round trip from the parking lot at Rosario. Elevation gain: 80 feet.* Cross the tombolo past the Maiden and go south to a grassy meadow overlooking Bowman Bay, then up to the top of Rosario Head with simply awesome views. Return via a central trail back to the Maiden or go to the north side of the head and pick your way carefully down a steep and rocky route to get back down. Crowds: moderate to heavy.

- **Pass Lake Loop Trail:** *2.2 miles roundtrip. Elevation gain: 400 feet.* Follows the northern shore of Pass Lake, then climbs up over an unnamed hill to descend down toward Rosario Road, then loops back to the Pass Lake parking lot. Crowds: minimal.

Insider: The Waterfall

There is only one waterfall in the park, and it's not on a trail. Follow the trail along Pass Creek heading toward the bridge. When the trail turns south toward the bridge, go straight about a hundred feet. You can hear the waterfall now, and you will see it on your right if you get close to the creek. It is only about 10 feet high in two drops, but when Pass Lake and the creek are full, it's a pleasant surprise that few will ever see. Dry in the summer, however.

Nearing the top of Rosario Head. West Beach on Whidbey Island stretches out in the distance.

- **Ginnett Trail:** *1 mile one way. Elevation change: 450 feet each way.* From the Pass Lake Loop Trail, follow the alternate route northward over a ridge, down into Heilman Valley, then up steeply to a ridge on Ginnett Hill. At the overlook at the end of this trail, enjoy dramatic views of Rodger Hill to the east, Pass Lake beyond Heilman Valley in front of you, and the unnamed hill to the west. Crowds: minimal.

- **Big Cedar Trail:** *0.4 one way. Elevation change: 300 feet.* From the bottom of Heilman Valley, take the side trail west to see the humongous Western redcedar tree. Wrap your arms around it, if you bring enough people! Continue on to the Pass Lake Loop Trail. A great idea is to combine this route with the others to make a large loop with little retracing of your steps except for climbing the ridge to Ginnett and back again. Crowds: minimal.

Sword ferns come cascading down a hillside along the Ginnett Trail near the intersection with the Big Cedar Trail.

- Tursi Trail: *1.0 mile to the park boundary, another quarter mile to Donnell Road. Note: there is NO parking at Ginnett or at the south end of Donnell. Elevation change: 200 feet up and down on park property, another 250 feet if you continue to Donnell.* Starts at the Ginnett overlook and contours north. An adventure of a hike. Wander past a quarry, along meadows, through clefts in rock, past a historical mining cabin and a mine, and through a variety of forests and glens. Crowds: None to minimal.

Trails on Kiket Island.

- Kiket Island Trail: *1 mile one way. Elevation change: 150 down then up then down again.* The main cross-island route from the parking lot on Snee-Oosh to Flagstaff Point. You have to see it to know it and appreciate it. Look for the large yew halfway across the island. Enjoy the grasslands at the west end, and the views of Deception Pass. Enjoy the abundant wildlife and quiet forests. The tombolo near Flagstaff Point just got buried in logs, but you can walk the beach instead. Crowds: minimal by design.
- North Kiket Trail: *0.7 miles one way. Elevation change: 150 feet.* Parallels the Kiket Trail as an alternative route out or back. I like taking it going out, as the steep portion is downhill this way. Enjoy old growth woods and views of Deception Pass framed by trees. Crowds: none to minimal.
- South Kiket Trail: *0.5 miles one way. Elevation change: 120 feet.* The easier route to return to the parking lot. Traverses through a maple - fir forest with some views to the south. A little problem with mud in the wet season.

Trails on other nearby islands.

- Skagit Island Perimeter Trail: *0.5 miles round trip. Elevation change: minimal.* A rough trail along the edge of the island, not always clear as to the route on the southwest side, but not hard to figure out where you are going either. Crowds: none
- Hope Island Trail: *0.3 miles one way. Elevation change: 120 feet up then back down.* Starts in dense forest, then the woods turn drier, then open and sunny with meadows of flowers on the south side of the island. There is no safe route from the meadows down to the beach. Crowds: none.

Dugualla State Park trails:

- North Trail: *1 mile from triangle near gate to Big Tree. Elevation change: Drops about 150 feet going south.* Follows the north side of the park on a road for half a mile, then a single track trail through open forest, down a ravine, and on to the Big Tree. Crowds: none to minimal.
- Beach Trail: *1.5 miles from the gate to the beach. Elevation gain: Loses about 300 feet.* The main trail in the park, actually a former dirt road for the first mile, running from the gate, between the two wetlands, then down to the Big Tree, then down further to the beach, coming out in the middle of the park-owned beach. The return trip is steep to get back to the marsh areas, then gently rolling.
- South Trail: *1.5 miles from where it leaves the Beach Trail to the Big Tree. Elevation loss: gains fifty feet a short ways in, then loses 150 feet to get to the Big Tree.* Goes around the south wetland, through an alder forest, then drops down through old growth to get to the Big Tree. Dirt road path for the first mile, then single track trail the rest of the way.
- South Loop: *0.5 miles one way. Elevation gain/loss: about 80 feet.* An alternative route from the South Trail to loop around on the dirt road instead of dropping down to the Big Tree, coming back out on the South Trail.
- Slingshot Trail: *0.3 miles one way. Elevation gain: about 60 feet down and up.* Goes around the east side of the wetlands, connecting the Beach Trail with the South Trail as a cutoff.

- Big Tree Trail, or Marsh Trail: *0.5 miles one way. Elevation loss or gain: 100 feet.* A misnamed trail as it does not lead to the Big Tree. It starts at the southwest corner of the north marsh, then parallels the Beach Trail to eventually join it a quarter mile from the Big Tree.

Horse Riding

Deception Pass has some limited but enjoyable horse trails in the park.

Hoypus Hill is perhaps the most commonly used area for horses. The Ducken Trailhead at the east end of Ducken Road provides ample room for horse trailers to maneuver and park, and then access to several miles of forested trails. The trails vary in quality, with mud being a problem in much of the Hoypus Hill area. Hoypus Point trails are off-limits to horses.

Dugualla is the other good location for horse riding in the park, but parking at the trailhead there is a challenge. The turnaround is not really one at all if you have a large trailer; it is just the end of a two-lane county road.

Jogging

If you want to get a few miles in, there are a few ideal routes to follow. Here are some of my favorites.

Lighthouse Point: start at Bowman, run up the headland, down to Lottie Beach, onto Lighthouse Point, running the loop and back to Bowman. For another mile of distance, now follow Bowman Bay north to the Rosario Trail, run to the top of Rosario Head and then back to Bowman again.

Pass Lake: starting at Pass Lake, run to Ginnett and back for an up and down and up, then down and up and down workout of several miles. Do the Pass Lake Loop as an alternative.

Goose Rock: it may not be very far, but it's a killer on the legs. Go from the south end up to the top, then down the north trail, then run the perimeter trail back to the south end again for a couple miles of intensity. Start at the park office for a handy access point.

Hoypus Point: Easy-peasy along the road but no distractions and great scenery. Put in as many miles as you wish, or go up on the trails with some tough stretches thrown in to get you winded or muddy or both.

Cornet Bay Retreat Center to Hoypus Point and back, mostly level and all paved but with little traffic, nets four miles.

Put them all together and you can come up with a half marathon without leaving the park.

Kayak Rentals

Anacortes Kayak Tours offers guided kayak tours out of Bowman Bay during the busy months of the summer season, and rentals for self-guided trips.

This professional business does a great job orienting visitors to the world of kayaking, and then paddling out of Bowman Bay and beyond Rosario to special areas near Sares Head. The tours take about a total of an hour and a half. Call for reservations at 800-992-1801.

They also rent kayaks and paddleboards at Bowman Bay for those wishing to take off on their own for outings around Bowman Bay.

An Anacortes Kayak Tours guide orients new kayak users to the techniques of safe travel in a sea kayak. They launch from Bowman Bay and head north to Rosario and Sares Head for an hour and a half total tour.

There are no kayak rentals at the park for getting to Ben Ure Island if you are renting that cabin, so arrange with the Anacortes Kayak Tours or any other rental company.

Kite Flying

The wind blows here a lot, so we see many, many kites at Bowman Bay and West Beach. West Beach is much better than Bowman because it has exposure to steady winds from all directions, and nothing to block a wind coming from Japan or Alaska.

Bowman is more sheltered from steady winds, and a little erratic in direction, but the broad field is still tempting.

Metal Detecting

Because the park is so rich in cultural and historical resources, most of the acreage is off-limits to metal-detecting.

Two hundred acres remain, however, for exploring for metal treasures at the surface. These are the West Beach area south of West Point, the Cranberry Campground campsites, the Quarry Pond campground, the Bowman Bay campground, and the Bowman Bay boat launch parking and day use area immediately south of that.

State Parks has reasonable limitations on this activity. Limit digging implements to ice picks, screwdrivers and probes not to exceed two inches in width and sand scoops not to exceed six inches in width and eight inches in length to be used only on sand surfaces. Any holes dug shall be limited to six inches maximum depth and shall be immediately refilled and the surface restored to its earlier condition.

Paddling near Lighthouse Point, with the light bulb structure visible in the upper left area of the picture.

Below, the cave near Lighthouse Point.

Model sailboat racing

A group of dedicated sailors gather twice a week, year round, to sail one meter boats in the park.

This generous and committed bunch of enthusiasts have several locations that they have used, but now focus on two or three areas at the most: Cranberry Lake just south of the swim beach, the east end of Cranberry Lake, and the pier at Bowman Bay. Bowman Bay is becoming their venue of choice.

Competitions with other sailors from around the West Coast are held on occasion with much fanfare, rivalry, and fun.

Visit www.dpmyc.org for more information.

Paddle Sports

Deception Pass is a mecca for paddle sports, especially sea kayakers, with miles of shoreline to explore, and water ranging from calm lakes and mostly calm bays to the fastest saltwater rapids in the state.

Some paddlers seek out the thrills of surfing in the whirlpools, standing waves, and turbulent eddies that the strongest tides and wind waves can create.

For quiet family paddles, launch at the west end of Cranberry Lake and explore its marsh lands to the south. Or try Pass Lake, and head away from the highway noise to a rocky bald near the northeast corner of the lake. Or stay in Bowman Bay, if the wind isn't blowing, for a saltwater experience paddling around the pier to a sandy beach or over rocky canyons under the water.

Intermediate paddlers can explore further from Bowman and head to Rosario and Northwest Island, or if it is slack tide, explore the many fingers of Lighthouse Point. One of them has a cave that you can almost paddle into, depending on the tide. Just be aware that you only have about an hour of slack before the tide creates more challenging conditions. Another option is to head out to Deception Island so long as you follow all the safety rules and understand that hazardous weather or tidal conditions can make this dangerous for the untrained or under-equipped.

> **Washington State Parks --**
> **Tips to safe boating adventures:**
> - Pick an activity level that matches your ability and be sure your skill level is suitable for the water and weather conditions before getting underway.
> - Always wear a properly fitted, U.S. Coast Guard-approved life jacket. Washington state requires all children 12 years of age and younger to wear a personal flotation device when boating.
> - Have a signaling device. Carry a whistle and a bright flashlight or flares.
> - Carry a VHF radio and/or cell phone (with charged batteries) in a waterproof bag.
> - Bring essential safety and rescue gear including navigation tools, and more than adequate food, water, and extra protective clothing.
> - Dress appropriately for the weather and water conditions - including water temperature. How long can you function in 50 degree water? Not long without a wet or dry suit.
> - Be visible – wear bright colors so others can see you.
> - Going in the water is always a possibility. Be prepared for unexpected emersion.
> - Learn how to self-rescue. Practice it in a safe place where others are around to assist you if needed.
> - Never use alcohol or drugs when paddling. They dull important survival reflexes and impair decision-making skills.
> - Children should never boat without the close supervision of an adult.
> - Always paddle in groups of two or more.
> - File a float plan with family and friends so they know where you're going and when to expect you back.
> - Enjoy boating the right way, with a training course to develop skills and safe operation habits. Paddle sports instruction is offered by local clubs, outfitters and many park and recreation departments.
>
> One great way to get started in learning safe paddling is to take the State Parks free Paddle Sports Safety Course. To get started, visit http://www.boaterexam.com/paddling/

There are many other intermediate options. Head to Cornet Bay and paddle over to Kiket Island and Skagit Island, or if you have time, down to Hope. At Kiket you can land on the south shore just east of Flagstaff. On Skagit, land at the northeast corner, but be careful of how the tide is moving to make sure you don't lose your boat. Hope has a beautiful beach on its south shoreline, perfect for an afternoon picnic after a paddle. These are lengthy paddles, and can be timed to go out with the rising tide and come back on an ebb tide.

A paddleboarder gets going on Pass Lake for an early morning exploration.

Stand Up Paddleboards, or SUPs, have become popular around here. We see them in all the areas of the park described above. Bowman Bay has kayak and SUP rentals.

My favorite kayak experience took place at midnight on a slack tide under a full moon in July. I paddled out of Bowman, around Lighthouse, through Canoe Pass under the bridge without moonlight, then around Pass Island and back out the main pass being followed by a moon shadow. There wasn't a breath of wind on this warm night, but every so often I would hear the breath of a seal as it checked out who this crazy person was sharing the night with them. They would look at me for a minute, then drop beneath the flat water out of sight. The world I knew so well was transformed into a magical alternative universe of beauty and glory. I paddled around in awe.

Please hear the message that these waters can be fatal if paddlers are ill-equipped or unprepared. Follow all of the safety precautions recommended by standard paddle sport experts. We have picked many people out of the water who failed to recognize their limitations and the power of this water. Since the year 2000, one third of all boating fatalities in this state involved paddle craft.

Picnicking

With such a variety of places to choose for a picnic, the hardest part of the meal may be deciding where to go. There are over 100 picnic tables in the park, and an infinite variety of places alongside trails, on beaches, on hilltops, in deep woods, or just sitting in a car with a fantastic view.

A simple picnic at a table at Rosario, a spectacular setting to make any gathering memorable. Picnic sites are scattered throughout the park.

Get here early for picnic tables at West Beach -- these can fill up by noon on busy days. The tables are between the parking lot and the beach, or actually the tables are on the beach, but also right next to the parking lot, making for an easy hike to a picnic table, and offering a great view and plenty to do. South of West Beach you can find more tables along the beach, but since you have to walk a short distance they may be available even on a busy day. Almost every table has a brazier nearby.

The swim beach also has dozens of tables, which also fill up quickly if it is swimming weather.

North Beach has several along the beach, but cars are hidden in the forest a hundred yards away, so the kind of crowd here is different.

Cornet Bay has very few picnic tables. They are not usually full unless it's the opening day of fishing or crabbing season.

Bowman has a couple dozen tables as well. This quiet side of the park is still busy for picnicking, so again get there early if you want to guarantee having a table.

Rosario has a small number of tables. You've heard this message before: it fills up quickly on nice days, so get here early to guarantee getting a table.

And Pass Lake has only one table. Being close to the highway noise, it is more often used by fishing folks for lake outing preparations.

Of course, you can also pack a picnic to just about any place in the park and make it your own special place.

Picnic Shelters

Popular for weddings, birthdays, or other social gatherings in our unpredictable weather, the ten picnic or kitchen shelters at the park get used year round.

If you need a shelter for your event, make sure you reserve it ahead of time. Look for 'day use facilities', then 'picnic shelters' on the web reservation page. They all have advantages and maybe some disadvantages as well.

East Cranberry (S1): near the park entrance, but with an acre of parking, a couple acres of grass, and a scenic setting next to Cranberry Lake, with a dock out over the lake. The shelter has a fireplace, wood cookstoves, lights and power. Large barbecues are outside. One plus for many is that you can have amplified music here for your event -- this is the only shelter where we allow amplified music.

North Beach (S2): right on the beach, but not very large. It's a great place to set up food, and then have people go through a line and sit elsewhere at tables or on the abundant beach logs. Parking can be challenging, especially when the fish are running in August or September in odd-numbered years.

Above: Sitting right on the beach, the North Beach shelter has amazing views of the bridge, Reservation Head, and the open water of the Pass. It is a crowded thoroughfare during late summer in odd-numbered years or whenever the sun shines.

Below: The shelter at Little North Beach.

Little North Beach (S3): not on the beach, although close to it, and small and shaded.

It is a shelter, and sometimes that's all you need, but its location and small size reduce its popularity.

The Bowman Beachside shelter is very popular for gatherings, with its large size, grand lawn outside, and unbeatable view.

Bowman Bay Beach-side (S4): very close to the waters of Bowman Bay, and very attractive, this shelter hosts many weddings and events for a good reason. It has three large wood-heat cookstoves, lights, and power. It holds half a dozen tables, and has a barbecue nearby. The restroom is close, but getting between here and the restroom or the parking lot is a challenge, as the ground is all grass, sloped, and somewhat uneven. It's close to the Bowman campground as well, which may be a blessing or a curse. Parking is limited here, so plan accordingly.

Bowman Bay ADA (S5): ADA means Americans with Disabilities Act, and is shorthand for easier accessibility. Not far from the parking lot, there is a graveled path leading down to this shelter. This one has a nice fireplace, three wood stoves, power, and nice lights. A couple

Classic CCC charm, restored beauty, and ADA access make the upper Bowman shelter very popular as well.

barbecues outside add to the options for cooking. It holds half a dozen tables. We renovated this shelter a few years ago to look like it did when it was built, making it a very attractive place for an event. It is a short stroll to the beach from here.

Rosario (S7): Another very popular shelter for weddings, not only for the setting of the shelter but also for the nearby Rosario Head setting. Many brides choose to use the shelter for the reception food and the Head or the nearby tombolo for the ceremony. This shelter has wood cookstoves and power. Barbecues and additional tables are just outside, as is a large lawn area. The beach is a short stroll away. Parking here is limited, so if you have a large group plan on getting here early, or carpooling, or having guests park outside the gate on the shoulder of the county road. Make sure they are not on the pavement if they do.

Cornet Bay (S12): Only room for two tables, but this shelter has gained quite a following, being right next to the action at Cornet Bay, on the beach, next to the dock, the parking lot, and the restroom, and not far from the boat launch. It's a simple shelter but useful in any inclement weather.

West Beach (S22): The nicest shelter on the inside, and a fantastic location between the swimming beach and the saltwater. It holds up to about ten or twelve tables. There are picture windows on three sides of the shelter. The pine paneling inside is just splendid in the evening with the lights turned low. The

The only fully enclosed shelter in the park other than those in the Cornet Bay Retreat Center, the West Beach shelter has beautiful golden pine woodwork and large windows that take advantage of vistas in three directions.

northern wall has a large screen for presentations. Some drawbacks include no parking nearby; and having to fight for parking spots at West Beach on a busy day; having hundreds of swimmers right outside the east doors; and no water in the shelter, although the restrooms are just around the corner. Two large ceiling mounted heaters warm up the room pretty well in the cooler months.

There are other small shelters scattered around the park, with room for only one table each. These can be found at East Cranberry, North Beach, and Bowman Bay.

Scuba Diving

Diving Deception Pass is dangerous. It should only be attempted by the most competent and prepared divers. Dives have to be timed carefully to take advantage of when tides are right for a drift dive from the cove, under the bridge, and back to the cove as the tide changes.

Black and white does not do justice to the rainbow explosion that fills the underwater world throughout Deception Pass. Photo courtesy of Jan Kocian, one of hundreds he has kindly shared.

However, because of this large tidal exchange, Deception Pass hosts some of the most spectacular colors and life in the Pacific Northwest. The walls and bottom are covered in a wild palette of colorful algae, invertebrates, and fish species, more than you will find anywhere else packed into such a special package.

The other popular diving location is Rosario. The bay itself is mostly sandy under the water, but the rocks around Rosario Head to the south and Sares Head to the north are fantastic. Some people motor out to Northwest Island, also offering great diving around this rocky land.

Please be careful.

Swimming

In summer, the fresh water is cool to almost warm, but, the salt water is cold. Go for it if you wish.

Cranberry Lake warms up into the lower seventies by late summer, and becomes a rainbow of swimming suits on people of all ages at the West Beach swimming area. This beach is one of the few available to the community, one of the few swimming holes in all of Whidbey or Fidalgo Islands, so it is popular.

There are buoys delineating an inner swim area and a deeper swim area. The beach is sandy, with some minor growth that gets thicker the deeper the water. Outside the buoys you will compete with row boats, canoes, kayaks, and an electric motor boat or two, but not many. Nearby are dozens of picnic tables, an outdoor shower to rinse off, the boat rental area, restrooms, and a food concession. It's all a hundred yards from the parking lot, connected by a paved trail.

A stone's throw away, and you don't have to throw the stone very hard, you can splash in the saltwater of Rosario Strait. The beach is cobbly, with more sand in the summer than the winter. Driftwood lines the beach, separating the cars from the beach. The water looks tempting, but not many people can swim in it for very long. Many go wading. Watch the tides, as the current can start moving by the beach fairly quickly, especially near the north end.

At the east end of Cranberry Lake, a dock tees out into the water. It usually has someone, or several people, trout fishing. If you wish to swim here, you can. In fact, this used to be the place to go swimming, sixty years ago or more. Many locals remember taking swimming lessons at this dock. But when West Beach was developed, the interest in East Cranberry waned, and now mostly fishing people use it.

If you do go swimming at East Cranberry, make sure you warn those who are fishing, and promise to stay on the opposite side of the dock. Unfortunately, the lake bottom here has a dense growth of vegetation. Someday, I hope to restore this beach to its former glory. It will take an investment of time and money.

Another busy day at the swim beach at the west end of Cranberry Lake.

Pass Lake occasionally has swimmers, usually long-distance swimmers looking for a mile-long swim or more, but it is mostly the haven of fly fishing aficionados.

Lottie Bay, Rosario, and Bowman also get a handful of people splashing around near shore, usually kids, and not for long. This water is cold!

Tidepools

Rosario used to be the best tidepools around. After they were decimated by cruel, thoughtless, and senseless teachers and students a couple decades ago, the tidepools are only now beginning to recover with baby steps.

The Rosario tidepools are coming back, though, little by little. Small sea cucumbers look like small orange slices among the gray rocks. Little seastars attempt life where there used to be an abundance of various species. Urchins hide in seldom seen crevices. We would love to have the pools full of vibrant vitality in the near future. Help us preserve and protect this special resource.

There are other rocks around the park that hold intertidal life as well, though without the numerous tidepool microenvironments that Rosario enjoys, where you can sit on your haunches and marvel at the life going on in a world of tide water just a few inches deep.

If Sammye or one of our other Beach Naturalists is there when the tide is low (and if the tide is low, there is a good chance that one of these dedicated volunteers will be there!) then don't hesitate to invite them to walk with you and pause at every new wonder you can encounter. They know where each animal may be found, as they get to know the critters as if they are old friends.

Because they are.

Former park interpreter Adam Lorio helps a wee visitor gain appreciation for the life in the tidepools.

Tidepool Etiquette:

- *Stay on the designated trail. Follow the rope!*
- *Walk with care. Seaweed is slippery, and just about every step you take is on some plant or animal.*
- *Leave all plants and animals where you find them. This is their home.*
- *The slower you go, the more you will see. The closer you look, the more you will find.*
- *Please do not lift rocks to look at what is underneath, as any animals under the rock may be crushed when you return it.*
- *Wet one finger before touching any animal, so you don't get your body oils on them. Use only one finger at most.*
- *Avoid handling soft-bodied animals, as they are under stress already by being out of the water.*
- *Leave attached animals attached. Do not pry barnacles, limpets, or other such critters from their homes as this injures them and can kill them.*

Weddings

Congratulations, you're getting married! And you are thinking that Deception Pass State Park is a memorable place for a wedding, yes?

Yes it is. Dozens of weddings take place here every year, sometimes several on the same weekend.

Call the park and talk to a staff person about your plans, preferably well in advance of your special day. We will walk you through what you need to do, how to make it special, what to think about if you haven't already, and other details so that the wedding day itself is nothing but a charming and enchanting ceremony and celebration.

You will be asked to complete a Special Activity Permit, which will ask how many people are coming, what your needs may be, your music plans, food services, parking arrangements, chairs, tents, tables, caterers, sensitive areas to avoid, etc.

And if you don't already have a place in mind, we can offer suggestions as to where you might enjoy having your wedding in the park. Just make sure to reserve the location up to nine months in advance.

The park has several locations that are popular for weddings, each with various features that attract some couples and not others. The locations listed below are used every year, most of them several times a year.

1. **Top of Rosario Head** A five minute uphill hike makes it challenging for some guests, but the setting is unforgettable. The weather must be perfect, however. Rent the Rosario shelter for the reception area. If hiking to the top of the head is out for some of your guests, have your ceremony near the Maiden. Love stories relate well.

2. **Overlooking Bowman Bay** near the CCC Interpretive Center. Easy access for nearly everyone, and a shelter nearby if it rains. A great choice.

The groom and bride celebrate as they walk out at the conclusion of a wedding ceremony at the Cornet Bay Retreat Center's amphitheater area. The Center is gaining popularity as a wedding venue for more than 150 people. Photo courtesy of Claire Brideau.

3. **North Beach** Another memorable view, easy access for most, and a shelter nearby. More rustic or relaxed of an experience than the others, right on the beach.

4. **West Beach Shelter** An indoor location that is just gorgeous, with an outdoor option that is also beautiful. Seclusion is limited, however, as the swimming beach is right next door, which may lend interesting background conversation to the vows. This area is excellent for the off-season.

5. **Pass Island** If you have a very small wedding party and don't mind the sound of trucks rumbling by, this location certainly has easy access and a memorable setting.

A wedding party overlooking the beach at Bowman Bay.

6. **East Cranberry Lake** The only place in the main park, besides the next setting listed below, that allows amplified music. Plus the benefit of a large shelter, large grass lawn area overlooking a lake, the most parking of any in the park, and scenic photo ops on the dock. It has a lot going for it, especially at sunset.

7. **Cornet Bay Retreat Center** A place all to yourselves, with room for 150 indoors or 200 outdoors, though parking is limited to about 50 cars on site. The retreat center has a private, beautiful bowl-shaped setting in the shadow of Goose Rock, with Mount Baker watching over in the distance. There are cabins and dorms for overnight stays for those guests who have come a long way and don't mind a rustic setting. Facilities include a full-size kitchen, large eating area, dance floor, outdoor fireplace, and lawn space for the kids to play while the adults are being boring.

Winter Sports

Well, once upon a time, and maybe someday again. Or maybe it is all just a memory now.

Winters in the Deception Pass area are rarely what most people would consider a real winter. Snowfall is light, and rare. Freezing temperatures are seldom down into the teens, Fahrenheit. Rarely even down into the twenties, for that matter.

But most every winter used to have one or two good freezes, and one or two good snow storms, a few inches anyway.

My first year here, in 2003, we had a snowstorm that left Cranberry Hill just begging to have kids go sledding down the road. My son Ben and I enjoyed many runs down the hill, along with another ranger family. A couple of people went skiing along the lake shore. A couple of brave souls wandered out onto the ice of Cranberry Lake, getting about halfway across before deciding to turn around.

Our lakes would freeze up for a few days every winter, it seemed. And our water pipes would have to be protected because we aren't used it. We normally turn off the campground water in November when cold weather threatens, and turn it on again in February when the danger is mostly past.

But in recent years, things have changed. The lakes hardly freeze, and with only a thin coat of ice when they do. Snow – we haven't had a real snow storm for two or three years now.

Maybe we will this year.

This could all be a random glitch in weather, not at all related to climate change. Or it could be the new norm.

I do know that our winters are wetter now, and our summers warmer and drier. The winter of 2015-16 set a record for the amount of rain. In 2015 we had to institute

We don't have many opportunities for skiing, sledding, snowshoeing, ice skating, hockey, or any other cold-weather dependent activities.

When it does snow, traffic snarls to a stop. Watch out at the bridge, as the approach on the north side can turn into a skating rink for vehicles.

But if it DOES snow, try the Cranberry Lake hill for sledding. It's pretty good. And any of the roads make for great cross country skiing if there is enough on the ground. Roads not covered by trees have the most.

As for the lakes, well, make sure the ice is truly thick enough. Everywhere you go. Or don't go.

Best of all, enjoy the new perspective, the candy coating of white on tree tips, the bright red of madrone against the white snow and a blue sky, the muffled sounds of life under the blanket of renewal.

a fire ban in June, a ban which lasted the rest of the summer. We have rarely had to begin a fire ban even in July; it's usually August if at all. Again, that could be an anomaly, and next year could be our usual dance with rain and sun thrown in all year long. That's how 2016 has been.

Which brings us back to winter sports.

So there I am,

wet suit on, phone in my waterproof pocket for use as a GPS and for communications, camera in another bag. It is a dead calm September afternoon, an hour before sunset. I launch at Bowman Bay, and paddle out of the bay to go see Deception Island. There has been fog the past couple of days, and the fog is lingering around the Pass and the headlands, but I can see Deception Island in front of me, and it's not far. I paddle with clean simple strokes, heading for Deception Island.

And then it disappears.

The fog settles in a little more. I can see Bowman Bay behind me, though, and I know exactly where the island is, and it's not far, and it's big, and it's close. I paddle straight toward it. And I paddle. And now Bowman Bay's headlands disappear into gray wisps as well. But I'm close to the island. I will hit it any minute, then turn around and there is no way I can miss Bowman Bay from here.

So I paddle. And paddle. And paddle. And paddle. I've been paddling far too long; somehow I missed it. So I turn around, and head back. After quite a few minutes, which would make sense, I see land on my right. Good, I'm approaching Bowman Bay. Uh-oh, that's not Bowman Bay, that's Deception Island, and I am approaching its seaward side. That's upsetting. How far out to sea had I gone? Oh well, just keep paddling, same direction, and I will hit the big target of Bowman Bay, or one of the headlands on either side. I check my phone's GPS and it shows that I am on target for Bowman Bay. It also shows that its battery is low, very low. Why didn't I charge the thing before I left?

The tide is now beginning to ebb, pushing me a little north, so I aim a little south to compensate. And I paddle, and paddle, and paddle. I should be seeing it. Then I do see land.

No way. It is the seaward side of Deception Island again, and I am approaching it from the seaward side. Now I'm really confused. Seriously, how did I do a 180, or actually a 360?

And now it's getting dark. The sun has set. There is still light, but it's all gray light, very even, very bland, the water and sky just one dark gray monotone all round me. I get my phone out, and yes, its battery is nearly dead. Now I have a choice: check the GPS on the phone, getting one final position, or call my wife and ask for help. Tough decision.

I call.

"Hey", I say. "I don't know where I am, well, actually, I know where I am, but I can't find Bowman Bay from here." Heavy pause. "Can you get some help coming my way?"

For me to ask for help, she knows it's serious. Then my phone dies. I never hear what she says.

A seal pokes his head up and watches me. Then she slips away. I never see her again. Will I ever be seen again?

I look at the tide, and see it going to my left. That means Fidalgo Island is straight ahead. I do my best to keep in a straight line. I paddle and paddle and paddle. I see land! Not Deception Island again, please... Nope, I recognize it as Northwest Island, a good half mile or more north of where I thought I was, but not bad. Now I can just follow the coast line to Rosario, then around the corner into Bowman Bay!

It is almost black now. I pass the tidepools, then Rosario Head, and turn into Bowman Bay. I keep following the north shoreline, well inside the headlands of the bay, at least half way inside. I can't get lost now, so I turn a little away from the north shore to strike out straight for the boat launch. I paddle, and paddle, and paddle. And paddle. I am sweating big time. I've covered many miles this evening. And the water and sky are one black liquid curtain now.

I pass some rocks in the water. There shouldn't be any rocks here; there are no rocks close to the boat launch or pier.

"Oh, no," I say, "I did it again." These are the Coffin Rocks, the rocky area at the west entrance of Bowman Bay. I have turned around YET AGAIN in the pitch black this time, and I am heading out to sea. I turn around, again.

This time I see a dim light where I think the boat launch should be. I aim for it. And I paddle. And paddle. The light is getting stronger. I paddle harder. The light gets brighter. I paddle harder. I hear voices. It's my wife, and my son Ben, and Ranger Shook, who has the spotlight on his park truck aimed out at the Bay.

I pull into the launch area, and my wife and my son give me a hug, which they regret because I am drenched – dripping wet drenched – in sweat. And very relieved. And embarrassed. And safe. And thirsty. And grateful for the help.

Yes, North Whidbey Fire and Rescue had responded to a report of a missing kayaker out near Bowman Bay. They knew who it was, and that made me feel very embarrassed. I am supposed to be on their team helping find boaters who get in trouble, boaters who may not have planned ahead as well as they should have. The rescue team had been preparing to launch their boat to find me when Ranger Shook notified them I was back.

Sometimes we take resources like that for granted. Knowing there are people ready and trained and equipped and willing to help makes me deeply grateful. And reminds me to never take that help for granted, and to be prepared for whatever problem may arise when on the water so that I don't need their help.

Like charging my batteries first.

Happening

"I've found that luck is quite predictable. If you want more luck, take more chances. Be more active. Show up more often."

— Brian Tracy

First day hike

As part of a tradition started elsewhere in the nation, Deception Pass hosts an annual "First Day Hike" on January 1. Each year the ranger- or interpreter-led hike explores a different part of the park. The hikes are suitable for people of all ages. Recent years have brought crowds ranging from 60 to 180 folks, hiking together to get out on the first day and do something outside that is a little strenuous and a lot of fun. It's a great way to start the new year.

The Foundation provides coffee, cocoa, and goodies at the end of the trail. It all costs nothing but getting up after New Year's Eve and getting to the park in the middle of the morning ready to hike. It's fun!

Previous hikes:
- 2012: Lighthouse Point
- 2013: Rosario Head from Bowman Bay
- 2014: Cornet Bay Retreat Center to North Beach, then Goose Rock
- 2015: Pass Lake to the ranger's house then to Ginnett
- 2016: Cornet Bay to Hoypus Point
- 2017: Where will it go?

Bellingham Series Marathon

For the past couple of years Deception Pass has hosted one of the Bellingham Trail Running events, a marathon, half-marathon, and kids' race that are all run entirely within the boundaries of the park, using winding routes of trails and roadways to get the necessary distance.

Currently this is taking place in early April.

Both races are now starting and finishing at West Beach, providing ample parking early in the morning and a scenic start for the long distance runners.

Visit their website at:
http://www.bellinghamtrail.com/p/deception-pass-half.html

Above: Runners begin the full marathon at West Beach, heading out to run nearly all the trails in the park.

Left: Part of the large gathering of hikers in the 2016 First Day Hike heading out to Hoypus Point.

Whidbey Island Marathon

Since about 2002, Whidbey Island has hosted a spring marathon that starts at Deception Pass and wends down Whidbey toward Oak Harbor. The race has at times started at Cornet Bay, but most recently has been starting at Pass Lake, giving runners a chance to cross the bridge (closed to traffic for the start of the race) as a majestic first mile.

A half marathon now starts at Cornet Bay on the same day. Both races exit Highway 20 on Ducken Road, just south of the Cornet Bay park entrance area.

Be aware of the start of these races if you need to get across the bridge, because the highway is shut down for about a half hour. It has been on a Sunday every year, around the middle of April, until this year when they tried a Saturday start. Popular opinion was that a Sunday start is better for the runners and for reducing traffic congestion.

Earth Day Cleanup

Every Earth Day weekend, local Lions' Clubs have their members come to the park to engage in whatever the need of the year is. In past years they have repaired bridges, constructed tables, built fences, pulled weeds, planted campsites, picked up litter, painted buildings, cleaned parking lots, and much more.

They are always willing to get more people helping, and they take care of their volunteers with food, drinks, and encouragement.

This park is so grateful to the Lions' Clubs of this area for dedicating a weekend every April to fixing and improving the park with dozens of volunteers. Here they are building a fence at the group camp.

Hope Island Weed Pulling

For about ten years now we have been taking an annual trip out to Hope Island to cut scotch broom and other invasive species from its meadows.

The island is a special place, especially in spring when the wild flowers are in bloom. It is so gratifying to see folks helping remove the forest of scotch broom and see the meadows become flower gardens again.

The Deception Pass Tours concession has generously offered the use of their large passenger boat to get us out to the island and back again for the past few years.

We spend about two hours on the island working up a sweat, then head back exhausted but well rewarded.

It is becoming a Memorial Day tradition now.

No, they are not looking for someone's contact lens. They are pulling new growth of Scotch broom on Hope Island. Each year's group has found that the previous year's efforts made a huge difference. But fire changes everything.

Salish Sea Native American Cultural Celebration

Since 2006, Bowman Bay has hosted the Salish Sea Native American Cultural Celebration. The Samish and Swinomish tribes celebrate their maritime heritage and culture with canoe rides, song, dance, and storytelling.

Riding a traditional canoe is part of the Native American celebration.

Tri-Island MS bike ride

On the second weekend of September we see as many as 2000 bike riders cruise through the park as part of the Bike MS: Deception Pass Classic. Deception Pass is a major destination and gathering area.

This event raises nearly $2 million dollars for Multiple Sclerosis research.

Fix-it Days

Although technically not a park event, Fix -it Days supports the park's operational budget. Created by members of Transition Fidalgo, and the brain child of Eric Shen, people bring things that need fixing, such as a clock, a lamp, a mixer or whatever to Fix-It Days at the Farmer's Market in Anacortes.

Volunteers who know how to fix things then fix the item if they can, and return it to the owner, charging only for any parts that needed to be purchased, and giving new life to items that otherwise may have ended up in the landfill.

In return, the owner donates what they wish to the Fix-it Days volunteers, who give it to the Deception Pass Park Foundation for operational improvements at the park. This event has donated hundreds of dollars each year to the Foundation.

Park Founders Picnic

It isn't an event yet. I believe it will be soon. I hope it will. Before the bridge, the Inter-Island Picnic gathered community members from Fidalgo and Whidbey Islands to celebrate the summertime and to encourage the future creation of a Deception Pass State Park. They were successful, and then the picnics ended.

I think it's time to revive these picnics, celebrate our common heritage, and commemorate the coming 100th birthday of Deception Pass State Park in 2022.

The Deception Pass Park Foundation has this as a goal. Me too.

Annual Open House

Although the park manager is always just an email or a phone call or a visit away from anyone, it's helpful for many to have a chance to hear what is going on at the park in a formal presentation, to find out what is planned for the upcoming months and years, and to weigh in on the directions being taken.

Every fall, usually in November, we have held an open house to summarize the past year's stories and share what we see for the future. We try to alternate hosting the event on either side of the bridge each year. The Deception Pass Park Foundation joins in and makes the event festive and fun.

Deception Pass Dash

In 2006, Bill Walker came to me suggesting a kayak race through the Pass in the middle of December. I laughed. A kayak race in stormy December through the dangerous waters of the Pass?

He said "Yes, I'm serious. People will love this."

And he was right.

The six mile paddle begins in Bowman Bay just before low slack tide. Kayakers (and now paddle-boarders and outriggers and other craft) head out to Deception Island, through the Pass, around Strawberry Island inside the Pass, then back out through Canoe Pass, back around Deception Island, and back into Bowman Bay, about a six mile paddle in winter weather.

In the years that races have been held the weather has ranged from sunny and balmy to frightful, sometimes with snow, or sleet, or high winds, or pouring rain, or some combination of all of the above. One was canceled due to a forecast of dangerous winds. Oddly, the forecast was wrong, and conditions were not bad at race time.

The race attracts people from all over the Pacific Northwest, who compete in various categories for the glory of victory or just for the opportunity to see if they can succeed.

Kayakers, outriggers, and paddleboards head out of Bowman Bay at the start of one of the Deception Pass Dash races. The sooner they return from the course, the less current they have to paddle against.

Organizers do an exceptional job of emphasizing safety as well as making the day fun for everyone. Rescue boats are on the water everywhere; aid crews are standing by. Participants must meet basic standards of equipment and protection to be allowed into the race.

Rainshadow Runs

Who would have imagined that a 25k and 50k foot race would be popular? In December?

Yes, those are not typos, 25 kilometers and 50 kilometers. Nearly 16 and 32 miles.

Registrations for the Rainshadow Running races at Deception Pass fill up almost the same weekend that they open, with several hundred runners coming here to run the many diverse trails of the park in one day. And then there is another race the next day, but only half as long.

Their websites for the two races are at:

http://www.rainshadowrunning.com/deception-pass-50k.html and
http://www.rainshadowrunning.com/deception-pass-25k.html

Bowman Bay Holiday (or Cornet Bay?)

The inaugural celebration was held in late December, 2015 as an experiment to see if it would be popular.

It was! Hundreds of people came out to enjoy the festive lighting of the buildings, fires blazing in the shelters, coffee and cocoa, crafts for kids, Santa sitting by the fire, and various cabins or campsites with activities or lighted displays

Members of the Foundation light up several of the buildings with holiday lights, host crafts in one of the buildings, and Santa in another. Local businesses decorate nearby campsites, adding more fun activities and holiday cheer.

We hope this event becomes a staple tradition for the weekend before Christmas.

It may be held at the Cornet Bay Retreat Center in coming years to meet the interest and provide bigger gathering areas out of the weather. And there may be a nominal charge in the future to help raise support for the Foundation's efforts. It's worth it.

Santa (volunteer Paul Tunstall) listens to the Christmas wishes of a child, and then poses with her for a photo by the fireplace at the Bowman Bay shelter.

So there I am,

getting into our park boat tied up at Bowman Bay, the wind howling out of the west, and the bay filled with a hundred kayaks ready to race through the Pass and back. White caps are breaking in the bay; out near Deception Island, I see larger rollers. The kayakers are ready to go. I am hesitant, wondering if the storm will intensify as the racers round the corner and hit the ebb tide.

My job is to be a safety officer for the Deception Pass Dash race. Started just a year or two earlier, the race is set in the middle of December. I thought the organizer, Bill Walker, was joking when he first proposed the idea to me as a winter event for the park. In December? Paddling six miles, going through the Pass twice? Really?

Oh, it will be popular, he predicted.

He was right. But this year is the first to have weather that would test not only endurance but seaworthiness. And not just for the kayaks – I am a little concerned how the park boat will handle these seas, with the wind still growing. Small craft warnings, they say. I'm in a small craft, 19 feet long, deep V hull built for tough water, but how tough? I gained a lot of boating experience in my younger years on the Sound in small boats, and up the Inside Passage and across the Gulf of Alaska in fishing boats. This will test what I knew about small boat handling.

I have a spotter with me to help look for boaters in possible distress. We stay ahead of the lead boats out to Deception Island, and then we hang around the western tip of the island as the flotilla of human-powered crayons bob and weave their way around the island and head east toward the Pass. Two kayaks flip over as they try to negotiate the turn. Another safety boat helps them get righted again, and they keep on their way. I follow the stragglers as they struggle through the seas. Two more flip off Lighthouse Point and they say they are done. I put them on board and we take them and their craft back to Bowman Bay.

I go back into the Pass to catch up to the last place boaters again. The seas are still rising, but the sun is coming out. The boats are doing okay now as they head into the calmer water under the bridge and around Strawberry Island inside. But they still have to come back out the Pass, out to Deception Island again, and then back to Bowman.

Sand from the Skagit River flows through the Pass and settles out when it hits the slower water outside the Pass, near Deception Island, making a shallow shelf. When winds blow from the west and the ebb flows from under the bridge, the shallow water between Deception Island and Lighthouse Point becomes a seething cauldron of mixed-up waters, waves coming in all directions at once, joining together to create constantly moving mini-mountains, dancing unpredictably.

I follow kayaks as they travel along the south shore of Lighthouse Point, then strike out for the south side of Deception Island. A couple give up before they attempt that penultimate leg into the teeth of the wind. Most paddle on, rising with each wave, then disappearing out of sight in the trough before the next. My boat does the same, losing all sight of land in the trough, then rising to meet the next wave, allowing me to get my bearings again. I look at my hands on the steering wheel and notice that my knuckles are white. Time to relax my grip, I say to myself. My hands do not agree. I look at my spotter, who looks worried. No worries, I say. We're doing great. Really. Could be worse, I think to myself, and sure enough, the rollers come in bigger than they were before.

A deputy is on a jet ski in that topsy-turvy world. We are doing our best to keep the kayaks in sight and help any in trouble, while keeping our heads above water. Then I see his jet ski flip over in a rogue wave. Now I know the conditions are tough.

The sun is blazingly beautiful now, and I detect that the power of the wind is abating. We have turned the corner in the storm. The last of the kayaks are also turning the corner of the island, heading back to Bowman. We do too.

When we land our boat and join up with the race party, we see that the attitudes are mostly jovial and celebratory. A few did not finish, and they realize it was beyond their abilities. The finishers know that they have been tested, that they have succeeded, and that they loved the experience. They can't wait to do it again next year!

I realize that's how I feel too.

Learning

*"In the end, we conserve only what we love.
We will love only what we understand.
We will understand only what we are taught."*

- Baba Dioum, Senegalese poet

Evening programs

Whether it's an evening interpretive program or a concert event, the amphitheater fills up on Saturday evenings for the entertainment and education.

What a great way to end a summer evening, sitting near a fire at the amphitheater and learning about a park feature or creature or historical episode.

Park rangers, interpretive staff, or knowledgeable neighbors share about a multitude of subjects during our weekend evening programs, usually starting at 7 p.m.

Subjects cover a wide diversity: history of the park, marine mammals, first person accounts of the ferry boat captain Berte Olson, star watching, beavers, slugs, animals of the night, kayaking, and so much more.

Times and subjects are published a few days before the weekend so campers and neighbors can plan on attending if it is of interest. The subjects are also advertised in the park's monthly e-newsletter, the *Current*.

Arts in the Parks

For many years now the National Endowment for the Arts has sponsored a series of cultural music events at Deception Pass, called Arts in the Parks. The events bring in musical styles from around the world to give listeners a view into the eclectic variety of cultural musical expressions.

These concerts are held in July or August at the amphitheater. They are often very popular, so come early if you want a seat. They start at 7 p.m., taking the place of the regular Saturday evening programs.

Junior Ranger programs

We care about our younger visitors too! For many years we have offered Junior Ranger programs at the amphitheater for children.

These are hands-on activities, stories, and adventures that appeal to a wide variety of ages and interests. Parents join in as an interpreter leads a craft based on a natural history subject. Programs usually start in the late morning or early afternoon, and last about an hour.

New Junior Rangers are sworn in by former AmeriCorps interpreter Sam Wotipka after they fulfilled their tasks.

Nature Walks

By Montana Napier, AmeriCorps Interpreter

"Let's take our hearts for a walk in the woods and listen to the magic whispers of old trees." - Unknown

When guiding a nature walk, my senses are heightened for the benefit of others. I watch for changes in the landscape; quickly, my eyes scan the forest floor for signs of life and activity. I take note that on a fallen log, a baby Douglas fir tree grows. The seedling, for that's what it is called, has taken root an old, dead log. This nurse log protects the seedling from being trampled on or shaded out. It also holds water, like a sponge, for the seedling to drink. Nutrients, which were once locked up in the old, living tree for hundreds and hundreds of years, are freed by decomposers. And on the roots of the seedling, truffles aid the tree in acquiring these nutrients, in exchange for sugar.

I lead children and adults over to the nurse log and show them a picture of a sprouting seed. Briefly, I tell the story of a Douglas fir tree and its long life in the forest. After many many years and experiences, our tree dies from windstorms and disease, eventually falls, and is now the log before us.

"The once great Douglas fir becomes a nurse log itself, and from its belly a new seedling rises up through the darkness of the forest," and then I point out the baby tree, only three inches tall, shooting up out of bright, green moss.

"Wow!"

"Oh that's so cute!"

Smartphones and digital cameras appear from thin air or oversized pockets and are angled at the tiny tree. Lights flash and clicking sounds fire as people lean into each other, elbow to elbow, trying to document a sight often overlooked. I wonder if they realize seedlings are everywhere in the forest, in a constant state of competition, struggling to reach sunlight and grow tall. For our seedling to exist, thousands of seeds were dispersed from their cones, and then over half of those seeds were eaten by rodents. Hundreds took root in a quarter-inch of moss or dirt, though most never lived beyond that first year.

I found this tree after a quick scan of the forest floor; hiding within red huckleberry plants and thick moss I see three more. My goal of nature walks is to encourage visitors to simply experience what is around them: to look at a tree from the top down, and verbally note what they

AmeriCorps interpreter Montana Napier illustrates a point on a nature walk with a living example. Photo courtesy of Bob Jepperson.

observe; to see signs of decay and rebirth in plant communities; to note how they feel beneath the shade of the canopy; to listen for the sounds of life, and of the wind moving through the leaves. I believe it is important to give up "old" ways of seeing -- looking singularly at one thing-- and try to experience the forest as a whole.

Oftentimes, people imagine a forest to be a collection of same-sized, living trees, so that is what they allow themselves to see. However, trees are to forests as bones are to our bodies; bones provide structural support for the body, and protection, as well as store nutrients, but the other stuff that makes up our body matters, too. After all, aren't we more than just a collection of bones?

I believe that modern humans need to broaden their scope, and see systems and natural processes versus sole objects, in order to cherish and protect their environment. To smell the fragrance of decomposing needles - feel the cool Earth beneath our palms, and use those experiences to learn how life works on this planet, in real time. To break free of our "old" ways of seeing, we have to take unusual steps, and sometimes that abnormality might be in the form of a nature walk.

Guided Tidepool Walks

Former AmeriCorps interpreter Carly Rhodes shares with a classroom having a field trip to the Rosario tidepools. Photo by Vince Streano.

Thanks to our AmeriCorps interpreters and a special thanks to our ongoing Beach Naturalists, the park provides guided hikes through the tidepools and Rosario Beach.

School groups are required to register for these tours so that we know they are coming, can give them preparatory information, and can schedule enough guides to make their visit meaningful.

After school gets out, we continue to have Beach Naturalists greet visitors to the beach, and to encourage them to follow the "rope trail" to keep human impact just along the trail.

We also provide detailed printed material for those who wish to learn more, and this often generates many conversations about the wildlife found here.

Former interpreter Adam Lorio shares a natural history object story with a family focused on what he is sharing.

Gracie the Gray Whale

When a large but deceased gray whale washed up not far from here one year, we obtained the necessary permits to have the skull brought to the park for cleaning. After a year or so, it was clean enough to put on a display trailer so that we could share it with anyone interested in learning more about this remarkable species that shares our planet.

Nicknamed Gracie, the skull amazes just about anyone who sees its immense size. Our interpreters have used Gracie to educate hundreds of school children and for visitors at special events such as evening programs or community picnics.

Former AmeriCorps interpreter Sam Wotipka lets kids handle the baleen of a gray whale to teach them about its feeding habits.

Large exhibits such as this can become a circus side show if handled improperly or insensitively. I am proud to see the respect that our interpreters and in turn our visitors develop for Gracie in using its life and death to transform our lives as well.

Visitor Centers

Although this park lacks a typical visitor center, it does have a couple of places where visitors can learn about specific topics of interest. And it has three small gathering places where you can get basic information and purchase guides to the park along with other park essentials.

The busiest information station is at the bridge. Here Deception Pass Tours staff join with Deception Pass Park Foundation members to offer information to anyone who stops by and asks. They have maps of the park, brochures about common attractions and activities, and some other items of interest such as sweatshirts for a cold day or t-shirts for souvenirs. The booth also sells tickets for the Deception Pass boat tours. It is open every day in the summer, most days during the shoulder season, and closed during the off-season.

Another busy information point is our welcome station, the entrance to the Cranberry side of the park. Although campers come here for registering for their campsites, it's also a great place to get park information of any kind, buy firewood, a map, a coffee mug, a hat, a sweatshirt, or a book about the park. It is open every day from 9 to 5 or later during the busy season, and only from 9 to 11 a.m. during the winter months.

One other information center can be found at the entrance to the Cranberry Campground, at our campground store. It is only open with limited hours, usually 4 p.m. to 8 p.m. during the summer months. You can get a map, firewood, or other basics here.

Bowman Bay Civilian Conservation Corps Interpretive Center

The largest center in the park houses two wings of photographs, displays, and exhibits showcasing the story of the CCC throughout the state of Washington. It uses the old bathhouse at the north end of the Bowman Bay day use area, south of the Bowman campground and right next to the water.

Our newest venture is to create a park-focused exhibit area at this center to highlight the many intact CCC features in this park.

Rosario Field Classroom

The other park interpretive center is at the Field Classroom near Sharpe's Cove. This building houses a small display of natural history exhibits, showing various plant specimens and wildlife displays. It also has an activity table for kids to draw, read, or write for fun. Volunteers allow this center to be open on weekends.

Above: The Rosario Field Classroom opened in June of 2016 after being refurbished from its bathhouse days. It has displays about natural history subjects.

Below: A visitor touches the fur of one of several mammals found in the park to see if he can identify it by touch and appearance. This display is in the Rosario Field Classroom.

Above: the Bowman Bay CCC Interpretive Center tells the story of the CCC in Washington state. New displays will focus on their stories in Deception Pass.

Below, some of the exhibits in the CCC Center.

Both of these centers are possible only because of the generosity of the volunteer members of our Deception Pass Park Foundation and Beach Naturalists.

Interpretive Trails

Deception Pass has two interpretive trails, both near Cranberry Lake.

The Dunes Trail, the longest of our interpretive trails, is located south of the West Beach parking area. It highlights the fragile environment of the sand dunes,

A large interpretive display at the overlook for Cranberry Lake along the Dunes Trail. Watch carefully for the small trail leading to this viewpoint.

starting with the foredunes and ending with an overlook to the wetlands of Cranberry Lake. Find over a dozen illustrated signs which were created by a local high school class.

Near the end of the trail look closely for a small trail leading to your right, toward the lake, to find an overlook with detailed stories about the wetlands of Cranberry Lake.

The other interpretive trail in the park starts across the street from our maintenance shop area. The quarter mile trail wends through the dry upland forest environment. A brochure guides hikers to help understand what they are seeing at numbered posts along the trail.

The beginning of the Forest Interpretive Trail, located near the four way intersection near our maintenance shop area.

Interpretive Signs

You can get a good working knowledge of the park just by reading all of the interpretive signs scattered around the park.

- Aircraft of the Navy: a large display sign immediately south of the West Beach parking area to show what airplane may be flying over your head.

- Beaver sign: on the trail between the East Cranberry picnic area and the Cranberry Road to the north, talking about our busy beavers.

- The bulletin board at the entrance to East Cranberry Lake tells the timeline of the history of this area.

- Cross section of a tree: An eagle scout, Matt Nortier, took a small piece of a tree we had to cut down in the park and turned it into a beautiful display showing a cross-section of the rings of the tree, all 498 of them. He then labeled the rings with notable dates in history. Find it inside the park office, waiting for a visitor center for proper display. It may be in the Rosario Field Classroom soon.

- Cornet Bay Retreat Center CCC tour: four signs at the retreat center illustrate the creation of the Cornet Bay grounds by the CCC. More pictures can be found inside the recreation hall at the retreat center.

- Cornet Bay restoration displays: two signs near the Cornet Bay beach restroom showing how the beach has been restored and the benefits of the restoration.

- Bridge display signs: three signs telling the story of island life before the bridge in this area, the construction of the bridge, and details about the bridge today. One sign is at the south end, one on Pass Island, and one at the north end.

- Large wooden sign at the bridge: between the highway and the parking lot at the south end of the bridge stands a tall wooden sign. One side facing south tells the story of Vancouver's experience at the Pass. The other side is an idealized picture of a large sailing ship.

- Plaque on Pass Island: The Daughters of the American Revolution affixed a bronze plaque to a large rock on Pass Island, near the parking lot. This plaque commemorates Vancouver's naming of the Pass on June 10, 1792.

- CCC Statue: Fifty of these statues of a CCC worker were created for having one in each of the fifty states. The statue for the state of Washington stands here at the northern parking lot at Bowman Bay, near the CCC interpretive center.

- Bowman Beach restoration signs: along the restored beach at Bowman, illustrating how the beach changed through history and what makes for a healthy beach.

- Rosario tidepool signs: on the beach trails leading to the tidepools we have signs discussing the fragility of the tidepools and how people can help care for them.
- Rosario field: along the main trail from the parking lot to the tombolo, a large interpretive display board shares information about tidepool zonation.
- Kokwalalwoot: four signs, one for each cardinal direction, placed around the Maiden and sharing the story of the Maiden of Deception Pass as told by the Samish elders.
- Kukutali Preserve: an interpretive display at the parking lot briefly tells the story of the Preserve. Other signs on the Preserve highlight special stories to be found around the island.

Above: members of the local chapter of the Daughters of the American Revolution restore the appearance of the plaque on Pass Island. The sign commemorates the exploration of Deception Pass by Captain George Vancouver. Photo courtesy of Fely Hersey

Below: Montana Napier looks at one of the displays in the Rosario Field Classroom.

So there I am,

in the summer in 2005, with great stories happening at the park, special events scheduled, new staff starting, historical lessons being learned, and volunteer projects underway, I have so many things to share with our neighbors as a new park manager, and no good outlet to share them.

So I type up a couple pages of nuggets in an email, add a title of -- hmmm, what should I call this? This is about the things currently happening in the park. We are famous for our current through the Pass. I'll call it the *Current*.

I email it out to a few dozen people who have contacted me over the past few months and expressed some interest in the park.

August rolls around, and I have lots more current topics to share. I decide to send something out again.

It becomes a way for me to share every month.

After three or four months, I realize I should put it in a document rather than just an email. I add some pictures. People like it and tell friends and it becomes a few hundred subscribers.

I ask if anyone wishes to create a logo out of the title, for the newsletter masthead. Local resident and graphic artist Barb Lyter calls and says she would love to; she says she loves the park, and has a graphic design business. She gives me some sample ideas, I choose one, and she refines it to make a catchy design.

I love it.

It has now been at the masthead for ten years and counting, every month headlining an outlet to share some of the many things going on around here.

Share your email address with me and you can be added to the list if you wish, so long as I am here.

Serving

> "To see the earth as it truly is, small and blue and beautiful in that eternal silence where it floats, is to see ourselves as riders on the earth together, brothers on that bright loveliness in the eternal cold—brothers who know now they are truly brothers."
>
> — Archibald MacLeish, American Poet

It takes a community to have a successful park. The staff at Deception Pass State Park love what they do. Most of them would make far more money in private industry, but they know that they are serving in a special place, and they feel called to make a difference here.

The fact that I have been here over a dozen years and I am still one of the most junior employees tells you how committed they are to making this a better place.

But it takes more than paid staff -- many more people are needed to care for these treasured places, to provide special events, to service such diverse features and structures, and to keep it all humming for the good of everyone, including our future generations.

Rangers

The iconic hosts at every park. The dream job of every four year old and every cubicle-dwelling downtown office worker. Wear a Smokey the Bear flat hat, talk to the squirrels, act like a tree all day. You can't really call this a job, can you?

Yes, it's a job. The scenery is incredible, and the work can be adventurous and meaningful, but like any job, it has stretches of menial tedium, frustrations, stresses, and challenges, dealing with over a hundred toilets a day, thousands of visitors not all of whom are sober or pleasant, miles of pipelines and roads and acres of roofs and grass, and tons of garbage, and smiling at yet another visitor asking "you can't really be full, can you?" on the Fourth of July weekend.

It's still a great job, meeting people and meeting people's needs, taking care of people in trouble and caring for grand treasures and cultural icons. We never know what the next hour will bring, but we love knowing that over the next few days, weeks, and years, the park will be better and the visitors happier because we made a difference.

Rangers are the all-around generalists in a park who do almost everything: collecting money, enforcing the law, rescuing those in need, cleaning toilets, mowing the lawns, painting the ceiling in the restroom, talking at the local Chamber meeting, or wearing any of a hundred other hats for work that needs to be done in the park. Deception Pass has half a dozen rangers, scheduled to try

Former park ranger Josh Lancaster helps a visitor find his way at North Beach with a trail map.

to cover seven days a week, 24 hours a day, but doing what we can with the time and tools we have.

Rangers are there to help you, but you won't often see them because they may be writing a report, accounting for money, fixing a shower, weed-eating a roadway, or fixing a flat on a lawn mower.

Construction and Maintenance staff

Maintenance Supervisor Mark Lunz oversees all of the maintenance projects in the park, usually by being fully involved in all of the work. Here he is re-roofing a building with historically appropriate shakes.

To truly keep the park running, we need maintenance staff whose primary purpose is to build and maintain facilities and equipment. Rangers may be the icon of parks, but maintenance staff are the workhorses who keep them functioning.

The infrastructure of Deception Pass is complex, aging, and frustrating. The job of our maintenance team is to make sure our visitors never know about that, as they find and fix water leaks, keep sewer pumps serviced and functioning, rewire ancient buildings to modern codes, build and rebuild buildings that were never meant to last this long, keep vehicles running longer than expected, and create works of wonder whenever they get a chance to build something new.

Take a look at the interior of the West Beach shelter, or the recreation hall at the retreat center, or the new cabins there, or the refurbished restrooms in the campground to see their handiwork. If the lights work, water comes out of the faucet, the toilets flush, and the roof is solid, it's because of them. If one of those things isn't right, we'll give them a call and it soon will be.

The park has four maintenance specialists, and we receive support from a team of maintenance specialists at the Northwest Region office as well.

Give them a blessing of thanksgiving if you happen to see one of them. Their hands will be dirty.

Office assistants

Like any business, our management is only as good as the quality of the paperwork to support it. Much of that is the work of one person, our office assistant. Fortunately, we have one of the best in the agency right now, a former ranger who handles numbers and other details with ease. With a revenue stream of over $2 million, and a budget of well over $1 million, her hands are full, but she handles it superbly.

This is a government agency, and there is paperwork, and it needs to be done with precision, accuracy, transparency, and timeliness. Our office assistant gets that credit.

I take personal pride that this park runs about as squeaky clean and transparent in our handling of revenue and your tax dollars as any you will find. We want to earn your trust every day.

Park Aides

The staff you will most likely see in your park visit will be park aides. These folks are mostly hired for the summer season to help with the tasks that most directly serve the visitor's basic needs: registering campers for their campsites, cleaning the restrooms, mowing the grass, trimming weeds, and hauling garbage.

They get paid far too little and work hard all day long at tasks that can be repetitive. They clean 18 full size restrooms every day, each with several toilets, sinks, and showers. They trim the edges of miles of roadway and every tree trunk in our day use areas every week or two.

Park Aide John Dinger trims the edge of the mile-long Cranberry Lake Road. Our park aides never run out of having too much to do and not enough time to do it.

Some are college students working for tuition money and experience. Some are retired folks still wanting to help and serve. And some are dedicated to the job just because it works for them.

We are so proud of every one of our park aides for keeping the park functional and operational.

Camp hosts

State Parks offers volunteer opportunities to camp in our parks for a month and earn a free campsite for that time by donating at least four hours a day.

Our hosts come from a wide range of backgrounds, mostly retired but not all. Some were executives in business in their earlier lives, some blue collar workers.

They all share the desire to make the park a better place by the work they do: helping campers in the campground, cleaning campsites, picking up litter, and helping with various projects such as mowing, weed-eating, making minor repairs, selling firewood, and more.

Call the park office if you are interested in joining this popular group.

Concessions

Concession operations are a way for private businesses to provide a public service on state park grounds that is mutually beneficial to park users, park management, and the business.

Currently the park has three contracted concessions operating in the park. Each contract is for a five-year period, with financial and visitor service benefits to State Parks and of course with benefits for the business as well.

Anacortes Kayak Tours operates guided kayak tours out of Bowman Bay. The one and a half hour tours  are a great way to experience the waters around Bowman Bay, Rosario, and Sares Head to the north. Skilled and friendly guides provide basic training in kayak operations and handling and stay alongside the group as they paddle. Make reservations by phone, online, or drop in at Bowman Bay if you like to take chances.

Deception Pass Tours has one hour jet boat interpretive boat rides out of Cornet Bay. The tour boat is specially designed for maximum visibility for the guests, with room for over 35 people at a time. A tour guide explains the sites seen along the way, including Ben Ure Island, the prison caves, the bridge itself, the marine life in the Strait of Georgia, and other subjects that are seen first hand. This is a great way to see Deception Pass up close and personal.

They have a ticket sales and souvenir store (with ice cream!) on Highway 20 east of the park, near milepost 44. And they have a small ticket sales and souvenir store in the parking lot at the south end of the bridge.

We also have a contract with a hay farmer to cut the hay in the fields around Pass Lake. This keeps the fields looking as they have for generations, as pasture, and it benefits the farmer with a source of hay to sell.

We hope to contract with someone to operate a food and beverage service near our swim beach, and a paddle boat rental nearby.

The concession websites are:

www.anacorteskayaktours.com

www.deceptionpasstours.com

SWITMO

A lengthy acronym for an even longer name, the Skagit Whatcom Island Trail Maintaining Organization, SWITMO has adopted this park to help maintain our trails.

At least twice a year they host work parties that bring in dozens of people to brush out trails and build or rebuild trails as needed and approved.

They are responsible for nearly all the new trails in the park in this century, including the Pass Lake trail, Tursi Trail, Dugualla's new trails, Quarry Pond trail, Discovery Trail connector, Bridge trail, and more. They also dedicate themselves to maintaining and improving trails throughout the park.

Some of their members come out almost weekly or as needed to remove trees that have fallen across trails. They exemplify the spirit of volunteerism, and hard work!

SWITMO volunteers grub the North Trail on Kiket Island in the Kukutali Preserve.

One of the many Navy groups who come out on a regular basis from Naval Air Station Whidbey Island to make the park a better place for everyone. The kindness and support of the men and women neighbors who serve in our Navy continues to amaze me, as does their service to our nation.

Volunteers

Over the past decade, this park has increased its annual volunteer workforce from about 2000 hours to 13,000 hours recorded in 2015. Thirteen thousand hours!

We love our volunteers, and I am personally grateful for everything they do to make this park a better place, whether it is weeding flower beds to giving interpretive programs to clearing trails to greetings guests to sweeping roads to cleaning campsites to teaching about tidepools.

The Navy, as a very good neighbor, has shared numerous squadrons and other groups to assist in special projects and in ongoing service activities. These fine hard-working women and men generously contribute much of their time to making this a better place. They have helped restore shelters, restore the park after a major storm, remove invasive weeds, build tables and structures, and pick up litter.

Local Lions clubs come to the park every Earth Day weekend to do an amazing amount of work. They have built bridges, planted campsites, built fences, built tables, cleaned storm debris, painted buildings, and whatever else needs to be done.

Scout groups contribute in many ways as well, picking up litter, tearing down dangerous beach forts, and cleaning windstorm debris out of campsites.

Eagle Scout candidates have contributed significant long-term benefits such as building footbridges, kiosks, amphitheater seating, tree displays, picnic tables, trails, and more. These projects give the scouts leadership skills and project management experience.

Our hosts, discussed elsewhere, are the eyes and ears of the park for our campers, helping where they can in our campgrounds, at the Cornet Bay Retreat Center, and the Cornet Bay boat launch.

Deception Pass Park Foundation

Park funding does not adequately cover our basic utility and maintenance costs, let alone our desires to provide educational programming and special protection projects at the park.

That's where the Deception Pass Park Foundation comes in.

Formed in 2005 by a group of park neighbors, the Foundation's mission is to provide support for education and resource protection at Deception Pass. Thanks to the dedication of many, this support group continues to grow and mature.

With the help of their members and community supporters, they have already accomplished many projects and brought ongoing education programs that continue today.

As a recognized 501(c)3, they are able to accept donations and honor the donors with tax benefits and well-deserved recognition. They are led by a Board of Directors comprised of those who take a deep interest in the success of the park and the educational objectives of the Foundation.

Helping the board are a multitude of members and other volunteers who support it financially and with their kind services.

The Foundation always has ways that you can help.

Here is a short list of some of their accomplishments:

- Restored Bowman Bay CCC shelter
- Formalized the Rosario Beach Naturalist program
- Provided ongoing funding of the AmeriCorps interpretive position
- Developed the Navy interpretive sign at West Beach
- Developed CCC photo exhibits and interpretive signs at the Cornet Bay Retreat Center
- Helped fund the Bowman Bay CCC trail bridge
- Continue to organize the Junior Ranger program
- Funded the West Beach Sand Dunes Interpretive Trail signs
- Funded protective and educational signs on Goose Rock
- Helped fund the CCC rock stove restoration projects at two shelters
- Helped fund the CCC fireplace restoration at the Cornet Bay Retreat Center
- Developed and funded the Tursi Commemorative sign at the underpass
- Created in-depth educational programming for the Deception Pass Institute
- Ongoing hosts at the Arts in the Parks programs
- Hosted the first annual Bowman Bay Holiday, the 75th bridge anniversary, and the 100th birthday for Washington State Parks.
- Funded safety rails along steep trails at Bowman Bay
- Funding and doing the work of preparing and opening the Rosario Field Classroom and the Bowman Bay CCC Interpretive Center

Future plans include expanding the Deception Pass Institute to offer more classes throughout the year, helping fund and construct a stage at the amphitheater, and working toward a visitor center and interpretive center for the park.

But there's always more to do. So join them, and help them preserve Deception Pass State Park and ensure that

A forest science class led by a college professor as one of the Deception Pass Institute featured classes. The DPI is developed and sponsored by the Deception Pass Park Foundation. Photo by Montana Napier

park visitors will continue to understand and enjoy its natural and historic wonders.

The Foundation would love to have anyone raise a hand to offer to help with an event, put up lights for the holidays, teach a class, keep financial records, coordinate volunteers, raise funds, staff a booth at a local celebration, sell merchandise or cook breakfast at an event, or any other task that you can spend a day or two helping out.

Give them a call. They will be excited to have you helping the park.

Pre-1935 vehicles crossing the bridge with all other traffic stopped at high noon, a part of the celebrations and ceremonies at the 75th anniversary of the bridge on July 31, 2010. This event, like many others in the park, was hosted by the Deception Pass Park Foundation. Photo by Brian Shelly.

Join!

To become part of the Foundation or to give your support, call, stop by, or visit their website at
www.deceptionpassfoundation.org

AmeriCorps

With the loss of our paid interpreter in 2010 due to budget cuts, we turned to the national AmeriCorps program for assistance in continuing naturalist work here at the park.

In 2011 we were awarded our first AmeriCorps intern, Sam Wotipka, who stayed with us for two years, went to MIT, then eventually came back to State Parks in the agency's Olympia offices to help manage the interpretive program around the state.

Since then, Jessie Osterloh, Carly Rhodes, Montana Napier and Dominique Saks have taken the mantle and continued to provide outstanding service to our park and our visitors.

Now they organize and lead the Beach Naturalist programs, the summer evening programs, Junior

Long-time Rosario volunteer and creator of the Beach Naturalist program, Sammye Kempbell shares her love of the beaches with some visitors who stop by the demonstration table above the tidepools.

AmeriCorps intern Dom Saks teaches a youngster about shells at the Rosario tidepool area.

Ranger programs, school group visits, tidepool talks, and other programs they create.

The Deception Pass Park Foundation provides the matching grants to fund these positions. The AmeriCorps interns only receive a stipend, so they are not even making minimum wage, but their enthusiasm and energy have always been phenomenal, and their talent far above what we ever even dream of.

Give them a big thank you if you enjoy one of their presentations or training events.

Beach Naturalists

Thanks to the efforts of Sammye Kempbell, long-time Rosario tidepool guide and mentor, we now have an annual Beach Naturalist training program.

Sammye created the initial training for volunteers to help lead visitors through the tidepools, share knowledge about the marine life found there, and help channel human feet to follow the rope trail rather than stepping on and crushing the plants and animals exposed at low tide.

Since then the program has expanded and honed in to be an ever-improving opportunity for people of all ages to get involved as stewards and caretakers of the tidepools.

During the month of March, our AmeriCorps staff provide four classroom sessions and a tidepool session or two to help new volunteers learn about the intertidal life in detail, and then how to share that with visitors of all ages.

> *"If we can light the spark of wonder and discovery in some of these kids, maybe they will go on to careers in natural science, biology, ecology, habitat restoration or land conservation.*
>
> *"They'll become advocates for the environment and stewardship.*
>
> *"Maybe they'll grow up to be kinder, more caring people.*
>
> *"If all they do is realize how nature renews their spirit, that alone is well worth it."*
>
> — Craig Johnson, Whidbey Island artist and educator

The Beach Naturalists then help guide visitors at the tidepools whenever the tide is low in the spring and summer. They also assist at the Rosario Field Classroom, helping visitors meander through the many displays to learn more about the entire park environment.

Many find it rewarding to help protect this fragile environment, and to connect with people as they share the stories about the plants, animals, and other discoveries in the intertidal zone.

What about you?!

How you can be involved:
- Subscribe to the **Current** e-newsletter to stay up to date with what is happening. Send your email address to me at jack.hartt@parks.wa.gov
- Become a Foundation member, contributing funds or your time and energy
- Help with projects, events, and celebrations
- Offer your expertise
- Share resources, including time
- Call the volunteer coordinator at the park and explain what you would like to do, or ask if there is any place where you can help.

Memorial Benches

Yes, I know, benches aren't people, but each of our memorial benches represents the story and memory of someone special and beloved.

Family and friends of loved ones have donated the money needed to purchase and install each of these benches. A small plaque honors the person in remembrance.

Each has been sited with care to provide a valuable resting place for visitors and a worthy view to remember and honor someone who lives on in our hearts.

Park staff work with the donors to make sure the benches are located in areas that fit within the cultural, natural, and historical context of the park so as not to damage park resources, while still providing a meaningful resting place that honors the memory of the loved one.

Memorial benches can be found at

- West Beach, near the beginning of the Dunes Trail
- Along the amphitheater road
- At the water's edge at the northeast corner of Cranberry Lake
- On Goose Rock, about halfway up the northwest trail

A bench with a marvelous view overlooking the entrance to Bowman Bay n the Rosario area, donated by Clive and Anne Clarke.

- At the Cornet Bay Retreat Center, just north of the Dining Hall
- At Cornet Bay, near the boat launch
- Along Hoypus Road, about a third of the way down
- Also along Hoypus Road, about two thirds of the way down
- At Hoypus Point
- At the overlook on Pass Island
- On the pier at Bowman Bay, with three facing in three different directions
- Along the shoreline at Bowman Bay between the pier and the boat launch
- Right at the Bowman Bay boat launch
- Just east of the field classroom at Rosario, along the trail.

Washington State Parks has a moratorium on adding any more benches, as permitting costs and time have skyrocketed, and for places like Deception Pass, we may now have a full complement for the park's needs.

One of the donated benches helps two park visitors enjoy the shade and the view from Cranberry Lake's shoreline. This bench was donated by Gayle Glass and her family in honor of her father, former park manager Johannes Christensen.

Profiles in Service

Darlene Clark,
Senior Park Aide,
registration booth

This is my 18th season.

I started here the day the entrance booth opened in 1998.

I used to open the park, using a flashlight early in the morning to read the numbers on the old combination padlocks to open the gates. I checked the campground, giving notices to campers who had not yet paid, then opened the entrance booth at 10 a.m. That's how I know the campground so well -- I checked every campsite every day.

I used to put out cones in every reserved site and a note on each site with the name of the camper coming in to each site. Things are a lot busier now!

I worked for 25 years as the parts department supervisor at Sears. After that, I took nurse's training at Skagit Valley College for a year, and took a job at the refinery for awhile. Parks called me with a job offer, but I turned it down. They called later with a higher-paying position, and I accepted it. I've been here every summer since.

I trained many, many people in this booth. I helped start the merchandise program at the park, and I have met thousands of campers.

People always ask me why I enjoy working here. After all, it is a very stressful job at at times. I love making campers and employees happy. I have made so many friends that I keep in contact with throughout the years. Loving what I do is my reward. And it helps to do what you are passionate about doing.

I love this park.

Eugene "Gene" Earnest
Volunteer

So this guy walks into my office several years ago. He offers to help get downed trees off our trails in the park. He seemed like a nice guy and after a chat to make sure he knew what he was doing, had help, and promised to cut safely, he and his helper Bob Blunk went out and cut a few trees off our trails.

And they came back a couple weeks later and cut some more. And more a couple weeks later. Pretty soon, they had all the trails clear. Every few weeks, they would check in and see if we had any more trees, and then they would go cut those too. And after every storm, they would be out there finding trees and cutting those off trails too. And this has continued now for umpteen years as Bob and Gene continue to be our go-to guys for removing trees off the trails of the park, Gene and Bob or Bob and Gene, chaps on, saws oiled and ready to go.

If I know of a tree across a trail, and staff can't get to it right away, I know these guys will. They've been cutting for so many years now they're almost a part of the forest. If you see a tree cut from across a trail as you are hiking, think about these two and the work they have done to make your hike easier.

Here's part of Gene's story:

Born Clinton, Maine, September, 1934. Worked on cutting fire trails at a new Boy Scout Camp in 1947. July of 1952 volunteered for the Navy during the Korean War.

In the spring of 1956, the birds were heading north and so did I, sticking my thumb out and hitchhiking to Fairbanks, Alaska. Started digging a ditch in permafrost the first day, soon went to the thaw fields for the gold dredges, but a few days later was hired by the BLM fighting wild land fires around the interior of Alaska.

Went to work for the Fairbanks Fire Department as a fireman. Became Acting Fire Marshal, but the job was too confining. Quit and went north to the Brooks Range with an old-timer to stake some claims. I fell in love with the country and hiked north to Wiseman, an old gold mining town of 9 souls. Bought a cabin from a miner and helped him with his placer mine.

That winter I flew in to Fairbanks. I was hired as Asst. Fire Chief on the DEW line at Point Barrow, the northernmost town in Alaska.

Decided to move back to Maine in 1967. Bought a 55 acre small farm, with timber and a trout stream. Started cruising timber for the Oxford Paper Company. Year and one half later I went into partnership in a logging operation. A year after, I started my own operation doing selective cutting and demonstrating logging equipment.

After many more ventures in Alaska, Washington, and Maine, I bought a home in Anacortes. Since retiring I have done the following: loaded logs on ships, located lines for the Nature Conservancy in Maine, cut and maintained trails in Mazama, volunteered with the Skagit Land Trust, built houses with Habitat for Humanity for 13 years, and cleared downed trees for the last 7 years or so for Deception Pass State Park and others. All the time at the Park, and most of the time at Habitat, Bob Blunk has been my hard working, enthusiastic, always interesting partner. He does the work and I get the glory

I have had a most interesting life and I value every minute of it, but I still want to see what is around the next bend in the trail.

Rick Colombo
Park Aide, Interpreter, Foundation Volunteer

After we lost our park interpreter due to budget woes, I mentioned in one of the *Current* issues that we were looking for a volunteer who might be interested in filling this need.

One of our readers passed on the suggestion to a neighbor of his, who turned out to be a dynamic force we have appreciated having around the park ever since. His energy and boundless enthusiasm are coupled with an outgoing personality and booming voice that gets everyone's attention. He then fills that opportunity with engaging insights into whatever subject is at hand. Add his handyman skills, willingness to weed-eat and clean toilets, and the drive of a former chief petty officer, and Rick Colombo finds his hand in a lot of what has been successful at Deception Pass.

In his words:

After thirty six years in the Navy, it was time to settle down. I always wanted to be a ranger. This park is close to where I live. My family is local. I lived 7 years on a boathouse in Cornet Bay. I was a Scoutmaster, a High Adventure coach, a scuba diver, and a fisherman.

I came to the park in 2011 as an interpreter for five months, paid by the Foundation. Then I became a camp host for a couple months, then a park aide, then a park aide the next year, which turned into a winter-long job as well for maintenance, then a summer park aide again for the past couple of years. I'm the secretary and treasurer for the Foundation now, too.

The interpretive side of the job is a big part of why I came here. I always wanted to learn more about the woods, the wildlife, the history. This is a great spot to do that. I love sharing about the outdoors, being outdoors. Living and working here, you get to know what's behind the corner; visitors don't know yet, and I get to share that local knowledge. I learned a lot in school and around the world. I can talk to anyone about anything. I gave fifty tours in Canada for a bus company. Some weekends nearly 40% of our campers are from Canada, and I can relate to the maple leaf with them. I know the places they are talking about.

I bring things to the park. I'm a jack of all trades. If it takes work, I can do it. I like working with the younger guys. Most people don't see me as 65. I see myself as a big kid. I enjoy the team here. Being a part of a team was what I missed most about being in the Navy, being part of something bigger than me. I feel appreciated here for what I do. I can be myself. Commitment is part of who I am. That outlet is here.

The best part of the job is the customer service, helping others. Bathrooms are not my favorite part of the job, but I know it has to be done to help our visitors. I get a sense of pride when people are satisfied with how the campground looks, or how a restroom is clean. I get immediate satisfaction from making things better. Here you see something that needs to be done and you get to do it.

I like the social end of the job -- you get to meet with customers. I love being on the staff because I can make a difference. It gives me a sense of purpose. I'm retired from the Navy but I still haven't sat down for retirement. I have a passion for parks.

It's hard not to like parks.

Ben Shook
Park Ranger

Ranger Shook was a rookie ranger in the ranger law enforcement academy when I started working at Deception Pass. I have always admired his integrity, his enthusiasm, and his service to others approach to life. He has a willingness to do whatever needs to be done, and gives a calm and no-drama response to every situation, even those that are highly dramatic. In other words, he is a professional, and a respected member of the park team.

Here is what he shared with me recently:

My family connections brought us here, and the park.

I met my future wife at Colorado Christian near Denver. I graduated with a history degree. I also had wildland firefighting training, so I wanted to combine those two somehow. Being a ranger was a perfect fit. I spent three years in Oregon State Parks, and then became interested in Washington State Parks. My wife's family was from Anacortes.

When Deception Pass State Park had an opening, I applied, as it was close to family and also such an interesting park. They offered me the job in 2003, and we've been here ever since.

I like the park because it's large; it has variety, and great natural resources. It's near the Olympics and Cascades, near the water, and has a variety of opportunities to do things. And for me as a history major, it has a fascinating history, and the extensive CCC developments.

I appreciate the job of being a ranger, tasked with being a steward. I watch over the park to protect it, and to help people enjoy it at the same time. I love being the steward of a great place like this. There is so much variety to what I do, from maintenance to search and rescue to helping people. I protect the park from people and protect people from the park!

It's been a fun ride here, seeing the staff change and morph through different combinations, sometimes with hiccups, but always making the park a better place and a better experience for our visitors.

Mark Lunz
Maintenance Supervisor

When I first came here, I recognized that Mark was one of those special people who want to do the best job they can, using the limited resources we have to their maximum, but who also works as a team player, someone who sees the bigger picture of the whole park operation, how we serve our visitors, and how our work and teamwork is a reflection of our character for all to see.

He has a great eye for details that make a project so much better in the end. He is one of the most talented and well-rounded construction workers in Washington State Parks.

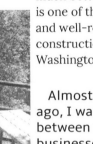

Almost twenty years ago, I was in transition between private businesses when a maintenance position opened at the park. I thought this would be a good fit for me. I found it fits me in a lot of ways.

The park has a lot of diversity. I can work on so many different projects and tasks, using so many of my skills. Being a big park fits me because there is so much to do.

You're always busy. There is a diversity of work. And it's all interesting. The only down side is trying to find ways to pay for things, for what needs to be done.

We have such great jobs, to come to work and see what we get to see here, one of the most beautiful parks in the system.

Pat and Barry Gum
Camp Hosts

Barry and Pat came to us as rookie hosts quite a few years ago – rookies for Deception Pass, but not to camp hosting. Their constant friendly badgering of us to let them work on more and more projects and to do ever increasing amounts of clean up and grounds-keeping eventually led us to recognizing that here were two people who loved to work hard and cared about making the park look better than when they started. Pretty soon we just gave them the keys to the truck and the equipment and trusted them to transform Bowman into a lovely place. And they have.

Here is what they shared:

We started hosting in the Eighties, actually. Working in the schools, we could do other things during the summer. We took our kids camping at Fort Stevens in Oregon, and our kids helped us volunteer in that park so that they could learn to give back. They were 3 and 5 years old to start. This was something different from our ordinary lives that we loved to do. When Pat became a school administrator we had to stay home during the summers. But she retired in 2008, and we were hosting again the very next day!

In 2009 we hosted at Jarrell Cove and then came up to Deception Pass for two months. Our kids were in the area, so it was a good fit for us as a family. When we first came here the staff treated us kindly but with caution. We wanted to do more, and they weren't sure if we could take it on and be trusted to just come get a truck and other equipment and stay busy using it all day and to work safely. It didn't take long before they saw that we could. It's encouraging to just be considered like part of the staff. We have a lot of freedom to do what we want to do, to be trusted to take care of this area.

This park is a beautiful place. We get to make it a better place, and meet wonderful people as well. Bowman Bay is really special. Many of the campers come back to the same campsites on the same weekend each year, and we greet each other as friends now.

We can say it looks better each year, partly because of the work we do, knowing it makes a difference, and also because of the work the staff here does. We love the Deception Pass staff. They make us feel like we are home. One of the maintenance employees came by on the last day of his work week just to check in with us and see if we needed anything because he was going to be gone for three days.

How sweet is that?!

Photos on page 177, clockwise from upper left:

- *Tim Hall and Jessie Osterloh installing an interpretive sign at East Cranberry;*
- *Joe Schmidt and Dale Chrisman roofing a CCC building;*
- *Ben Shook and Jeri Lancaster building a dumpster screen;*
- *Mark Lunz and Jim Aggergaard fixing a sewer pump;*
- *two volunteers planting at Cornet Bay;*
- *Marv Wold and Mark Lunz building a new campsite.*

From Eeww, or Owww, to Ahhh...

My mantra for the park team has been to make the park "park-like", to build supportive teamwork, and to provide great customer service.

Sometimes all three came together at the same time. Someone on the staff or a visitor or volunteer will share a problem, and with our heads together we come up with a solution.

So there we are,

looking at the toilets at the South Bridge parking lot. It's my first week as the new manager (many years ago now). I see stainless steel sinks, stainless steel mirrors, and stainless steel toilets in each stall, but none of the toilets have any seats. Even if I really have to go, I wouldn't use these! Eeewww.

We ask why there are no seats, and some reply that the seats might get vandalized. I say if I needed a toilet and found one without a seat, that might put me in a mood to do vandalism. We put seats on the toilets and wait to see will happen.

So far, no toilet seats have been vandalized. But our visitors are happier, I am sure.

There was a garbage can at each end of the South Bridge parking lot, with garbage scattered around each can. The team suggested that if our goal is to have a clean park and parking lot, then we should get rid of the garbage cans. A couple people gasp. It will be a mess, they say. The others reply that it's a mess now. Let's give it a try, they say.

We pull the cans. 98% of the mess disappears.

From there, across the parking lot, we look at people walking through the lot to get onto the bridge. The most direct route takes pedestrians right through the vehicle entrance from the highway. Cars would turn into the lot in a blind, high speed turn from the highway to avoid getting rear-ended by someone following behind them looking at the view instead of the car bumper directly in front of them.

We think a barrier along the sidewalk extending from the bridge to the middle of the parking lot will get pedestrians out of the throat of the car entrance to a place further in where cars will have slowed down.

But it takes me seven years to put the pieces into place, with park staff then able to install the extended cable railing to solve the problem.

Why so long? I have excuses, but none of them would hold water if someone had been hit by a car in the meantime. At least it's better now. No 'owwws'.

Some problems are not as obvious.

I had hiked the 'social' trails on Pass Island several times -- always in the daylight. I got a call one morning from a man who said he had parked on Pass Island late the previous evening, and had strolled out onto the trail northeast of the turnout on the island. The trail is wide and inviting as it enters the woods -- then dead ends at a 180 foot vertical drop-off to the water below. In the dusky light, he barely saw the edge in time. That would have been an owww.

We put up a fence the next week.

The West Beach area has a service road leading from the parking lot to the restroom and concession building. A gate blocked the road to keep unauthorized vehicles from driving down along the beach. But it also forced hikers to get around the gate somehow to walk to the restroom or Dunes Trail. We decide to put a post in the middle of the road instead of a gate across the entire road. Instantly it is a welcoming change for beach users, an 'ahhh' moment.

Every day our team looks at needs and finds ways to make the park better. I have always been impressed with the insights these professionals have in the little things and the big things, finding better ways to clean a toilet, light a building, improve our cost accounting, reduce costs with our garbage service, fix broken water lines or pump systems or pilot lights or whatever it may be to keep the park functioning safely and efficiently.

We want to remove the eewws, prevent the owwws, and allow visitors to have satisfied ahhhs.

Our goal is to make each visitor's experience magical so that they don't notice anything out of place or not working properly or causing them frustration.

If we do our jobs well, most people won't notice. They just go "ahhh..."

Caring

*"Unless someone like you cares a whole awful lot
Nothing is going to get better, it's not."*

— *Dr. Seuss, in* The Lorax

People come and go. Park buildings go up, older ones come down. Features change, new features get added. But the park itself remains. The park that was here 10,000 years ago is basically the same landscape that we see today, with trees in slightly different places maybe, and beaches shaped in new ways, but we would recognize what we would see back then.

That is the beauty of parks. Our world grows, changes, and moves on, but there are constants, and one of those constants is knowing that parks like Deception Pass are a dependable part of our heritage and will continue to be a part of our future.

Parks are forever.

The tribes still call this land home. They know their ancestors are still here; they know their roots are planted deeply here.

As a non-tribal person, I too know that this land is my home, that the memories of family times together will live on, and that my grandchildren will always be able to come back here and know the land of their grandfather.

My role as park manager is to first do no harm, to let Deception Pass roll on into the future as the landscape of hope for all generations. We make plans to improve the park, but they are always tempered by what they mean for preserving what is best, preserving and cherishing the heart of this place.

The future has many promising and beneficial developments and improvements coming. The future is always bright with hope.

But there are also some concerns approaching us which will arrive just as inevitably, causing challenges and changing our use of the park and perhaps our enjoyment. The park itself is changing constantly, reflecting the changes in our planet, our culture, and our future.

Cornet Bay Moorage

We have plans and possible grant funding to replace the pier and docks at Cornet Bay with modern facilities that are healthier for the environment and which will be better for boaters as well.

We hope to be able to connect the outer docks and the inner docks, and extend the amount of dock space to increase opportunities for moorage for our many boaters. The new design will be better for the eelgrass beneath the docks as well. Some of the moorage may have power outlets. Reservations for dock space are also a possibility.

Look for this in 2017.

100th birthday

It's coming. Not many years from now, the park will turn 100 years old as a State Park.

In 1922, the United States Government transferred over 1700 acres of the former military reservation land to the state of Washington for a new state park. Called Deception Pass, the new state park was one of the earliest parks in the state park system, a system that itself had started just nine years earlier.

After the House and the Senate agreed earlier in the month, President Harding signed the approval on March 23, 1922. The State Parks Committee accepted the property on April 17 of that year, and the Whidbey and Fidalgo communities had an area-wide celebration on July 20 at the park.

I hope there will be a year long celebration in 2022, hopefully culminating in a July 20 party at the park. We have much to celebrate, and much to look forward to in the next 100 years for Deception Pass. Can we start now?

Kiket Changes

The Swinomish Indian Community and Washington State Parks have a mutual goal of preserving and protecting the natural resources of Kukutali Preserve while allowing low-impact recreational use.

Very little is planned for the area, to keep the island natural.

We now have grant funding to build a small shelter at the west end of Kiket, in the lawn area, to allow small groups of visitors to enjoy a gathering for a picnic or small ceremony.

We also want to build a trail on the Fidalgo Island side to take visitors from the parking lot down to the lagoon without having to walk along a roadway that is shared with two residences. Along with the trail we hope to create minimal interpretive signage to introduce visitors to the great stories that surround us.

The view west from Kiket Island toward Skagit Island with the bridge in the distance.

One of the greatest unnatural features of the island that still remains from the days of earlier development is the causeway of fill that joins Kiket Island and Fidalgo Island at the tombolo, keeping Kiket from being an island.

The waters of the sea used to flow across this spit at the highest of tides. Neighbors recall their grandparents routinely boating through the gap between Kiket Island and the lagoon area. That is why Kiket was named an island, and not a head or point or other moniker for connected land masses.

Early in the twentieth century, the owners filled in the gap to allow vehicles to drive onto the island. The boulders of this fill remain to this day.

In our efforts to restore the area to its natural health, we have a chance to reintroduce the natural water connection to make Kiket Island an island again.

The Tribe and State Parks are looking into the probable ramifications of restoring the flow of water here. It will make vehicle travel a tide-dependent affair, as we will have to wait for a low to medium tide to cross the channel, as is done at Lone Tree Point just to the south. It will require hikers to consider the tide when they visit the island to avoid having to remove their shoes and socks on the return trip. Fortunately, high tides are most prevalent during the nighttime during the summer months.

The benefits include restored sediment movement in the area, restored fish migration patterns, improved beach structure on both sides of the island, and improved natural processes we may not even know about.

Visitor Center

Most parks of any size and substance have a visitor center, a gathering place where visitors can come learn about the park, become oriented to what there is to discover, meet with staff to make a personal connection, and find maps, books, or other materials to make their visit more profitable, memorable, and engaging.

Deception Pass lacks that center. Some visitors meet an employee at our booth when they sit in their car to buy a pass to enter the Cranberry area. And some stop at the booth at the bridge to buy tickets for the Deception Pass Tours ride, but that is a crowded area and the booth is too small to share more than a brochure.

Most visitors never see a staff person except maybe someone cleaning a bathroom. And there is no easily accessible place for visitors to go to learn about the park and gain that grounded feeling of knowing what is available to them.

We tried to buy a store sitting on Highway 20 near Cornet Bay Road, but we lacked the priority of funding that we needed. With nearly three million people coming here every year, this is one need that I hope will be met in the near future.

Keeping CCC Facilities Alive

When the Civilian Conservation Corps built the many structures in Deception Pass, they probably had no expectation that the buildings would outlive them. The facilities were built well, but with inherent weaknesses that started the clock ticking on their longevity: rafter ends exposed to the rain, foundation logs sitting on concrete at ground level, rock foundations that crack with age and weathering.

Every building except one is still standing and still in use.

The only way to make this happen is a constant effort of maintenance and repair. Grants, historical preservation monies, and the Deception Pass Foundation have been generous in supporting these efforts financially. Volunteers and park staff have been generous with their time to provide the intense labor necessary to make the projects successful.

In 2002, park and region staff, supported by Field Preservation School students, rebuilt the East Cranberry Shelter. In 2008 several roofs were replaced with authentic shakes split and installed by the SWITMO members and park staff.

In 2011 a generous donor, Ted LaGreid, provided funding for a stonemason to replace two failed rock fireplaces and chimneys, and the Foundation provided funding to repair the stone amphitheater fireplace at the retreat center. At the same time HDR Inc. of Seattle and park staff rebuilt two shelters at East Cranberry under the tutelage and hands-on labor of preservation expert Harrison Goodall.

In 2012 a capital project funded the restoration of the former bathhouse at Rosario, converting it into a field classroom.

In 2013 and 2014, we renovated the upper Bowman shelter with new roof perlins and rafters, a new roof, new windows to replace Plexiglas windows installed in the Seventies, and a new look as the brown paint on the logs was stripped down to its original golden glory and preserved with clear stain.

In 2013 the small shelter at the retreat center was rebuilt by the Field Preservation School.

Alex McMurry and Bud Betz use a crosscut saw to cut a roof support post for a CCC shelter. They are using historical methods for authentic repairs.

In 2014 and 2015 the Bowman beach shelter was rebuilt as well, along with re-roofing the Rosario Shelter and the CCC garage and residence on the Cranberry side.

Many more structures remain in need of capital investment to protect their integrity and extend their useful life. The two CCC residences are in the most critical condition. These historical landmarks are stout, but only through proper renovation will they survive to be one hundred years old.

We hold the keys -- or the purse strings -- to the future. We must invest in our heritage to keep it alive, meaningful, and vibrant for the future.

Lake Quality

The past few years have seen dramatic problems with the health of both of our lakes. Will this continue in the future? Will it become worse? Will we be able to use the lake in summer anymore?

Do planted fish contribute to the nutrient overload of the lakes? Does climate change become a growing factor in the future as warmer lakes support more cyanobacteria? Will the use of Cranberry Lake for swimming and boating change from a tradition to a rare event?

Are Canada geese part of the problem? Although these are native birds, we now have far more geese residing here year round instead of migrating through. Where we once had a handful of geese, we now have flocks of 80 to 100 at a time, pooping a pound a day -- each -- onto the shorelines and into the waters of Cranberry Lake. However, these birds are not a factor at Pass Lake.

We are working toward finding answers. Scientists and citizens are coming together here and elsewhere to get answers, and hopefully solutions. You may be able to help us find these answers.

We need to find out more, or the lake may be closed for much of the year.

Forest Health

Imagine a senior citizen assisted-living center. Most of the people staying there appear to be fine as they wander the halls and eat meals together. But the reality is that they are seniors, and we tend to have health issues as we age.

Our trees throughout much of Deception Pass are senior citizens. They look fine from a distance, big and strong, but if you look closely, you see that these ancient marvels are elderly and struggling with health issues.

This affects the future of Deception Pass for camping and for the structures in the park. Nearly every campsite in the Forest Loop has an old tree nearby. Many of the sites in the Lower, Middle, Back, and Bowman areas also have senior trees nearby.

Rockport and South Whidbey State Parks had to close campgrounds to protect campers. Here we closed our group camp, and changed Bowman and the Forest Loop to be open only during the busier months.

Forest experts monitor the trees every year. There will be an inevitable point in the future when a closure may be necessary.

We also face other forest health issues. For example, for tens of thousands of years, forest fires would occasionally burn through our forests, removing debris on the ground and creating a diversity of habitats.

As a park, we work to stop forest fires as soon as possible to protect park resources, park visitors, and developed neighborhoods on the park's boundaries.

Park neighbors and interested friends explore a remnant tree plantation at Dugualla State Park, left over from the days before it became a park. Dr. Rob Fimbel, Washington State Parks forester, discusses options to restore this area of the forest to natural health.

Now we have forests that are laden with debris, ready to burn intensely if a fire ever does get going, and creating the possibility of a conflagration. The park's limited size reduces the potential for an explosive fire, but the potential is there.

Another little-known issue can be fixed if we want. The lands we acquired from the Department of Natural Resources, Hoypus Hill and Dugualla, were once logged over in patches and then planted like a tree farm, with large areas seeded at the same time with the same kind of tree, Douglas fir.

Fifty years later or more, these plantations look homogeneous and relatively lifeless. They are unnatural.

We could let them go on like they are, and in a few centuries they would start to become more natural forests. Or we could modify them now, removing some of the even-aged trees, creating snags for wildlife, openings for other plant species to grow, and planting different species to allow for variety and diversity in plants and wildlife.

It would take a little effort, but the results would be the right thing for achieving healthy forests for the generations to come. It takes a lot of work to restore a park to look like untouched nature!

Bowman Pier

As popular as this pier is, the reality is that the pier is on its last legs, literally. The pilings holding up the pier have been there for seventy years, and may not last much longer. Some of the beams above them have also reached a ripe old age.

Finding the money to make these costly repairs will be a challenge. Some say we should just let the pier go away; some others want a newly-designed pier to improve our boating services and other opportunities. And some say just fix what we have, as it is comfortable and good enough. Money or the lack of money may drive the final decision.

Power Generation

Our park burns nearly as much energy as a small town each year, with all our campsites, heated cabins, shops, sewer pumps, and other powered facilities.

We consider alternative opportunities any time we hear of one. Several have been suggested, and we have found funding to do some minor retrofits, but we could do so much more. For example, with one grant we were able to upgrade older fluorescent lighting to more efficient lights, including LED lighting in places. We have changed a couple buildings from baseboard heat to ductless.

One neighbor had the numbers figured out to put a wind turbines at West Beach. The Snohomish PUD and a group of Naval Academy students have put forth initial thoughts about tidal turbines in the Pass for power generation. Extensive studies will have to be done to show that the clean energy outweighs any danger to the marine environment or park aesthetics for these.

Solar may solve some of our needs in the near future, if we can find adequate funding through grants or other sources to get started. Any solutions that reduce the park's carbon footprint make perfect sense and cents.

Carrying capacity

> "Conservation of wildness is self-defeating, for to cherish we must see and fondle, and when enough have seen and fondled, there is no wilderness left to cherish."
>
> - Aldo Leopold

How many people can Deception Pass State Park hold? If you count how many parking stalls it has, you can get a ballpark number of possible attendance.

How many should it allow at one time? Now we are talking politics and park management. Is there a limit to the number of people that can be in the park before the values of the park become degraded? The answer is obviously yes, but what that number is can be debated forever.

More people in a landscape means more impact on the recreational experience, more degradation of natural and cultural resources, and an increased need for infrastructure such as restrooms, waste receptacles, sewer systems, and parking stalls to serve the needs of the visitors which in turn further impacts our resources.

Our current management accepts the size of the parking lots in the park as our level of acceptable carrying capacity. Each area has a finite number of parking spaces. The facilities are scaled to be able to handle the people that would be in the park if all of these parking spaces are full. The past decade has seen an acceptance of this level of use, with no significant degradation of recreational experience or resources being obvious. Visitors have enough room to enjoy the park, enough space to not be in conflict with others, and enough facilities to handle physical needs.

On sunny afternoons we sometimes stretch these limits, and have to close certain areas to any further visitors to keep from being overrun.

Growth Management

There are several issues that will be exacerbated by one particular growing concern: our population growth.

When I was young, our state had just over three million residents. Right now we have nearly seven million, more than double the number from fifty years ago. If we add another couple of million people, what pressures will be brought to bear on our natural lands and our undeveloped lands, either through residential needs, power needs, and the ever increasing pressure for developing further recreational space at the expense of natural landscapes and cultural resources?

Recycling

My biggest failure as a park manager, in my mind anyway, has been the inability to have any consequential waste recycling.

It's not through a lack of trying, or discussions with those who know how. It has just been making it economically viable in a climate that requires an intensive hands-on effort to perform the sorting when I don't have enough staff to even keep the restrooms as clean as our visitors deserve.

Breakthroughs in recycling systems are not far away. We may have a solution available to us even now, so I am hoping to at least make a dent in the next year.

Development

Death by a thousand cuts, one of my mentors once described it. Adding a little building here, a parking lot there, a new trailhead here, a restroom there, and before you know it, the park is not the same park that you started with.

Changes came to Deception Pass haphazardly over the span of many generations. The various tribes opened up most of the beach and seashore areas for long houses and summer camps hundreds of years ago. Taking advantage of these openings, pioneers and homesteaders built residences in the same places, and opened up the woods further with roadways, docks, and sawmills.

In the Thirties when the CCC built the park use areas and the associated structures that went with those areas, they took natural advantage of the existing developments to create a unified park setting. East Cranberry, North Beach, Cornet Bay, Bowman Bay, and Rosario became even more popular destinations with parking lots, restrooms, and shelters to accommodate the needs of visitors.

The bridge obviously added to the mix by bringing a major highway right through the heart of the park and joining Whidbey to the rest of the world by road instead of ferry.

Bigger changes occurred when we added campsites to meet this growing demand, taking over a hundred acres near Cranberry Lake to not only build roads and campsites, but also install water, sewer, and power lines right through the roots of old growth trees. We also added a road and a monster parking lot right on the beach at West Beach, changing that environment forever.

And then a fish hatchery at Bowman Bay eliminated an untold amount of wetlands, and erased the beach by covering it with boulders and a pier.

Building three hundred campsites in the park, along with the pavement, utility lines, and tree removal required for that many sites, changed the park dramatically.

Building parking lots for nearly a thousand cars here at one time has an impact on each visitor's experience because so many people are here vying for the same recreational resources. And still we have to turn away visitors because we didn't build parking for two thousand cars.

These changes are beneficial to us in many ways. They add to the park experience and allow more people to enjoy the park.

They also change the natural environment of the park, and thus the actual experience of each visitor.

There comes a point, the thousandth cut, where we realize that the original landscape can no longer be recognized, where we have eroded and damaged the park landscape and experience to the point of not being what we want anymore.

It's all a matter of values. Special interests want to use the park for their needs, and see any limitations on the use of the land as a restriction against their enjoyment. Whether it be RV campers, boaters, motorcycle riders, mountain bikers, historians, picnickers, rockhounds, geocachers, kayakers, hunters or drone fliers, everyone wants to enjoy parks in their own way.

Where we draw lines defines which user groups get satisfied and which don't, or what kind of balance we prefer.

Each development proposed for the future needs to be viewed in the light of the original park intentions, our current values in parks and recreation, and what the future needs of the children of our grandchildren will be.

Some changes in the dozen years I have been here include several miles of trails throughout the park, changing some campsites to cabins, adding four campsites where we once did not own the land, removing three group camps from old growth forests, restoring two lengthy sections of beaches to original habitat, and adding several hundred acres of new park land around our edges.

At the same time, we have aimed to improve and restore the structures and infrastructures throughout the park without changing their footprint or impact on the land.

Future improvements must be weighed against protecting all the resources we value.

Finances

In the past, parks were considered a community value, and our taxes paid for their support and upkeep.

Now, the Washington State Parks and Recreation Commission, like many other park agencies, has been asked to raise almost all of the money it needs from park revenues: camping fees, day use fees, reservation fees, boat launch fees, moorage fees, special activity permit fees, and others.

The danger in this approach is that it rewards finding ways to make money in parks. On the surface, that seems reasonable, perhaps, but when the survival of a park depends on how much money it can raise out of its resources, you can see the temptation to become a revenue generating park rather than a heritage preserving park. Steps may be encouraged, and taken, that sacrifice our long term benefits for short term profits.

Deception Pass has been considered for high-end upscale motels, restaurants, and private moorage docks at places such as West Point, the playfield at Bowman, the Retreat Center, and Cornet Bay.

We have had zip lines proposed to cross from Bowman Hill to Goose Rock, and across Heilman Valley. We have had a motel company want to take over the Retreat Center to bring in high-end lodging instead of kid-friendly bunkhouses. We have had one business want to build a breakwater and marina at Bowman Bay.

These kind of developments would bring in serious money, and all we would have to give up is public access to the most popular places in the park. When profit is the motive, these proposals become tempting. The cost of such ventures would be the lost beauty of the area, and even more importantly, the lost values of a land dedicated to us all, free to explore, free to enjoy, and free of modern development for all time.

A state park should not be run like a business, where profit is the goal, as this leads to decisions that may sacrifice the park values for the profit values. Parks are a social and ecological value; that is why they should not have their profit margin as the priority of park management.

> "Our parks are sources of strength and pride to our people and nation. They serve as places of common ground linking us spiritually and physically to each other and to the natural world to which we are all connected. To open the doors of commercialization in our parks is disrespectful to the past generations of people who fought to protect these lands, and shows a lack of regard for future generations who are rightful heirs to these unique places."
>
> Theresa Dix, Washington State, 2006
>
> "In these days of budget crunches, the lure of turning public assets into a way to make money is alluring. The free market is seen as a panacea for seemingly every aspect of government service, in the minds of some. Don't get me wrong. The free market is a wonderful thing and in the appropriate circumstances can lead to greater efficiency and productivity. It's just an atrociously bad idea for public parks, corrections, law enforcement, fire and other fundamental public services.
>
> "Our system of parks was built upon the notion that they are for everyone, not just the privileged few with money. They have, for the most part, been kept free from the commercialization that has overwhelmed our society and they are places of distinctive beauty that citizens have been able to enjoy and appreciate. In these times in which the pace of society is frenetic and one has very few places to escape the constant drumbeat of marketing messages, parks are more necessary than ever.
>
> "If parks are required to make a profit, the fundamental character of these unique public assets will change, and not for the better."
>
> Rufus Woods, Publisher, Wenatchee World newspaper, 2012
>
> "To be blunt: Parks are not businesses. They are socialism. That was the whole point, starting with the founding of Yellowstone in the late 1800s — to shield a few of the country's wild places from capitalism.
>
> "It's not that capitalism is evil. It's just that the twin, unique goals of parks — preservation forever of the resources and access to all the public — are not exactly capitalism's strong suits.
>
> Danny Westneat, Seattle Times newspaper, 2012

Bridge failure

No bridge lasts forever. The Deception Pass Bridge is over eighty years old as I write this. It is in fair condition; I hope I'm in fair condition at the age of 80.

But with the loads and traffic it bears daily, its future is unknown. Repairs may extend its life for some time, but eventually it will either have to be replaced or a new span will need to be built elsewhere. One good alternative route is from Strawberry Point on Whidbey Island to the northern tip of Camano Island. This route would save an hour of time each trip for many and collectively save millions of dollars in the fuel we burn to go from Everett to the middle of Whidbey Island right now.

The expense of either of those alternatives is hard to comprehend in today's construction world, especially in an environment as precious and challenging as this one.

Imagine the park without a bridge.

Earthquake/ Tsunami

It's not if, but when. This area is subject to earthquakes of a severe and devastating magnitude every few hundred years. It has been a few hundred years since the last one, in the year 1700.

The park is exposed to a possible earthquake-generated tsunami out of the west; lowland areas could be inundated. We have over 1500 people sleeping in the park each summer night. Over 1000 of them are in the potential path of a tsunami, on the low ridge exposed to the Strait of Juan de Fuca.

We try to plan for events such as these just in case. But we can't prevent them. They will happen someday.

Climate change

We live in a changing world. Our changing climate is an unknown that can change everything about our life and our planet.

Even moderate sea level rise will change Deception Pass. West Beach is near the high tide line right now; higher tides could breach the beach and change Cranberry Lake into a saltwater marsh. Restrooms at Bowman Bay and Cornet Bay would also be susceptible to higher water. Moderate changes were considered in the newest facilities. The most recent king tide of 2016 came within inches of flooding the Cornet Bay restroom. A two foot rise in the sea level will inundate all of these areas.

Weather changes may affect the park in untold ways. Summers may be drier, winters wetter and windier. Fires may become a problem, as will flooding and vegetative changes because of the new climate, which will also change wildlife in unknown ways.

We have already begun to see the changes predicted by computer modeling for the Northwest. Our winters are wetter, warmer, and windier. Our summers are drier, and also warmer.

But even more concerning, the ocean is warming and becoming more acidic. What this means for the future can only be guessed at in hushed tones by those who study such things. How will this affect the Salish Sea, and our entire ecosystem?

Three numbers frame the discussion. If we grasp the meaning of these three numbers, the purpose and direction of the climate change discussion is clear. Those numbers are:

2

565

And 2,795

All proper scientific studies and models indicate that 2 degrees Celsius is the most the planet can climb without devastating consequences. Considering the change and damage at the current 0.8 degree rise we have already achieved – half of the summer sea ice in the arctic gone, the oceans 30% more acidic, droughts causing food and humanitarian crises – even a 2 degree rise might be far too much.

565 is how many gigatons of additional carbon we can pour into the atmosphere to stay below a 2 degree rise. Some say that the rise to 1.6 degrees is already in motion even if we stopped burning carbon now, but computer models say our planet can absorb another 565.

And 2,795? That's the existing number of gigatons of carbon in proven coal, oil, and gas reserves held by companies and countries worldwide, which they intend to process and sell for us to burn. That is five times beyond the 565 number, five times beyond survival of life as we know it. Will we?

What will Kokwalalwoot think of these changes?

What will our grandchildren think of these changes that we have wrought? What are we doing today about the trajectory in which we are heading?

Please do your part to work toward protecting our planet and maintaining a habitat that allows humans to survive and thrive along with the other planetary organisms, fellow organisms who depend on us to not destroy their home, our home, the only home we all have and share.

Seagulls are a part of this park's culture. They inhabit the beaches, looking for flotsam of the sea, a dead crab, a piece of clam, a peck at a wounded fish, or a taco wrapper blowing in the wind.

In the winter they look noble, banking on the breeze, purposeful in flight, mostly alone. In the summer they are busy hustling for food, standing near picnic tables looking for scraps that may fall off and be forgotten.

When summer starts to fade into fall, the seagulls start congregating in the West Beach parking lot. They sit there, lethargic, goal-less, standing, waiting, looking forlorn and of no purpose on the planet. A car drives by, and they move out of the way if they have to, but otherwise they don't even turn their head for the passing car.

Eventually the seagulls disappear, one by one, not to be seen again, except for a handful who are dancing with the wind, flying into the winter, seemingly strong and mostly alone. I always wonder where the others go, why we never see most of them again.

So there I am,

entering the park early in the morning, and I see an older man pushing a bicycle near the park entrance, with a few belongings on his bike. He is disheveled, wearing a plaid woolen jacket, worn out pants, a dirty button up shirt underneath. His hair is scruffy and mostly white, on his face and on the top of his head.

For the next few days and months I see him a lot, always near the park entrance. The first times we find him we realize he is sleeping in the shelter at Cranberry Lake, then just hanging out for the day time. We remind him he cannot sleep in the shelter, or anywhere in the park if he is not registered into a campsite. So now he leaves the park as dusk falls.

We all get to know him as Patrick. He is about my age or thereabouts, so an older gentleman, and Irish according to his name and accent. One of my rangers checks his identification and finds out he is not wanted anywhere. The double entendre doesn't hit me until much later.

Over the next few months we have a few short talks, how he had come from Bellingham because he couldn't find a place to live there. I see him wandering the park during the day, riding his bike with his belongings in the basket on front. He will sit at the beach, or hang out at the dock. In the evening he will be near Cranberry somewhere. Occasionally we will see him early in the morning crawling out of an area just outside the park, or somewhere inside the park. We find that he often camps at the foreclosed tavern across the street, or in the woods between the highway and our Quarry Pond campground.

Then it gets colder. We find him a couple times in the early morning sleeping in a campground restroom. I tell him that he will have to find some place legal to live, as we can not let him sleep in our restrooms. He understands, he says. We have this talk several times, actually. And he disappears for a short while. We still see him around the park, but not at night. He still has no tent, and he still wears the same clothes he had when I first saw him here six months ago, the same clothes every day.

I talk with housing people around the county, but no one has any solutions for shelter.

Now it is getting very cold at night. Our camp host in the campground tells me that he is getting complaints of someone sleeping in the restroom late at night, and our campers are concerned for their own safety. I find Patrick the next day and tell him that he needs to find a shelter for the winter. I emphasize to him that he cannot sleep in the restrooms, as it frightens campers who see him in the middle of the night spread out across the floor next to the toilet.

I ask Patrick if there is anything we can do to help him find a place. He says no, he'll figure it out.

I tell the campground host to call me if he ever finds Patrick sleeping in the restroom at night.

I get a call from my camp host that very night, at two in the morning. I drive over to the campground, and see Patrick sleeping in the middle of the restroom near the urinals. I wake Patrick up, and tell him he will have to leave in the morning and not come back into the park as he is upsetting and frightening campers and breaking the law and the trust I had in him.

He swears at me under his breath, and leaves right then.

I never saw him again.
I still wonder.

Finding

"In wilderness I sense the miracle of life, and behind it our scientific accomplishments fade to trivia."

— Charles Lindbergh

Best Places

Best Place to Kiss

Anywhere.

You both want to kiss? Why not now?

You want a better answer than that? Nope, I still think anywhere that you both are in the mood. And if you are in the park with a loved one, you should be in the mood.

Best Place to Propose

1. Anywhere he or she will say yes
2. Nowhere else

Okay, those two rules are a given. But with the right preparation, a few places will be more likely to encourage that yes answer. It all depends on who you are as a couple, whether adventurous or confined to a wheel chair or more into boats or heights or crowds or solitude or whatever it may be.

A few places in the park seem to just say "propose here". These are not listed in any priority as every relationship is unique. And no, I have not had the opportunity to try any of them. Let me know if they work.

And be sure to consider the ramifications if she or he says no. Most of these locations have critical drawbacks if the proposal does not go well. The next several minutes may not be comfortable.

- ♥ On top of Rosario Head, under the wind-whipped tree or at the edge. If you are at the edge, be careful how you get down on one knee. Extra points for being at sunset.
- ♥ In front of a crowd at a music event at the amphitheater. This truly depends on the right couple at the right time in the right way with the right music..
- ♥ On a rowboat in the middle of Cranberry Lake. Definitely be careful how you get down on that knee.
- ♥ On the very top of Goose Rock. Make sure jets are not flying overhead.
- ♥ On the point at Kiket Island.
- ♥ At the overlook at Ginnett.
- ♥ At the end of the pier at Bowman Bay.
- ♥ At the Ben Ure Cabin.
- ♥ South of the West Beach area, along the Dunes Trail or along the beach.
- ♥ At West Point at sunset.
- ♥ At the meadow on the south side of Lighthouse Point.
- ♥ On the dock at East Cranberry
- ♥ On a Deception Pass Tours tour or an Anacortes Kayak Tour out of Bowman Bay. Again, make sure she will say yes. That would be an awkward place for a no.

Best Place for Watching Sunsets

Sunset quality varies in many ways. One depends on where the sun is setting -- is it in the northwest, west, or southwest? Some areas are good year round, some just at specific times of the year.

But wherever the sun, even more important is if there IS a sun to see, and the ideal layers of clouds to give it intensity and "God-rays" and reflections off the water.

Some of my favorites:

- West Beach, especially if you want people. In particular, West Point at West Beach, near the old searchlight base or the rocks just east of there.

- Hoypus Point, at March 21 or September 21, when the sun sets under the bridge as seen from halfway down the old roadway toward Hoypus Point. There will be a crowd of photographers there on those days if the sun is shining.
- North Beach near the equinoxes or late summer. The glow of the driftwood, the curve of the beach, and the sun framed perfectly give it the wow factor.
- Rosario at any time, whether you get the curve of the beach from the north boundary area, or the view from the head looking in any direction.
- Bowman Bay, with different kinds of sunsets depending on the time of year. The equinoxes puts the sun through the gap above the tombolo at Rosario.

- Goose Rock
- East Cranberry with the dock in the foreground.
- The bridge, of course. Get creative, avoid cliches, but even the classic shots are classic because they are beautiful. You can't miss.
- Lighthouse Point, any time of year. The trees make great frames.
- Kiket, especially near the equinoxes.

Best Place to Watch a Sunrise

Although a little colder than watching a sunset, it's also a lot less competition, with few people up early enough to see and care about finding a great sunrise.

Some of my favorite places:

- East end of Pass Island (see page 188)
- West end of North Beach, looking back toward the bridge (see page 20)
- Hoypus Point
- Goose Rock
- The bridge, of course. Depending on the season, there are some great views to the southeast of winter sunrises from the Canoe Pass areas, and to the northeast of summer sunrises from the main span.
- South side of Lighthouse Point looking back toward the bridge, except in spring or summer.

Best Place to Find Quiet

There are only a few places in the park that I have found where highway noise is almost non-existent. An occasional motorcycle or loud powerboat may intrude, and certainly aircraft may fly over at any time, but for quiet (and solitude, a natural byproduct) these places stand out:

- Hoypus Hill's back side, facing toward the east. Here you will find old growth forest, a long distance to the highway, and far from the maddening crowds.
- Heilman (aka Naked Man) Valley, between Pass Lake and Ginnett Hill. You can actually hear the noise turn off as you drop into the valley from Pass Lake.
- Kiket Island's southwest side.
- Hope and Skagit Islands too, and Deception Island and Northwest Island west of the pass.
- West Beach (yes, West Beach) when the wind is out of the west and it is winter. Or go into the dunes in summer, unless the jets are flying.
- West side of Rosario Head.
- Ginnett Hill, unless the neighbor's dog is acting up. The rest of Ginnett is pretty good too.
- Dugualla State Park, pretty much anywhere.

Best Place to Go for a Hike

There is no <u>best</u> place, of course, but there are a bunch of great options. These are my personal favorites.

- Lighthouse Point: Classic, fun, adventurous, great views, great sunsets and sunrises, interesting side routes.
- Pass Lake to the North Boundary (Tursi Trail): One of the least visited trails in all of Deception Pass, and one of the most magnificent if you don't need a view of saltwater.
- Bowman to Rosario Head: A wonderful stroll through madrone along the south facing slopes above Bowman, then the dramatic finish at Rosario Head.

- Rosario Head: short and sweet! The view from the top is unmatched, with a nearly 270 degree sweep of water all around you. (See photo above)
- Kiket Island: see Kiket Island's description. One of my newest favorites now.
- Hope Island: you need a boat, but hiking from the north bay to the south shore brings spectacular views when you get to the meadows.
- Dunes Trail: simple, short, and paved. And a world apart from the hustle and hubbub of the rest of West Beach. I like going backwards, south on the lakeshore, north through the foredunes. The interpretive signs are an added bonus.
- Goose Rock: I like every angle of this hike. To make a round trip back to a car, it's easiest from the bridge, but most interesting to me by parking at the park office and hiking up the south side, down the north side, and then either all the way around the perimeter trail, or down the west side and back south again. The south side is steep but with great views as you climb. Also fun at midnight with a full moon. Be sure to visit both summits.
- Dugualla Loop with the beach side trip, which makes for a hike of several miles and great variety.

Best Place to Hike with Young Children

Children are such a blessing. They get us to slow down, look at details we may otherwise miss, and see things from the ground level instead of from five or six feet up in the air. Although wee ones have short legs and short attention spans, they can add to your experience at the park with adventures designed for them.

Whatever hike you take with your little ones, make sure it provides fun and relaxation. They need praise, patience, and playfulness, as outdoor writer Maureen Keilty describes it. Keep it interesting with variety and fun. Here are some suggestions:

- Bowman Bay to Lottie Beach: just carry them over the steep headland portion if you need to, or go at low tide and walk the beach. Two of my grandchildren have loved this hike at the ages of 1 and 3. The pier is a memorable bonus of adventure. The playground at the end (don't start with it) puts the day over the top.
- West Beach: It's a beach. Add a child and your job is done. Play in the sand, throw rocks, chase waves, have a picnic, swim or wade at the swimming hole, dig holes, make sandcastles.
- Rosario: skip rocks into the bay, make a small fort in the logs, check out the tidepools, and finish by coloring or reading a book in the Field Classroom. Extra points if you can hike to the top of Rosario Head, but extra caution as well to keep everyone safely away from the edge of the bluff.

Best Place to Take a Photo

Great photography is a matter of the placement of your feet: be in the right place at the right time. The problem may be though that you have limited time, and the time you are here is the only chance you have.

This is a scenic park. Exceptional photographs can be made just about anywhere. You can find old growth, meadows, rocks, people, the bridge, boats, wildlife -- the list is endless and delightful.

However, there are a few places that offer classy stock photos that can't miss if conditions are right. Even these places need the right lighting, effects, and quality of composition and technical skills, but if you have these it's hard to miss.

- North of the bridge, about a hundred yards west of the bridge entrance. Choose the right lighting, either at noonish when the fog is partially obscuring the bridge, or the evening a month or two before or after the solstice when the sun turns the bridge golden.
- East end of Pass Island: sunrises are spectacular here with good framing

- East end of North Beach: I like the sweep of beach to the west in the evening sunset March through September, or a moonset on occasion. Also the view of the bridge from the beach is classic.
- West end of North Beach: capture the sunrise over the Cascades through the bridge. Or capture any of the views along the beach.
- Lottie Point: classic view up to the bridge, especially with foggy or sunset conditions. Go to the far east side.
- Lighthouse Point: this is one place you can't miss, at almost any time of the day, somehow, somewhere, anywhere on the point.
- Bowman Pier: such great opportunities. Look for them
- Rosario: again, hard to miss here.
- West Point: Great for storms, people, wildlife, beaches, the lake.
- East Cranberry: great shots of the lake at sunset, or along the lakeshore in the morning
- Hoypus Point: Walk a quarter mile along the road/trail from the gate to see a full-on perspective of the bridge without having to get in a boat.
- Kiket Island: both tombolos offer great views.

Insider: Sun Under the Bridge

If you are here during one of the equinoxes, around March 21 or September 21, find time to get to the Hoypus Point trail. Walk down a quarter mile to the first bench, and you will be able to watch the sun set directly beneath the bridge.

If the sun is out at all, you will not be alone to capture that view. I have seen over fifty people with their cameras on tripods waiting for that perfect frame.

Itineraries
for those with limited time:

If you only have a limited handful of minutes to explore the park, what should you experience? I will give you some suggestions, although these are purely subjective. But so is everything else in the guidebook, so use the suggestions or make your own plans as you wish.

Just 10 minutes:
Stop at the north end of the bridge, about 100 yards before you get to the bridge. Then stop at Pass Island and walk out onto the overlook. Time's up.

A half hour:
Drive across the bridge, then head to Rosario. Park in the parking lot, walk to the Maiden, then to the top of the bluff.

An hour:
Go to Rosario as above, then the bridge as for the 10 minute stop, then drive through the old growth forest on your way down to North Beach and hike to the shelter area at North Beach. Look back up at the bridge, across to Lighthouse Point, and west to the Strait. Your time is up.

Two hours:
All of the above, then a visit to West Beach and a hike out to the point, then down and around the Dunes Trail.

Or go to Bowman Bay and hike out to Lighthouse Point. It doesn't take two hours to make the hike (I have run out to the point in just a handful of minutes during one rescue), but if you enjoy it as much as I do, the two hours won't be enough.

Four hours:
All of the above, and then a choice between either taking the Deception Pass Tours boat for the one hour tour under the bridge and out into the strait, or a one and a half hour tour in a kayak out of Bowman Bay. Either way, you will see the park from a different perspective. Or a third option, hike to the top of Goose Rock. Or drive out to Kiket and hike out to the point. Or tour the CCC interpretive center at Bowman and hike out onto the pier. Or hike out to Lighthouse Point. I just gave you six options for the last couple hours. I don't know which one I would do, honestly. You need more time.

A one night stay:
Okay, now you can do at least two or maybe even three of the options listed above, plus you get to enjoy s'mores around a campfire, catch a sunset from the bridge, walk the beach late at night, go fishing or crabbing or birdwatching or look for beavers in the early dawn and still have time for a great breakfast and another option or two.

Two nights:
Now you have time to choose nearly all of the options above, plus check out Dugualla's trails and beaches, or hike to Ginnett beyond Pass Lake, or explore the quiet solitude of old growth at Hoypus, or take a bike ride down to Hoypus Point, or a kayak trip out to Hope or Skagit. That might be a good choice for the second night -- spend it on an island. Or in the cabin at Ben Ure.

After ten years, I have done all of these and more, and I still find myself struggling to choose which opportunity I am going to take advantage of today, because I enjoy them all, in different seasons, in different weather, with different people or alone.

Each experience is never the same, and each person who experiences the park is never the same again either.

Park Stats

Size:
Over six square miles, about half on each side of the bridge

Shoreline miles:
about 17 linear miles

Highest Point
Ginnett Hill at 709 feet. At only 484 feet, Goose Rock is the fourth highest hill in the park, but the highest in the park on the Whidbey side.

Campsites:
329 total

- Quarry Pond 62 sites total
    5 cabins, 49 utility sites, 7 standard sites, one hiker/biker site
- Cranberry Campground: 235 sites total
    146 standard sites, 84 utility sites, 5 hiker/biker sites
- Bowman Campground: 20 sites total
    18 standard sites, 2 utility sites
- Bowman Bay Cascadia Marine Trail site: 1 site
- Skagit Island Cascadia Marine Trail sites: 5 sites
- Skagit Island: 1 non-designated site (open to all)
- Hope Island: 5 boat-in campsites

Volunteer hours
- 11,000 hours in 2015

Islands:
8 islands, plus a small portion of two others
- Northwest Island
- Deception Island
- Pass Island
- Strawberry Island
- Ben Ure Island (80% is park-owned)
- Kiket Island
- Skagit Island
- Hope Island
- Northern end of Whidbey Island
- Southwest end of Fidalgo Island

Staff:
15 permanent staff, of whom 13 are year round:
- 1 manager
- 6 rangers full time
- 1 ranger, seasonal
- 4 maintenance staff
- 1 office assistant
- 1 senior park aide, year round services
- 1 senior park aide, half time, booth operations
- AmeriCorps interpretive staff: 1 or 2, less than year round, no guarantee year to year
- Summer aide staff: 11

Annual Operating Budget
About $1.6 million this year

Annual Revenue
About $2.3 million, probably more next year.

Attendance
2.7 million in 2014
2.6 million in 2015

Awards

King 5/ Evening Magazine, 2016:
Best place to watch a sunset–FIRST PLACE
Best roadside attraction–FIRST PLACE
Best State Park–FIRST PLACE
Best Campground–FIRST PLACE
Best Ranger–FIRST PLACE (Jim Aggergaard)

TripAdvisor: Certificate of Excellence

Best of Whidbey: Numerous annual awards

Yelp: 4.5 stars

Emergency Help

For any emergency, or illegal behavior such as rowdy campsites next door, someone dropping rocks off the bridge, etc. **Call 911**

Park Entrance Station (primarily April through September) 360-675-2417

Park Office 360-675-3767

On-duty Ranger: 360-914-0118

AEDs: one is at the entrance station, and one is with the on-duty ranger.

Island Hospital, Anacortes
Follow Highway 20 to Anacortes onto Commercial Avenue. Turn left on 24th, go one block.
360-299-1300

Emergency Department
Follow Highway 20 to Anacortes onto Commercial Avenue. Turn left on 26th, go one block.
360-299-1311

How to connect with park staff

In an emergency, or if the campsite next door is loud at midnight, or you got stuck behind a locked gate or you are on a trail and you have no idea which way to go, call 911.

For less than emergency conditions, such as needing a jump or shower tokens or a breaker reset, here are some ways to get our attention:

360-675-2417 rings at our entrance station, which is staffed from about 9 to 9 during the busiest season, 9 - 5 during shoulder seasons, and only 9 - 11 a.m. in the off-season. Someone might not answer there if he or she is already busy with customers at the station.

If so, the phone will ring at the administrative office across the highway. We are not at that building with any predictable hours, as we use that building for paperwork and meetings. Someone is there maybe 50% of the day. Or you can call the office directly at any time and leave a message. The number is 360-675-3767. Extension 21 goes to the ranger desk, 23 to the assistant manager, 25 to the maintenance office, 26 to the manager, 27 to the administrative lead, and 31 to the park interpreter.

The ranger on duty carries a cell phone, which we call the Duty Phone, which you can call if you need basic assistance such as a jump start or assistance with a faulty toilet or a registration issue. Call 360-914-0118. Sometimes the ranger is on a loud mower or away from the park so leave a message if no one answers.

Email works for less than immediate needs. Email us at deception.pass@parks.wa.gov.

To find us in person, you can try at the entrance station, or the administrative office, or the maintenance shop at the intersection where you can go either to North Beach or West Beach.

Park staff have six square miles to cover, with over 320 campsites and eight islands, so it's usually easier to call than trying to drive around to find us. We want to be visible all the time, but it's a big park and there are not a lot of us around here.

We are here to help you, and care for this park.

Nearby services

- Laundry: Oak Harbor and Anacortes, 9 miles either way.
- Souvenirs, shirts, maps, mugs: at the welcome station at the park entrance, at the booth at the bridge during the busy months, and at the campground entrance store when it is open.
- Gasoline: Soundview Shopper, one mile south, or Harold's Market, two miles north.
- Firewood: in the park! Visit the store at the entrance to the Cranberry Campground, or go to the Welcome Station at the East Cranberry entrance.
- Fishing licenses: Ace Hardware stores in Oak Harbor and Anacortes.
- Groceries: Soundview Shopper and Harold's Market have the basics; Anacortes and Oak Harbor have large chain grocery stores.
- Hardware: Anacortes has an Ace and a Sebo's; Oak Harbor has an Ace and a Home Depot.
- RV repairs: minor repairs are available in Anacortes and Oak Harbor; both have Les Schwab service centers and major auto parts stores, along with minor repair facilities. Full RV service is available in Burlington.

Other Nearby Parks to Visit

- Sharpe Park, north of Rosario: A gentle trail past a quiet reed-filled lake, then left to dramatic mossy bluffs high above Rosario Strait, or right to more headlands and views.
- Mt. Erie, north of Deception Pass: A road lets you drive up to the top for some awesome views from the highest point of Fidalgo Island, especially south over Lake Campbell, the many islands of the park, Whidbey Island, and Mt. Rainier and the Olympics beyond.

The view south from the top of Mt. Erie, 1200 feet high, looking over Lake Campbell in the foreground, Kiket, Skagit, and Hope Islands on the left, and the dark woods of Hoypus Point and Hoypus Hill on the right.

- Washington Park, Anacortes: an amazing feature in the city of Anacortes, with a three mile one-way loop road leading to tree-framed meadows and beaches facing north, then west, then south. Trails meander through the forests, campsites nestle among the trees. And the road doesn't open to cars until 10, allowing early-rising joggers and hikers to enjoy this gem with the wildlife.
- Cap Sante: the large headland overlooking the waterfront of Anacortes. Great views of the town and the islands to the east.
- Tommy Thompson Trail, Anacortes: Connecting downtown Anacortes with the March Point area, this former railroad trestle is now for hikers, bikers, and strollers. It crosses Fidalgo Bay, providing a perspective that is always a pleasure to experience.
- Ebey's Landing, near Coupeville: The drama of the interplay of bluffs, beaches, and views is indescribable. It must be experienced. Hike north on the bluff, then down to Peregos Lagoon and back along the beach.
- Fort Ebey, near Coupeville: Preserved because of the military bunkers, but a must-see because of the huge meadow sloping gently down toward the Strait of Juan de Fuca with views north, west, and south.
- Fort Casey, near Coupeville: Forts, views, kite flying, a lighthouse, and beaches. And more.
- Padilla Bay Interpretive Center, north of Bay View: Well-designed interpretive stories about the natural riches of the Padilla Bay estuary.

Other Notable Local Sites

- Snow Goose Produce, on the Conway/Best Road shortcut (humongous ice cream cones, natural goods and produce)
- Christianson's Nursery, Best Road (large size, good people)
- The Bread Farm, Edison (north of Bay View): great natural bread products, cash only
- Skagit Valley Food Co-op:(downtown Mt. Vernon): the area's best selection of natural foods and products

Local Theaters

- Anacortes Cinema, Anacortes
- Blue Moon Drive-in, Oak Harbor (yes, a drive-in!)
- Oak Harbor Theater, Oak Harbor
- Lincoln Theater, Mount Vernon (eclectic, old style)
- Cascade Mall Theaters, Burlington
- Pickford Theater, Bellingham

Good Eats

- Frida's, Anacortes (quality Mexican)
- Gere-a-Deli, Anacortes (quality sandwiches)
- Majestic Inn, Anacortes (quality, period)
- Thai Season, Anacortes
- Anthony's, Anacortes (large chain, but they do a great job, right on the waterfront)
- Sweet Rice Thai, Oak Harbor
- Christopher's, Coupeville
- Fraser's Gourmet Hideaway, Oak Harbor
- Il Granaio, Mt. Vernon (authentic Italian)

Nearby Public Golf courses

- Swinomish Links, Anacortes: plain and open but well maintained and friendly
- Gallery Golf Course, Oak Harbor: military course with rolling tree lined fairways and great views of the Strait of Juan de Fuca
- Whidbey Golf and Country Club, Oak Harbor
- Avalon, Burlington: 27 holes, firm greens, native tree lined fairways

Viggo Mortensen rests while waiting to shoot a scene at Rosario in the movie "Captain Fantastic".

In the Movies

It's no wonder that movie producers take advantage of the scenic attractions of the park for dramatic movies.

The Postman, filmed in 1997, used the tombolo at Rosario for the final scene. Starring Kevin Costner, this post-apocalyptic movie was not well received. Perhaps it is because they covered Kokwalalwoot to shoot the scene.

The Prodigal, a 1983 Billy Graham evangelical movie, starts with a pretend campsite scene near West Beach, and shows aerial footage of Fidalgo Island before heading down to the Seattle area. Hope Lange, John Hammond, and Joey Travolta have roles in the film.

The Ring (2002) a horror movie with images of the bridge. I'm not into horror. Stars Naomi Watts.

Captain Fantastic, released in 2016, directed by Matt Ross, starring Viggo Mortensen among others. Viggo's red suit and pants make a stunning visual outdone only by the beauty of Rosario Head and a large funeral pyre for the scene near the end of the movie. That was a long, hot, gorgeous day. It's about a dad raising and homeschooling a family of six kids, and it's about being honest, true, and dedicated to what you believe. I loved it.

Commercials

Several commercials have been filmed here, usually four or five a year. You can google Deception Pass advertisements and get some interesting results.
Some of the memorable examples:

Pemco: The insurance company created several humorous outdoor scenarios at West Beach to show that us folks in the northwest are just a little bit different.

Reebok: Two men bungie jump off the north span of the bridge. If you haven't seen it, I don't want to spoil how it ends, but the company ended the use of the advertisement shortly after it aired because of the uproar of complaints about it. You can still find it on Youtube.

Carhartt: In 2014 we shot several scenes in the park, including the bridge, the Forest Loop, and West Beach. Maintenance worker Marvin Wold gets a cameo up in a tree; the oil drilling scene is actually at West Beach after sunset in the winter.

Car advertisements: probably the most common item advertised here, along with clothing. Many of the shots have been popular. My favorite is a man taking his dog for a drive; the views include Cranberry Lake and the bridge.

The camera-carrying car on the left is filming the moving car on the right as they drive north across the main span of the bridge for a car advertisement.

Some **historical videos** of the bridge can be found at these two websites. The first focuses on the bridge itself shortly after its opening; the second talks about Whidbey Island, showing the bridge and a special shot of East Cranberry lake before moving on elsewhere:

http://www.washingtonruralheritage.org/cdm/singleitem/collection/whidbey/id/231/rec/4

http://www.washingtonruralheritage.org/cdm/singleitem/collection/whidbey/id/233/rec/14

For an outstanding **video about Kokwalalwoot** produced by Don Hedstrom in cooperation with the Samish Indian Nation, visit this site. This one is superb.

https://www.youtube.com/watch?v=760xf-dCrGc&index=4&list=UUApzGqYC2uOpKKx8WNXU1dQ

Suggested References

Publications

Cascadia Marine Trail Guidebook, by Washington Water Trails Association, 2007, 152 pp.

Christmas Clams by Ray Mitchell, 2012, edited by Todd Mitchell, Honeybee Press

Current e-newsletter, distributed monthly, describing what is happening at the park and other related information. Subscribe for free by sending an email to jack.hartt@parks.wa.gov

A Day in the Park with Ranger Jack, by Susannah Hartt. 2013. A children's book illustrating the typical work of a park ranger at Deception Pass State Park. 28 pp.

The Exploration of Whidbey, Fidalgo and Guemes Islands and the Origin of Fidalgo and Guemes Island Place Names, compiled by Terry Slotemaker, 2002, 35 pp, Anacortes Museum

The Geology of Fidalgo Island, by Terry Slotemaker, 2007 and 2010, 52 pp., Anacortes Museum

A Geomorphic Classification of Puget Sound Nearshore Landforms, by Hugh Shipman, 2008, 42 pp, US Army Corps of Engineers Seattle District

The Geomorphology of Puget Sound Beaches, by David Finlayson, 2006, 55 pp, University of Washington

Getting to the Water's Edge, by Pedersen, Schmidt and Neumiller, 166 pp, 2006, WSU Extension Office Island County

A History of Washington State Parks: 1913 - 1988 1988, Washington State Parks and Recreation Commission, 184 pp

101 Things to Do on Whidbey Island, by Deb Crager, 2011, 218 pp., Rockwater Press

Kukutali by Theresa Trebon, 2013, 56 pp

Land Use, Environment, and Social Change: The shaping of Island County, Washington, Richard White, 1980, 1992; 234 pp., University of Washington Press

The Maiden of Deception Pass - A Spirit In Cedar, by Ken Hansen, 1983, 22 pp, Samish Experience Productions

Long Journey to the Rose Garden by John Tursi, 1989, 198 pp, Fidalgo Bay Publishing

Natural Grace: The Charm, Wonder, & Lessons of Pacific Northwest Animals and Plants, by William DIetrich. 2003. 236 pp. University of Washington Press

The Natural History of Puget Sound Country, by Arthur Kruckerberg, 1991, 470 pp, University of Washington Press

Natural Skagit: A journey from mountains to sea, Skagit Land Trust, 2008, 126 pp., Premier Graphics

Northwest Trees, by Stephen Arno and Ramona Hammerly, 1977, 160 pp, The Mountaineers

Our Ways: Testimonies of the Swinomish Way of Life, Mitchell and Lekanof, Honeybee Press

Pig War Islands, by David Richardson, 1971, Eastsound: Orcas Publishing Company

Plants and Animals of the Pacific Northwest, by Eugene Kozloff, 1976, 264 pp, University of Washington Press

Seashore Life, by Eugene N. Kozloff. 1973. 282 pp. University of Washington Press

The Sibley Guide to Birds, by David Sibley, 2000, 544 pp, Knopf

The Swinomish Totem Pole: Tribal Legends, by Sampson and Whitney, 1938 and 2011, 56 pp, Union Printing Co.

Thirteen Moons, by J. Michael Thoms and others, Swinomish Indian Tribal Community

Two Hands and a Shovel, by Jack Hartt and Sam Wotipka, 2013. An illustrated exploration of the work of the Civilian Conservation Corps at Deception Pass State Park. 330pp. Hundreds of black and white photographs from the 1930s era as many of the park's features were being developed by the CCC.

A Walk at Bowman Bay, by Jack Hartt, 2015. A children's book following a little girl and her family as they explore the trails and beaches at Bowman.

The Washington State Park Story, by Ruth E. Pike. College class manuscript, about 1956. 16 pp

Whelks to Whales, by Rick Harbo, 1999, 245 pp, Harbour Publishing

Whidbey Island: Reflections on People and Land, by Guss, O'Mahoney, and Richardson. 2014. 196 pp. History Press

Web sites:

The Deception Pass Park Foundation has a comprehensive site for park information, maps, descriptions, activities, volunteer opportunities, and more.
www.deceptionpassfoundation.org

On Facebook: Deception Pass Park Foundation. Posts about Foundation activities, volunteer projects, educational opportunities. "Like" us!

Also on Facebook: Deception Pass Park. Posts about the park itself, wildlife, changes, adventures.

Washington State Parks' official webpages for Deception Pass: **parks.state**.wa.us/497/**Deception-Pass** or www.parks.wa.gov/411/Deception-Pass-State-Park

Kukutali Preserve:
http://www.swinomish.org/resources/environmental-protection/kukutali-preserve.aspx

"The shortest distance to far away." The local tourism group has excellent information about the Island County area in general. Go to www.whidbeycamanoislands.com/todo/deceptionpass

Washington Trails Association: reviews of hikes at www.wta.org

Information about Coast Salish tribes at http://coastsalishmap.org/start_page.htm

Samish Indian Nation
www.samishtribe.nsn.us

Swinomish Indian Tribal Community
www.swinomish.org

Geology of the Pacific Northwest
http://commons.wvc.edu/rdawes/PNWindex.html

Geological maps of the state of Washington that allows you to zoom in and interact on specific parcels in detail:
https://fortress.wa.gov/dnr/protectionis/geology/

Naval Air Station Whidbey Island (NASWI)
https://www.facebook.com/NASWhidbeyIsland?fref=ts

Fidalgo Island blog
wildfidalgo.blogspot.com
One of my favorites for the local area, blogger Dave Wenning combines excellent photography and frequent insights into the life and stories of the park and Fidalgo Island area.

Practical wildlife information:
Wdfw.wa.gov/living

Whidbey Audubon Society
www.whidbeyaudubon.org

Another Rewarding Video

The documentary "**The Maiden of Deception Pass: Guardian of Her Samish People**" tells the story of Kokwalalwoot and how tribal history continues to inspire generations of Samish people.

The movie debuted on Earth Day in 2016. It runs about 30 minutes long, delving into the traditions of the Samish people, the struggles they faced with recognition and assimilation, and the new life of the past couple of decades, a life witnessed and perhaps assisted by the story pole at Rosario.

Tribal chair Tom Wooten said that the carving helped bring together the tribe when it was put up more than 30 years ago, and now he hopes telling its story again will achieve the same thing.

"I hope it lets people know who we really are and that we are still here," Wooten said.

Find it at the Samish Indian Nation headquarters offices.

About Washington State Parks

The people of Washington State have always been leaders in the parks and recreation movements of the nation. Less than twenty five years after becoming a state, Washington had already created a state park system, three years before the national park system.

The legislature created the State Board of Park Commissioners in 1913, before we even had any state parks. Two years later, the first two parks had been accepted. By 1922 there were seven, including Deception Pass. The Board was now called the State Parks Committee.

Park acquisition was a diverse and unpredictable activity. Sometimes parcels were acquired from the federal government, as in old forts or military reservations, or from gifts of individuals or even towns or counties, such as Osoyoos or Twin Harbors. Some were set aside by the State Land Commissioner, some from logging companies, some from power companies or tax delinquent properties.

And some park lands were purchased, some at reduced prices due to the generosity of owners, some at full price.

The Civilian Conservation Corps created many of the iconic park facilities that we know and love today, such as the shelters at Deception Pass, the tower at Moran, the Vista House at Mount Spokane, and the Swinging Bridge over the Spokane River in Riverside State Park. These developments spurred further use and interest in our park system.

In 1947 another name change reflected a new management approach when the legislature and governor created the Washington State Parks and Recreation Commission, the name by which the agency is still known today. (It is not a 'parks department'; the director is appointed by the Commission, not the governor, who appoints department directors.)

Now the oversight of the agency was in the hands of governor-appointed volunteers from around the state.

Funding has always been a challenge for the Commission. Funding had come from driver's license fees in the earliest years, but usually from general fund tax dollars.

A series of statewide bonds in the 1960s and 1970s, supported by large majorities, provided boosts in park acquisition monies and park development funding.

Although State Parks has never enjoyed the stable or adequate funding of more prominent agencies, they have always gotten by. Unfortunately, this often meant not being able to maintain facilities for the long term, as adequate maintenance of aging infrastructure and buildings takes large investments of capital and staffing.

The legislature authorized a parking fee in 2003 designed to meet these maintenance backlog needs. Many such needs were addressed, but public sentiment against paying for access to park lands took the fee away in 2006.

The system was in for an even bigger shock during the recession of 2009, which eventually led to the loss of 90% of the general tax fund support the agency had been receiving. With such a drastic cut in funding, the legislature created the Discover Pass in 2011 as a user-fee to provide alternative funding for parks.

The Discover Pass has been generally accepted as a reasonable approach, especially since State Parks receives

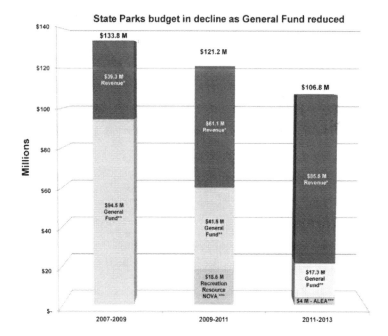

Overall funding for State Parks has dropped, as this graph shows. More specifically, tax support has dropped precipitously, as shown by the light gray portion of each column above. The darker portion indicates how much of the park budget must be raised through fees. Illustration courtesy of Washington State Parks.

very little general fund taxes for our parks. Users of the parks pay for nearly all park operations, through either the Discover Pass, or camping fees, or other field-based revenue.

Reduced staffing has led to reduced services and a much greater dependence on volunteers and donations for basic operations.

In spite of these challenges, the Washington State Parks and Recreation Commission continues to be recognized as one of the best systems in the entire nation, with some of the most treasured parks and recreation areas, some of the highest per capita use, one of the lowest costs to operate per citizen or per visitor, and with vocal support by the state's communities for all of the parks.

The system is loved and beloved, as attested to by the continuing growth in attendance and active support for parks throughout the state across the spectrum of politics.

State Park Budgeting 101

State Parks has several budgets to help it provide the lands, development, and services that make for a well-rounded state park system.

Several funds are appropriated specifically for land acquisition. These funds, including the Washington Wildlife and Recreation Program, provide funding for acquisition of lands only. These funds cannot be used for park operations or maintenance, as they come from a budget designed to protect appropriate lands around the state that are critical for recreational use or resource protection.

The legislature also creates a capital budget each year for developing capital facilities, usually structures, infrastructure, or grand-scale utility developments far beyond the limits of typical operating funds.

Parks also receive funding each year from grants, some of which are dedicated to State Parks and some of which face competition with other recreational agencies for limited funds. These grants may come from federal, state, non-profit, or other opportunities. Many of our recreational facilities, such as boat launches and beach restorations, have been funded through this process.

Our operating budget is separate from the above funding sources. The significant majority of our operational funding used to be from general taxes. Revenue from camping and other park fees went back into the general government funds to be distributed as needed throughout state government.

After the recession of 2011, tax-based funding for State Parks steeply declined, from nearly 90% of the budget down to about 15%. The legislature directed State Parks to work toward becoming financially self sufficient.

While that is not feasible, this has led State Parks to be more proactive in pursuing a host of revenue-generating ideas beyond the Discover Pass, such as cell phone tower installations, business leases, variably priced campsites, park-operated camp stores, and increased public-private partnerships.

But at the heart, at the core of State Parks are the priceless places set aside for us all, protected for all time, reflecting our values and our connections with this good earth. The money is just details.

What is untouched is unloved. Touch these places forever with your adventurous spirits and understanding hearts. And let your feet dwell in the park as your beloved home.

Partial list of known Deception Pass State Park managers:

Rutherford, 1924
Al Ditmeyer - CCC era
Harry Buckley, Bowman Bay side, 1935
Harold Rauch
Chester Thomas
Vern Yoakum, 1944-1949
Johannes Christensen, 1949 to 1954
A. Vince Henry 1957 to 1961?
Harry Walker, late Fifties to mid-Sixties?
Bruce Hawley late Sixties to early Seventies
Wallace "Wally" Girton, early Seventies
Robert "Bob" Little, early to mid-Seventies
Howard Adams, mid-Seventies
Ralph Mast, mid-Seventies to 1983
William "Bill" Overby, 1983 to 2003
Jack Hartt, 2003 to

So here you are,

at the end of a journey with me exploring some of the life and depth of Deception Pass State Park.

Thank you for letting me join you for that journey. I hope you can help me make it better with your ideas, stories, and insights. And I hope your next visit to the park now has an added dimension of depth and understanding.

Thank you for joining me in this journey through time, this walk through the wealth of stories at the park, this simple peek at where we are, how we got here, and where we are going. Hy'shqa. I raise my hands to you.

Now it's your turn.

Make use of what you know, what you have learned, and what you have planned.

Go.

Get close to this park's wild heart. Share it with friends and family, or experience it in quiet solitude.

Explore.

And share your hopes for the future of the park, your birthday wishes for when it turns 100, and your ideas to make it even better in its second century.

Sign up for the **Current** newsletter to stay in touch with what is happening at the park. The monthly e-newsletter captures the trends for what is planned and the activities going on throughout the park. Stay current.

And do what you can to play your part in caring for this special place. Opportunities abound. Get involved. You know what you can do.

And I hope you say hello if you find me standing on a cold beach early in the morning to watch the sunrise, or resting in a sun-baked meadow on a winding trail, or catching the sunset from the tip of a rocky point, or paddling under the bridge with the water reflecting a sky filled with stars and dreams.

I hope to see you here.

About the Author

My life began in the Ballard area of Seattle, where I grew up looking out over Puget Sound from my bedroom window. I spent much of my school-age years exploring Seattle's beaches, sometimes when I was supposed to be in school.

I attended the University of Washington, receiving a Bachelor of Science degree in Forest Management, with a specialty in outdoor recreation. My senior thesis for the outdoor recreation program focused on Washington State Park's management of its shorelines. How ironic.

I spent summers working for the UW's Fisheries Research Institute in Alaska, as a volunteer leader for the Student Conservation Association at Mount Rainier, for the United States Forest Service in the Cascade Mountains, for the National Park Service at Rocky Mountain National Park in Colorado, and for Recreational Equipment, Incorporated (REI) in Seattle.

After graduation, I began a career with Washington State Parks that has allowed me to live and work as a ranger at Sun Lakes, Camano Island, Cape Disappointment (when it was called Fort Canby), Ocean City, Olmstead Place near Ellensburg, Fort Worden in Port Townsend, and as the manager at Riverside State Park in Spokane before coming to Deception Pass in 2003.

In this career I became the agency's first Master Instructor for law enforcement training and the first agency fitness instructor.

My wife and I also raised a family of six children, all of whom grew up living in parks. It has been a different kind of family life than most.

I enjoy being with family and friends, hiking, writing, flying, photography, basketball, golf, lilacs, music, hot weather, warm blackberry pie, and sunsets.

Photo of Jack Hartt by Vince Streano, *local professional photographer and good friend of the park.*

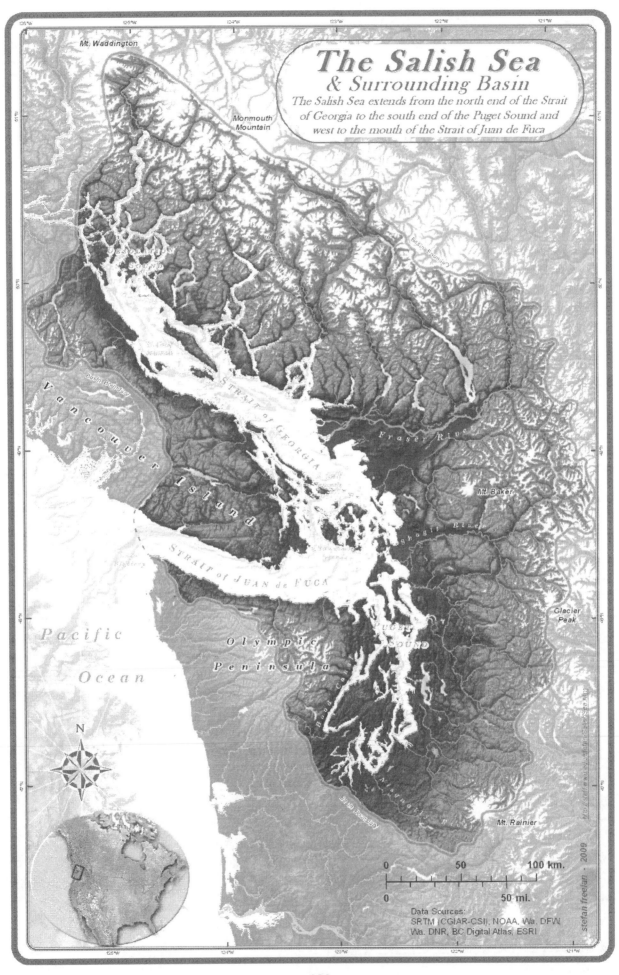

Maps

"Adventure is not in the guidebook, and beauty is not on the map. Seek and ye shall find."

— Terry Russell, *On the Loose*

Above: The overall map of the park layout, showing park lands in a darker shade. Map courtesy of OpenStreetMap.

Left: a beautiful representation of the entire Salish Sea, showing the entirety of the drainage basin feeding Puget Sound, the Strait of Georgia, and the Strait of Juan de Fuca. Deception Pass State Park lies almost at the center of the Salish Sea, at the north end of Whidbey Island. Illustration created and kindly shared by Stefan Freelan.

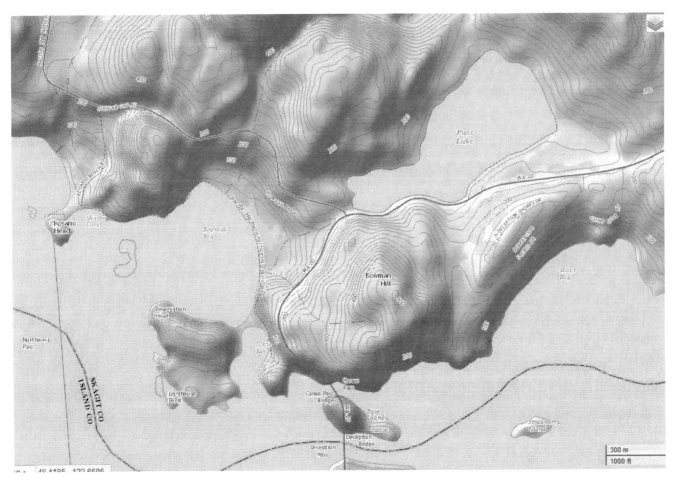
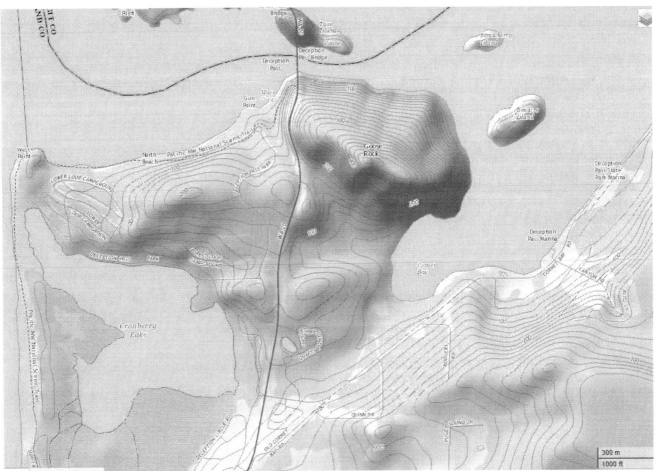

Opposite page, top: a topo map focusing on the northwest corner of the park, showing Rosario, Bowman Bay, Bowman Hill, and Pass Lake areas.

Opposite page, bottom: a topo map showing the southwest corner of the park, showing West Beach, North Beach, Cranberry Lake, Goose Rock, and Cornet Bay.

Below: A topo map of the Hoypus Point area, also showing Kiket, Skagit, and Hope Islands.

All three illustrations courtesy of OpenStreetMap.

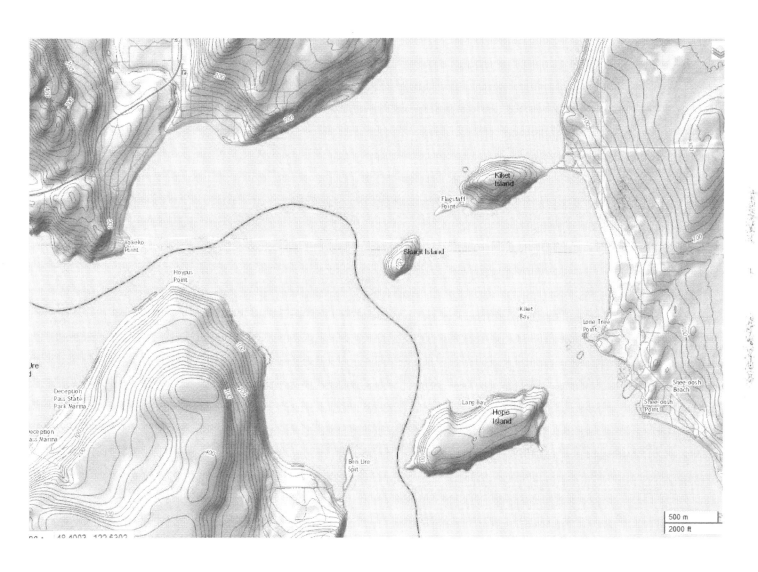

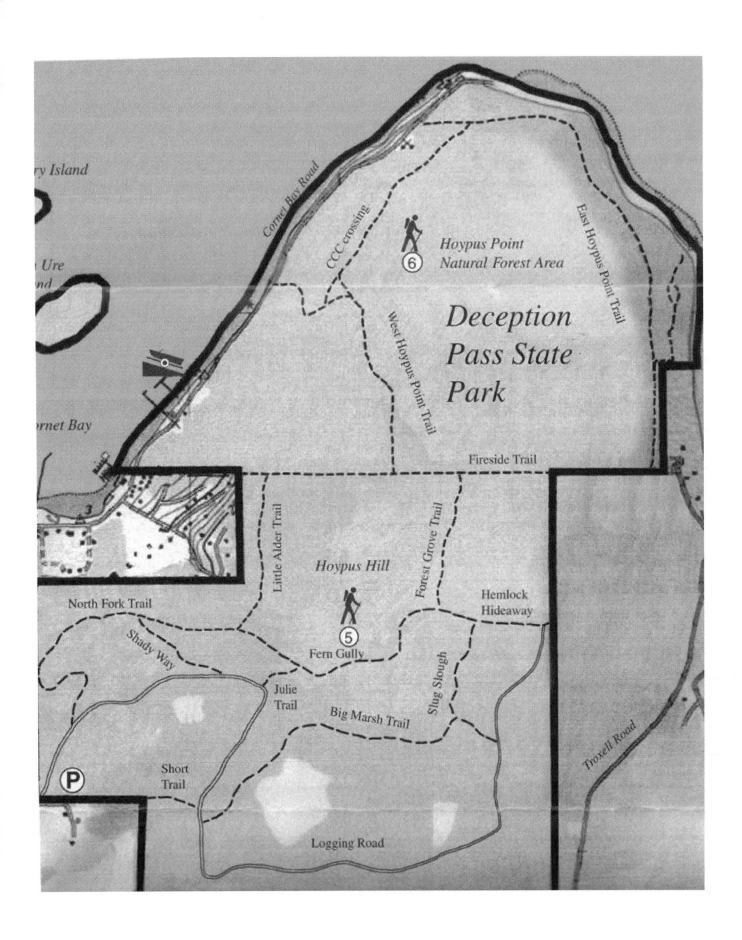

Left. part of an out of print park map showing the Hoypus area trails with their trail names. Since the map was made, we have acquired the land east of Hemlock Hideaway to allow the trails to connect with East Hoypus Point Trail to the northeast. Illustration created by Jim Bruner.

Below: Kukutali Preserve on Kiket Island has three main trails to explore. Future changes may include a trail from the parking lot to a lagoon overlook, and the possible removal of the eastern tombolo to make Kiket truly an island again, but still accessible by foot except at the highest of tides. Illustration courtesy of Washington State Parks and the Swinomish Indian Tribal Community.

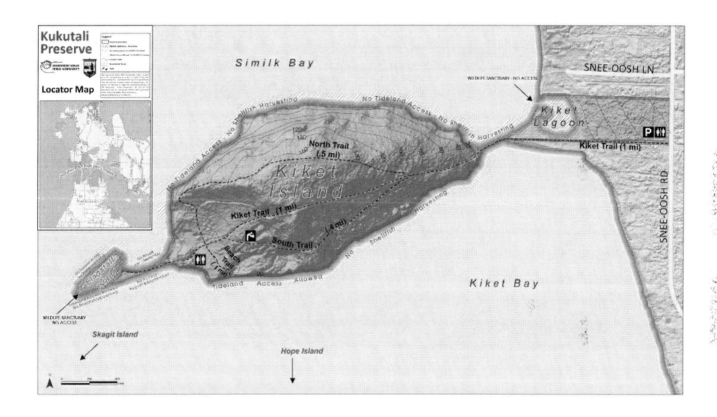

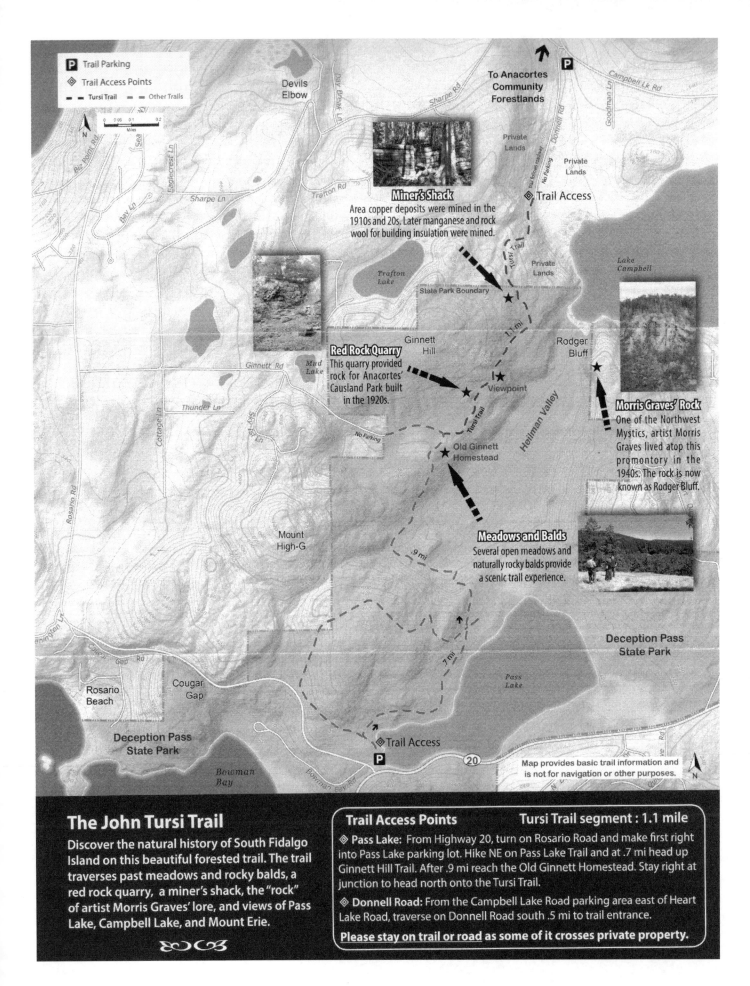

Left: The Skagit Land Trust publishes this map of the new John Tursi Trail, which connects the north boundary of Deception Pass State Park with the Anacortes Community Forest Lands to the north via a short county roadway. Illustration courtesy of the Skagit Land Trust. Contact the Land Trust for a free color copy.

Below: a drawing of the layout of the the prison camp on Bowman Hill, showing the quarry that was mined, the buildings where rock was crushed and then screened, the raft at the water's edge, and the sleeping quarters and wharf far to the east. The "future quarry" shown on the map was never mined. Little evidence now remains of the structures. Illustration courtesy of Washington State Parks archives.

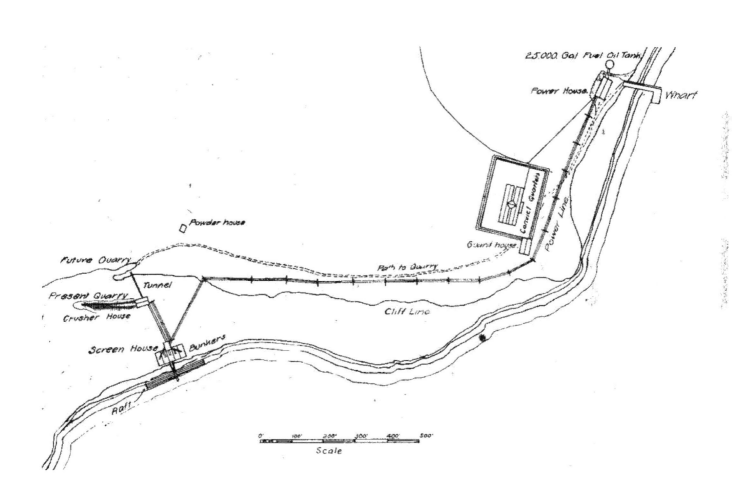

Right: the topography under the water in Cranberry Lake. The roadway follows the northern shore at the top of the map. The arrow points to the boat launch. Illustration courtesy of the State of Washington.

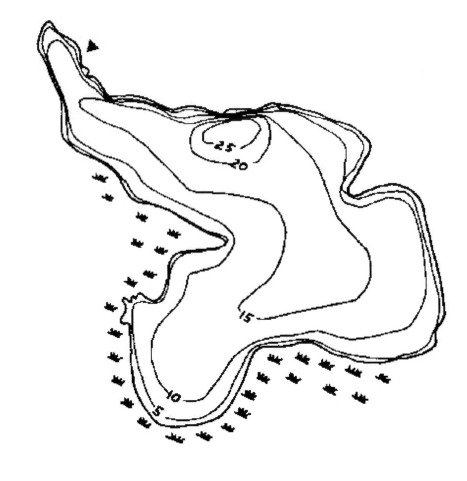

Right: the topography under the water in Pass Lake. The parking lot is at the far western edge of the lake. The arrow points to the boat launch. Illustration courtesy of the State of Washington.

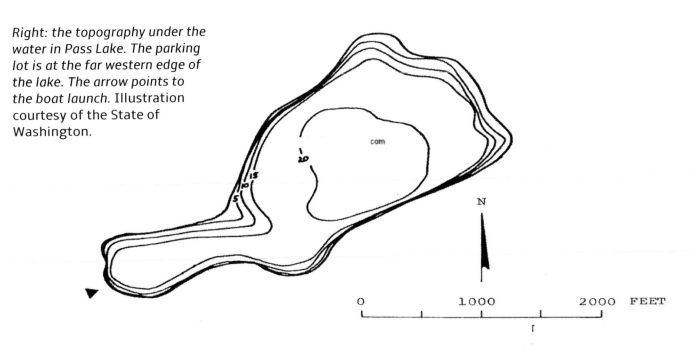

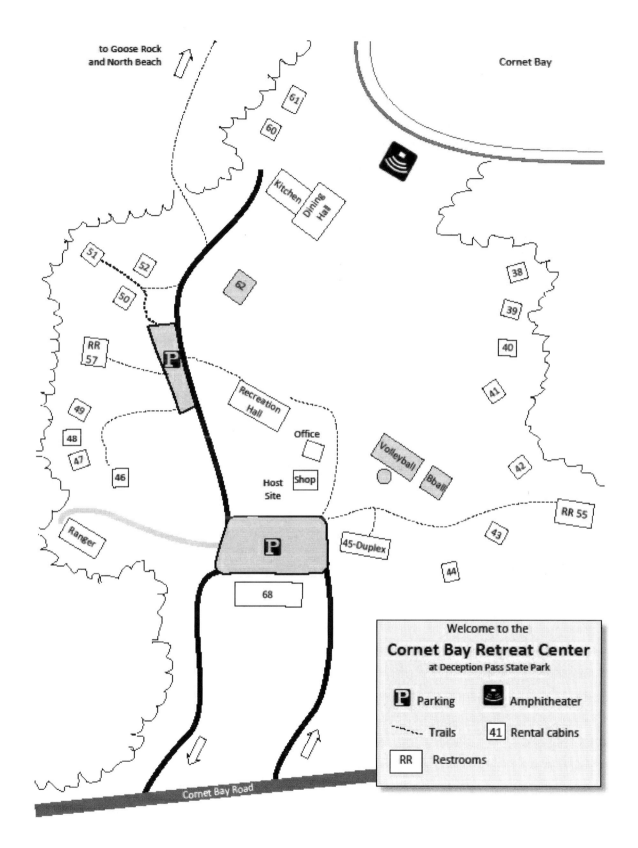

The Cornet Bay Retreat Center layout, showing the cabins, lodges, and other features of the camp.

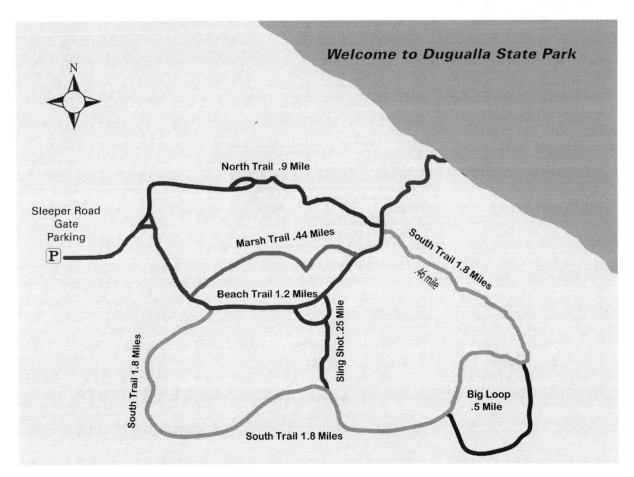

Two maps of the Dugualla State Park area, one showing the trails and mileages, the other showing the topography and trails. Above illustration courtesy of Island County Health Department. Illustration below courtesy of OpenStreetMaps.

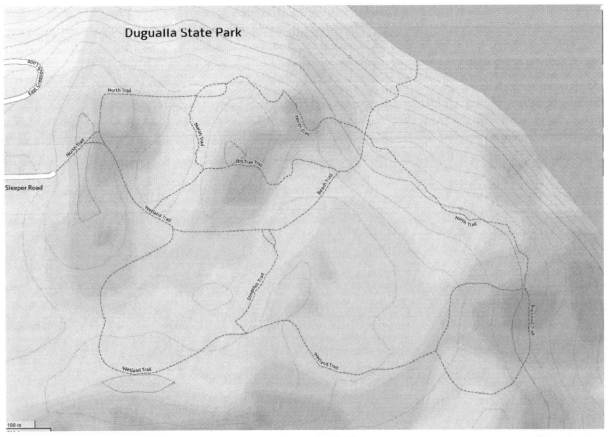

Photo locations not identified in text:

Page	Location in Park:	Page	Location in Park:
ii	North Beach	149	Kiket Island
x	Pass Lake - Bridge trail	150	Goose Rock
xiii	Lighthouse Point trail	156	Pass Island
xiv	Canoe Pass	163	Canoe Pass
0	Lighthouse Point trail	178	North Beach Road
4	North Beach	183	Bowman Bay from Rosario
4	Lighthouse Point trail	186	Bowman Bay from Lottie Beach
6	Pass Island	188	Pass Island looking east
12	Pass Lake area	190	East Cranberry Lake
40	Coyote: near Pass Lake	203	Cranberry Lake, northwest shore
40	deer: Kiket Island	204	North Beach
47	Sailing ship off Lighthouse Point	217	Little North Beach
116	Rosario toward Reservation Head	221	North Beach, west end
140	West Beach	222	Reservation Heat toward Rosario
147	Rosario	224	Rosario Head

Index

A

Abbey, Edward   121
Adams, Brian   xii
Admiralty Inlet   10, 47, 48
Aggergaard, Jim   xiii, 175, 195
Alaynick, Susan   xii, 33
alder   22, 24, 28, 64, 117, 120, 136, 138
Alderman, Allison   24
algae   20, 23, 32, 35, 94, 96, 124
Allmond, Doug   49, 63
Almy, Amos   xi
AmeriCorps   xi, 76, 157, 158, 159, 169, 170, 195
amphitheater   4, 10, 48, 66, 79, 81, 99, 104, 106, 110, 135, 146, 157, 168, 169, 171, 181, 191, 193
Anacortes   xii, 16, 49, 50, 51, 55, 58, 60, 67, 71, 81, 87, 97, 104, 117, 153, 173, 191, 196, 197
Anacortes Community Forest Lands   xii, 59, 118,
Anacortes History Museum   xii,
Anacortes Kayak Tours   112, 139, 167
Audrey Hartt   xiii, 114
Aydelotte, Captain John xiii

B

Bailey, Barbara   73
Bailey, Bill   xi
bald eagles   38, 116
balds   8, 25, 30, 43, 105, 140,
banana slugs   37
barnacles   20, 35, 71, 94, 132, 145
bats   35, 40
Bauer, Wolf   ix, xi
Beach Naturalists   17, 35, 43, 72, 145, 159, 169, 170
beach strawberry   21
bear   40, 165!
beaver   11, 40, 102, 157, 161, 194,
Ben Hartt   xii, 146
Ben Ure Island   11, 22, 23, 27, 33, 48, 50, 51, 74, 75, 81, 91, 92, 108, 110, 127, 139, 167, 191, 195
Ben Weiser   113
Bennett, Barbara   xii
Big Cedar Trail   117, 137, 138
bigleaf maple   22, 24, 27, 48, 71, 118, 120, 138
bioluminescence   42
blackberry   32, 205
blackberry   32, 205
Blank, Rick   xiii, 71, 122
Bligh, William   47
blue-green algae: see cyanobacteria
Blunk, Bob   xii, 172, 173
Bowman Bay   ix, xii, 2, 10, 11, 14, 17, 22, 23, 27, 28, 32,36, 37,38, 39, 40, 41, 45, 49, 53, 55, 59, 54, 55, 67, 68, 69, 71, 76, 78, 81, 92, 97, 98, 112-116, 125, 126, 128-132, 134, 135-137, 139-140, 143, 146, 148, 151-155, 160-161,167, 169, 171, 181, 183, 184, 185-191, 192, 194-195, 199, 202, 209
Bowman Bay Holiday   154, 169
Bowman Pier   182, 194
Bowman, Amos   49
Bowman, Dunnell   49
Brand, Jay   xiii
Broughton, William   47
Bryan Hartt   x, xiii
bull kelp   32
Burt, Candice   xiii

C

Camano Island   185, 205
camas   25, 30
canada geese   38, 96, 181
Canoe Pass   38, 50, 60, 61, 62, 110, 114, 136, 141, 153, 192
Captain James Cook   47
Captain Kellett   48
Carrasco   47, 81
Carson, Rachel   1
Cayou, Rosie   xi
CCC   see Civilian Conservation Corps
cedar   22, 24, 25, 28, 43, 45, 46, 64, 68, 72, 114, 117, 137, 138
Charlie Hartt   x, 78
chickaree   41
chitons   20, 35
Churchill, George   xii
Civil War   1, 48, 49
Civilian Conservation Corps   xi, 53, 55-61, 63, 65-66, 68-69, 72, 76, 78, 79, 81, 101, 102, 104, 112, 1115, 135-136, 143, 146, 160, 161, 169, 175, 180, 181, 183, 194
Cladoosby, Brian   xii, 76
clams   36, 107, 132, 187
Clark, Darlene   xiii, 172
climate change   97, 147, 181, 195
Coast Salish   1, 67, 200
Colombo, Rick   xi-xiii, 19, 173
Cornet Bay boat launch   2, 70, 73, 79, 81, 107, 168
Cornet Bay Retreat Center   2, 15, 30, 38, 40, 55, 66, 70, 78, 79, 81, 90-92, 97, 98, 105-106, 135, 139, 143, 146, 151, 161, 166, 168, 169, 171, 181, 184, 215
Costner, Kevin   198
cougar   40, 55, 115,
coyote   40
crabs   20, 35, 43, 65, 71, 73, 89, 92, 107, 113, 125, 129, 132, 142, 187, 194
Cranberry Campground   2, 14, 15, 70, 83, 91, 94, 98, 102, 129, 130, 131, 140, 160, 195, 196,
Cranberry Lake   2, 11, 21, 27, 32, 37, 38, 40, 41, 45, 55, 56, 59, 60, 61, 65, 74, 79,96, 101-103, 105, 126, 127, 129, 133, 134, 140, 142, 144, 146, 147, 161, 166, 171, 181, 183, 185, 187, 191, 198, 209, 214
Current newsletter   157, 163, 170, 173, 203
Currents   11, 46, 48, 122, 126, 144
Curvers, Let   xii
cyanobacteria   23, 96, 97, 132, 181

D

daphne   32
Darwin, Charles   42
Dawes Act   46, 75, 81,
Deception Island 8, 11, 105, 116, 127, 140, 148, 153, 155, 192, 195
Deception Pass Dash   xii, 153, 155
Deception Pass Park Foundation   xii, 3, 58, 59, 73, 77-79, 104, 151, 153, 154, 159, 160, 168-170, 180, 181
Deception Pass Tours   xii, 127, 152, 159, 167, 180, 191, 194
deer   35, 40
Department of Natural Resources   8, 33, 69, 182, 34, 69, 83, 108, 200
Dewey   49, 50, 52
DeYoung, Doug   xiii, 172
Dioum, Baba   157
Discover Pass   81, 91-92, 111, 119, 127, 201
Discovery Trail   22, 135, 167,
divers   144
dogs   75, 96-97, 128, 132, 193, 198,
Doran, Molly   xii
Doran, Terry   xi
Douglas fir   21-24, 26, 28, 33, 41, 120, 137, 158, 182,
Douglas squirrel   41
Dr. Seuss   179
Drinkwin, Joan   xii
Dugualla   3, 10, 22, 24, 25, 28, 30, 33, 36-38, 69-70, 78, 81, 120, 125, 138-139, 167, 182, 193, 195, 216
Dunlap family   75

E

eagle scout   79, 161, 168
eagles   xv, 38, 107, 116, 122
Earnest, Gene   xii, 172
Earth Day   80, 152, 168,
East Cranberry   55, 59,76, 78, 79, 90, 98, 101, 102, 133, 135, 142-144, 146, 161, 181, 183, 191-192, 194, 196, 198
Edwards, Laura   68
eelgrass   20, 179

Eliot, T. S.   101
Eliza   47
Elora Hartt   xiii
Emergency Help xiii, 34, 52, 94, 95, 99, 196
English ivy   33
Evans, Brian   xiii

F

Fidalgo Island   1, 2, 7, 10, 17, 32, 40, 45-52, 59, 60, 63, 75, 107, 118, 128, 144, 148, 153, 179, 180, 195-200
Fidalgo Fly Fishers   xii
Fidalgo, Salvador   47
Fimbel, Rob   xi, 83, 182
Finsen, Fred   51-52
Fire   xv, 13, 23, 24, 26, 28, 29, 31, 33, 34, 51, 93, 94, 99, 119, 128, 131-132, 147, 154, 157, 172, 181-182, 185, 196
First Day Hike   151
fishing   xv, 2, 15, 25, 41, 45, 51, 52, 64, 65, 73, 89, 91, 94, 96, 101, 104, 112, 116, 125, 129, 133-134, 142, 144, 155, 194, 196
Fix It Days   153
flowering currant   29
Forest Interpretive Trail   135, 161
Fort Casey   49, 51, 60, 197
Foster family   74
frogs   35, 37

G

geese   38, 87, 96, 97, 122, 181,
Geocaching   134, 184
Ginnett   8, 24, 25, 27, 32, 34, 39, 49, 74, 77, 105, 116-118, 125, 137-139, 151, 191-193, 195,
Ginther, Brett and Terica   xii
Glass, Gayle   xii, 65, 171
Gobert, Tanisha   xi
Goodall, Harrison   xii, 79, 181
Goose Rock   2, 8, 16, 22, 24-25, 27-29, 43, 51, 56, 78, 94, 104-106, 111, 125, 129, 135, 139, 146, 151, 169, 171, 184, 191-195, 209
Governor Gregoire   76
Governor Stevens   46, 74
Gracie the Gray Whale   159
grand fir   22-24, 26
great blue herons   38
Group Camp   31, 67, 76, 90, 101, 134, 152, 181, 184
Gum, Pat and Barry   174, 175
gumweed   21, 31
Gun Point   49
Guss, Elizabeth   108, 199
Gustafson, Derek   xi, 85

H

H.M.S. Bounty   47
Hall, Louis   74
Halpin   49
Hanks, Tom   42
Hanna, Bruce   xii
Hansen, Ken   67, 68, 199
Harrington, Harold   xii, 73
Harris, Todd   xiii
Harrison, Scott   xii, 51
Harvey, Marsha   xi
Haugen, Mary Margaret   73
HDR, Inc.   77, 79, 181
Hedstrom, Don   198
Heilman Valley   22, 28, 30, 34, 40, 49, 63, 74, 117, 137, 184, 193
Heilman, Amelia   63
Heilman, Claire   63
Heilman, Kathleen   xii, 63
hemlock   22 - 24, 26, 31, 48, 136
herb robert   33
Hinkle, J. Grant   55
Hobson, Greg   xii
holly   32
Hope Island   8, 11, 17, 23-25, 26, 32, 33, 36, 37, 71, 119, 120, 126, 130-132, 138, 152, 193, 195, 196, 209
hornets   36
Hoypus Hill   2, 22, 25, 28, 29, 36, 69, 74, 77, 81, 108, 125, 132, 135, 136, 139, 182, 192, 196
Hoypus Point   2, 8, 11, 22, 24, 25, 27, 38, 48, 52, 73, 74, 77, 94, 98, 107, 108, 111, 125, 126, 132, 133, 135, 136, 139, 151, 171, 192, 194, 195, 196, 209, 211

I

invasives   32, 33
Itineraries   194

J

JJ Hartt   xiii
Jenga   113
Johns, Lucie   xii
Johnson, Chris   xi
Johnson, Craig   170
Johnson, Estelle   xii
Johnson, Jill   xii
Jordan Hartt   xiii, 105, 196
Joy, Gene   xii
Juan de Fuca   47
Junior Ranger   157, 169, 170
juniper   23, 27, 120

K

Kataleya Hartt   xiii, 196
Kaufman, Lisa   xii
Kauvel, Kimberly   xii
Kayakers   2, 10, 11, 51, 74. 95, 106, 108, 112-114, 119, 120, 126, 130, 139, 140, 141, 144, 148, 153, 155, 167, 184, 191, 194, 195
Keilty, Maureen   193
Kempbell, Sammye   xi, 43, 71, 72, 145, 170
Kiket Island   2, 8, 11, 16, 23-25, 27, 28, 36, 38, 40, 46, 48, 75-76, 81, 94, 111, 118-119, 125, 130, 132, 136, 141, 167, 180, 191-196, 209, 211
killer whales   41
kingfisher   38
Kiver, Gene and Barbara   xii
Klope, Matt   xii
Kocian, Jan   144
Kokwalalwoot   46, 67, 68, 81, 162, 186, 198
Kukutali Preserve   22, 32, 75-76, 81, 91, 118, 119, 162, 167, 180, 199, 200, 211

L

LaGreid, Ted   79, 181
Lancaster, Jeri   xiii, 177
Lancaster, Josh   165
Lang, Paul   52
Lazzeri, Larry   xii
Leahy-Mack, Heather   xi, 71
Lee, Jean   xii, 150
Lee, Julian   xii
Leopold, Aldo   182
lichens   23, 31
Lieber, Richard   125
Lighthouse Point 7, 16, 22, 23, 25, 28, 29, 38, 39, 50, 51, 112, 113, 114, 126, 136, 139-141, 151, 155, 191-194, 197
limpets   20, 71, 145
Lind, Jay   xii
Lindbergh, Charles   191
Lindsay Hartt   x, xiii, 113
Lopez Island   10, 47
Lorio, Adam   xi, 20, 41, 43, 71, 73, 145, 159
Lottie Bay   11, 22, 37, 77, 113-114, 136
Lottie Point   23, 38, 114, 129, 136, 193, 194
Lovell, Jim   42
Lubbock, John   7
Luft, Max   59
Lunz, Mark   xiii, 69, 74, 77, 166, 174
lupine   21
Lutz, Mira   xi
Lyter, Barb   163

M

Machin, Rick   xii, 118
MacLeish, Archibald   165
madrone   22, 27, 28, 48, 137, 147, 193
Maiden   33, 46, 49, 67-68, 137, 146, 162, 194, 199, 200
March Point   46, 49, 197
McCrumb   xi
McMurry, Alex   76, 181
Melcher, Duane   xii
Melcher, Joan   xii
Memorial benches   113, 171

Menzies, Archibald   48
Merriman, Liz   xii, 59
Mitchell, Todd   xi
Morse, George   60
Mortensen, Viggo   198
mosquitoes   36, 120
Mount Baker   47, 74, 106, 108, 127, 146
Mount Erie   33, 34, 48, 63, 78, 108, 116, 117, 118, 126, 130, 193, 196
Mount Erie Fire Department   xiii, 33
Mount Rainier   47, 196, 205
Muir, John   19
Mukilteo   45, 87
mushrooms   31
mussels   20

N
Naked Man Valley   63, 117, 192, 193
Naomi Olivia Hartt   xiii
Napier, Montana   xi, 158, 162, 169, 170,
Narvaez   47, 81
Nautilus Construction   xii, 78
Navy   11, 42, 70, 77, 95-96, 107, 161, 168, 169, 172, 198
nettles   22, 30, 108, 136
Newberry, Ron   xiii
North Beach 2, 4, 11, 14, 15, 22, 24, 25, 27, 28, 36, 38, 39, 42, 45, 48, 49, 55, 59, 60, 62, 65, 66, 76, 77, 78, 79, 90, 97, 98, 102-105, 110, 111, 114, 125, 129, 130, 133-135, 142, 143, 146, 151, 165, 183, 192-194, 209
North Cascades   7, 8, 105, 107, 128, 194
North Whidbey Fire and Rescue   xii, 33, 95, 148
Northwest Island   116, 127, 140, 144, 148, 192, 195
Northwest Straits Foundation   xii, 80
Nortier, Matt   161
Noyes, Mike   xiii
nudibranch   20
nurse logs   158

O
Oak Harbor   49, 73, 97, 152, 196, 197
ocean spray   21, 23, 29, 123
O'Conner, Jim   xiii
octopus   1, 20
O'Hara, Charley   xi
Old growth   xv, 15, 21, 24, 25, 28, 49, 63, 69, 74, 82, 84, 102, 107, 108, 117-118, 120, 129, 130, 134, 135, 138, 183-184, 192-195
olive colored flycatcher   39
Olsen, Mae   68
Olsen, Vic   68
Olson, Berte   52, 60, 157
Olympic Mountains   7, 8, 12, 13, 88, 89, 115, 196
Open House   73, 153

orcas   41
oregon grape   23, 24
Osterloh, Jessie   xi, 170, 177
Overby, Bill   xiii, 202
owls   38-39
oystercatchers   39

P
Pacific Northwest Trail   118
Pacific yew   24, 28, 118, 138
painted turtles   37
Palmer, Lex   77, 79
Park Founders Picnic   153
Parmley, Bob   xiii
Pass Island   10, 25, 33, 48, 60, 61, 89, 94, 108, 109, 111, 123, 136, 141, 146, 161, 162, 171, 176, 192, 193, 194, 195
Pass Lake   2, 14, 15, 22, 24, 28, 32, 33, 37, 38, 40, 41, 48, 49, 55, 60, 63, 64, 76-78, 87, 89, 96, 97. 98. 116-118, 125, 126, 133, 136-142, 144, 151, 152, 167, 181, 192, 193, 195, 209, 214
Phelps, Berniece   xi, 69
plankton   8, 20, 42
porcupines   41
Port Townsend   19, 87, 96, 205
Porter, Brian   xi
President Andrew Johnson   49
President Barack Obama   87
President Franklin Roosevelt   55, 60
President Warren G. Harding   55, 179
Prison   49, 50, 81, 127, 167, 213
purple loose strife   32
purple martins   39
purple shore crabs   20, 35

Q
Quarry Pond   13, 14, 16, 22, 70, 72, 76, 78, 81, 91, 92, 94, 97, 98, 105, 118, 125, 128-131, 133, 135, 140, 167, 187, 195
Quimper, Manuel   47

R
Rachel Hartt   x
rainshadow   12, 13, 89
Rainshadow Running   xii, 154
ravens   39, 122
red elderberry   22, 24
red huckleberry   30, 31, 158
red-throated loons   39
Reservation Head   113-114, 136, 142, 193
Rhodes, Carly   xi, 104, 159, 170
rhododendrons   29, 105, 135
Richardson, Vince   xiii
Ritterbusch, Paige   xiii
river otter   41, 113, 122
rockweed   20, 32
Rogers, Bud   xii

Rosario 1, 2, 7, 8, 10, 11, 15, 19, 20, 25, 28, 30, 32, 33, 36, 38-42, 45-47, 49, 53, 55, 68, 71, 78, 81, 88, 89, 92, 97, 102, 108, 112-114, 115-116, 126, 129, 130, 132, 136, 137, 139, 140, 142-145, 148, 151, 159, 160-162, 167, 169-171, 181, 183, 191, 192-194, 196, 198, 209
Rosario Field Classroom   33, 53, 78, 93, 115, 159-161, 169-171, 181
roses   22, 23, 30, 117, 122, 199
Ross, Matt   198
Ruh, Bill   xiii
Russell, Terry   207

S
Saks, Dominique xi, 170
salal   21-24, 29, 31, 116, 136
Salish Sea   3, 8, 12, 21, 22, 32, 46, 65, 70, 74, 81, 103, 107, 152, 185, 207
salmon   15, 20, 22, 45, 51, 58, 65, 75, 94, 104, 107, 133, 134
salmonberry   22, 30, 31, 117
Samish   xi, I, 25, 45-47, 67, 68, 115, 152, 162, 199, 200
Sand dunes   21, 98, 103, 161, 169
Sand Dunes Trail   23, 28, 98, 125, 134, 161, 171, 176, 191, 193, 194
sand lance   22
sand verbena   21
Schmidt, Sarah   xii, 199
Schorr, Erik   xii
Schorr, Megan   xii
scotch broom   xii, 33, 120, 122
Scott, Jay   xii
sea cucumber   20, 71, 145
sea lettuce   20
sea urchin   20, 43, 72, 115, 145
seals   41, 141, 148
seastars   20, 43, 71, 145
Seattle   12, 14, 19, 36, 49, 51, 60, 61, 63, 64, 74, 77, 78, 84, 87, 88, 97, 181, 185, 198, 199, 205
Sharpe's Cove   38, 42, 49, 53, 78, 115, 126, 160
Sharpe Park 196
Sharpe, Thomas   49
Shaw, Barb   xii
Shaw, George Bernard   45
Sheldon, Joe   9
Shelly, Brian   xii, 169
Shen, Eric   xii, 153
Shepherd, Doug   xii
Shipman, Hugh   xii
Shook, Ben   xiii, 34, 94, 148, 149, 168, 174, 177
sitka spruce   21, 22, 26
Skagit Island 11, 23, 25, 27, 91, 92, 107, 119, 126, 130, 138, 141, 180, 192, 195
skunk cabbage   22, 30
Slotemaker, Terry   xii
Smith, Norma   73
Smith, Ted   xi

snails   20, 35
snakes   35, 36, 121
soil 8, 12, 13, 16, 22, 23, 24, 25, 27, 28, 29, 30, 31, 37, 43, 75
spurge laurel   32
Sandvik family   74
Stapert, Jason   xiii, 94
starflower   30
stinging nettles   see nettles
stinky bob   33
stonecrop   23, 31
Strait of Georgia 47, 67, 207
Strait of Juan de Fuca   13, 47, 102, 115, 185, 197, 207
Strawberry Island   38, 51, 81, 108, 111, 122, 123, 153, 155, 195
Streano, Vince   xiii, 159, 205
Sullivan, Maggie   xii
surf smelt   22, 92, 107, 133, 134
Susannah Hartt   xiii
Swainson's thrush   39
swim   2, 10, 11, 38, 41, 56, 59, 65, 66, 74, 78, 96, 97, 98, 102, 103, 105, 119, 127, 129, 130, 132, 140, 142, 143, 144, 146, 167, 181
Swinomish   xi, 25, 36, 45, 46, 68, 74, 75, 81, 118, 119, 132, 152, 180, 197, 199, 200, 211
SWITMO   xii, 70, 77, 78, 167, 181
sword fern   22, 24, 29, 97, 138

T

Taffy Hartt   x, xiii
tansy ragwort   33
Terrell, Scott   xiii
thimbleberry   23
ticks   13, 36
Tidepools   8, 10, 19, 20, 35, 36, 43, 71, 72, 78, 92, 94, 115, 121, 145, 148, 159, 162, 168, 170
Tides   1, 10, 11, 16, 17, 20, 35, 43, 67, 71, 113, 114, 133, 140, 144, 180, 185, 193, 211
Tobin, Shawn   xi
Treaty of Point Elliott   45, 46, 81
Trebon, Theresa   85, 199
Trust for Public Land   76
Tursi Trail   25, 28, 59, 78, 81, 116, 117-118, 138, 167, 193, 213
Tursi, John   xi, 58, 59, 104, 199
turtles   37

U

Underpass   58, 77, 104-105, 125, 135, 169

V

Vancouver, George   x, 1, 10, 47, 48, 81, 111, 161, 162
Varner, James   xiii
Vaux, Bob   xii, 121
Visitor Centers   4, 59, 159, 161, 169, 180

W

Wagner, Nathan   79
Walker, Bill   xiii, 153, 155
wallaby   84
Wasserman, Larry   xi
water hemlock   33
waterfall   137
Watilo, Eric   xi, 133
Watkinson, Bryce   xiii
Wenaas, Barry   xii
Wenning, Dave   xii, 200
West Beach   2, 10, 11, 15, 21, 30, 35, 38, 41, 51, 59, 65, 74, 81, 89, 94, 97, 98, 102-103, 104, 112, 125, 127, 129, 130, 132, 133, 134, 137, 139, 140, 143, 144, 146, 151, 161, 166, 169, 171, 176, 182, 183, 185, 187, 191-194, 198, 209
western grebe   39
Whidbey Camano Land Trust   xii, 74
Whidbey Island   2, 7, 8, 9, 10, 11, 14, 40, 48, 51, 52, 55, 60, 61, 87, 88, 96, 105, 107, 115, 118, 129, 137, 152, 153, 168, 170, 195, 196, 198, 199, 200, 207
Whidbey, Joseph 48
white crowned sparrow   39
Whittet, John   xiii
Wilkes, Charles   48, 75
Willis, Russ   64
willow   22
Wold, Marv   xiii, 15, 69, 74, 83, 84, 177, 198
Wooten, Tom   xi, 200
worms   20
Wotipka, Sam   xi, 76, 77, 150, 157, 159, 170, 199

Y

yellow archangel   33
yellow jackets   see hornets
Young, Steve   xii

Z

Zillig, Jane   xii

So here I am.

It's the end of a lot of pages, and also nearing the end of a lot of years of life and service for me here at Deception Pass State Park. I see the park with nostalgic eyes now. In a short time, all these places I write about I will be seeing as a visitor rather than as my blessed assignment. My work will be finished, my hand in the accomplishments complete, the book closed for me.

And yet the contributions of each of us will remain as part of the legacy of the park. Stories will be told of that guy Jack who did this or didn't do that, for better or worse. Generations to come will not know my name, but they will see the handiwork of something we did as a team while I was here.

This park is lovingly cared for each day by a team of employees who obviously care about what they do, knowing that their work has meaning because the park gives meaning to the lives of today's visitors and the generations to come. I take pride to be a part of this exceptional team.

And it is lovingly cared for by hundreds more in practical ways each year, volunteers who give their time, their energy, their creativity, and their devotion to serve our park, our community, and our planet. They know this park is one small place where their service is needed, and appreciated, and valuable, and an investment in the future.

And this park is in the hands and hearts of so many more. It is cherished and treasured by millions, and has become a part of the fabric of all of our lives.

I am honored to have this opportunity. I am blessed each day to be here. I am humbled by my shortcomings, knowing others could have done far better. But regardless, I have done what I could, the best that I could, and that gives me joy.

Someday, someone else will come in and take my place, and do a great job, taking the park several steps beyond what I could even imagine.

Many have come before me, and then moved on. Eventually I will join them, like the waves of the sea, rolling on without end.

But we will not be gone, no.

Every part of this park is sacred. At night, when the park is silent and you think its shores and woodland trails deserted, they will throng with the returning hosts that once filled them and still love this beautiful place.

Love stories never end.

Made in the USA
San Bernardino, CA
02 December 2016